GLOBALISATION AND INDIAN ECONOMY

GLOBALISATION AND INDIAN ECONOMY

BHARAT JHUNJHUNWALA

KALPAZ PUBLICATIONS

DELHI-110052

Globalisation and Indian Economy

Rs. 720

ISBN: 81-7835-599-X

Published in 2007 in India by
Kalpaz Publications
C-30, Satyawati Nagar,
Delhi-110052
Phone : 9212729499
E-mail: kalpaz@hotmail.com

Lasser Type Setting by: Rudra Computer Graphics, Delhi
Printed at : Salasar Imaging System, Delhi

Contents

Preface

This book has its origins in a request from Kalpaz Publications that they wouid like to bring out a collection of my published articles in various newspapers.

As I went through the first printout of the compilation, it became clear that these articles were written over a time span of 13 years. What was relevant in 1995 is no longer relevant in 2007. Thus I have reorganized the articles in three sections:

- *The journey so far.* This section contains articles that were relevant for India in the nineties at the beginning of globalization. At that time India was in a defensive mode. It was necessary to protect and support Indian companies to take on the might of Western MNCs. India has since overcome that challenge. The resistance to speedy opening up of the Indian economy to FDI and free trade put up by Swadeshi economists like me and the Left Parties led to slow opening. That provided breathing space to Indian companies and enabled them to emerge as MNCs in their own right in the middle of this decade.

- *Asian century.* This section contains articles relevant to the present times—the first decade of this century. India has started to emerge on the world stage. The mainstream assessment is that victory is still 20-50 years away. I hold, however, that India may dominate the world economy and emerge as No 1 on the world scale in much less time—say by 2015. These articles suggest policies India must follow to attain that goal.

• *Just world economic order.* India's dominance will initially come by adopting the predatory tactics hitherto employed by the Western countries. This will lead to Indian victory but not to the establishment of a just and peaceful world in keeping with our philosophy of *Vasudev Kutumbakam.* This section discusses the issues that we must start thinking as we assume the role of global leader.

The difference of approach at the three levels will become clear by a few examples.

Foreign Direct Investment

• *The journey so far.* Till about 2003 this author vehemently opposed FDI so that Indian companies get space for upgrading and acquire the capability to challenge the might of MNCs.

• *Asian century:* Beginning about 2003, India's outward FDI is rising fast. We are acquiring foreign companies. Consequently India may emerge as the chief global 'exploiter' in some time. We may bring world wealth to India via profit repatriations etc. The opposition to inward FDI has, therefore, now changed into support for outward FDI.

• *Just world economic order.* The next challenge will be to establish an outward FDI regime that is just. India must promote migratory outward FDI that helps develop other countries.

TRIPS

• *The journey so far.* TRIPS is opposed since it allows technology-rich Western MNCs to extract technology rents and impoverish India.

• *Asian century.* The transfer of R&D activities by various MNCs to India and the acquisition of frontline technologies by Indian PIOs in Western countries open up the possibility that India may emerge as the key technology innovator in the next decade. India will then stand to gain by embracing TRIPS.

• *Just world economic order.* The final challenge is to dismantle TRIPS and make available new technologies free or at a low cost to all countries.

Free Trade

• *The journey so far.* This author opposed free trade since there was a danger of Indian producers being swamped by low-cost hi-tech manufactures from other countries. There was a need to practice 'optimal protectionism' to protect as well as cajole Indian industries to upgrade.

• *Asian century.* India is now in a position to face global free trade and swamp the world with low cost manufactures. We now stand to gain from free trade.

• *Just world economic order.* India must encourage and support other developing countries in adopting optimal protectionism so that they are not swamped by Indian manufactures and can protect their own industries.

Foreign Aid

• *The journey so far.* The case was for increasing unattached aid. India needed the capital and technological support to stand in the global economy. India must accept aid selectively.

• *Asian century.* India needs aid no longer. The aim should be to educate other developing countries how to prevent donors from destroying domestic economy by killing self-esteem of the local entrepreneurs. India must give unattached aid on a large scale and help other developing countries.

• *Just world economic order.* India must put forth the case of dismantling all foreign aid and providing money to developing countries through better terms of trade so that their self-esteem is not hurt.

Capital Account Convertibility

• *The journey so far*. CAC must be opposed because it would abet outflow of our capital. The rupee was declining hence domestic investors stood to gain by sending their capital abroad.

• *Asian century*. We must encourage our investors to invest in foreign countries and capture the world economy. CAC is thus beneficial. There is no danger of outflow since the rupee is rising.

• *Just world economic order*. We must support only migratory capital flows so that we do not extract resources of other countries and also do not allow our resources to be extracted. Thus CAC should be restricted suitably.

I hope these examples will show how the argument changes with the emergence of the India Story. I have edited the articles and tried to explain the context. I request the reader to keep this in mind otherwise the articles may appear to be mutually contradictory.

The term 'developing country' has been used for India in the period covered under *The journey so far*, and other developing countries at a similar level of development today. The term 'emerging economy' has been used for India and China in the first decade of the 21st century. The terms 'West', 'developed country' and 'rich country' are used synonymously for OECD countries, inclusive of Japan.

This book is about India's role in the global economy. My friend Jaya Govinda Charan Das has pointed out that she will be able to discharge the role outlined here only if she is able to solve the problem of domestic inequality. I agree wholly. However, the subject matter of this book is focussed on international economy hence I hope to deal with this question elsewhere. The same applies to the need for educational and cultural reforms. India's ability to practice the philosophy of Vasudev Kutumbakam rests ultimately on the spread of this thinking among her people. I hope to deal with this question subsequently as well.

I have not been able to provide detailed references to many reports and web pages referred in the articles. However, I have provided enough detail that the reader can locate the concerned page with a small effort. I beg the reader's pardon for not being able to provide this service.

V V S Narayana Saladi has helped in editing this book and it has become more readable due to his efforts.

I hope this book will help India to follow global dharma in the coming time.

Lakshmoli Pomaletha **Bharat Jhunjhunwala**
Via Kirti Nagar
District Tehri 249161

PART - 1

THE JOURNEY SO FAR

1

Emerging Crisis in the Economies of Developed Countries

The model of globalization being adopted towards the beginning of this century assumes that developed countries will continue to lead the global economy. This is not likely to happen. On the contrary, economies of the developed countries are soon likely to stagnate. But that does not mean that developing countries will automatically be able to tilt the scales in their favour. The developed countries can spin and cause the developing countries to voluntarily accept the suzerainty of the developed countries even though there is no basis for continuation of their dominance. It will require concerted effort on the part of the developing countries to tilt the scales in their favour.

Limits of Growth

Mainstream economists mostly focus on the need to increase investment, such as in infrastructure. It is assumed that demand is plentiful to make use of these investments in roads etc. But the crisis of banks in 1999-2000 indicates that explicit policies are needed to generate demand. Investments can go bad otherwise.

The problem started with long-term capital management (LTCM) in the U.S. and was followed in quick succession by GITIC in China, Renong in Malaysia and UTI in India. Fundamentally the problem is that of bad income distribution and lack of demand which starts a chain reaction leading to run on financial institutions. More intensive regulation of the banking structure cannot solve the underlying problem of weak demand. Instead of believing that financial regulation is the panacea, we must all address the problem of income distribution which alone holds the solution to the crisis.

Long-Term Capital Management was a hedge fund based near New York. It had on its staff two Nobel laureates of economics– Mayron Scholes and Robert Merton. It attracted large sums of money from leading financial investors. It made huge amounts of money by borrowing cheap and investing dear. It used sophisticated computer models to locate profit opportunities. With a capital of mere $2.3 billion it had borrowed heavily and accumulated an investment portfolio of nearly $125 billion. The debt-equity ratio was more than 50, as compared to 2 that is considered appropriate for normal manufacturing companies.

Neither the Nobel laureates nor the sophisticate computers were able to predict the decline in the value of its global investments, however. The global prices fell suddenly in 1999. The result was huge losses which wiped out LTCM's entire capital and create a possibility of liquidation and panic selling of its remaining vast portfolio. According to U.S. Fed chairman Greenspan, this could have "triggered the seizing up of the markets... and could have potentially impaired the economy of many nations," including that of the U.S. In order to avoid such a situation, the Fed persuaded major investors to put in a further $3.5 billion to rescue LTCM from its immediate problems.

What is noteworthy is that everything was 'normal' except the fall in the value of its investments. The problem arose not because LTCM had high debt, or that it was 'unregulated'. The problem arose from the fact that its wizards failed to predict the slowdown in the global economy.

The problem in Malaysia too was precipitated by a recession in the economy. Renong Bhd was much involved in rail and toll-road operations. The income from these infrastructure operations declined as the economy slowed down. As a result it was unable to repay its debt on time. The government backing for the debt that was falling due; and also tax exemptions on toll roads were to expire soon. The government intervened and $3 billion of Renong's debt was restructured. Its creditors had to accept bonds instead of cash. Once again, the origins of the problem lay not in debt itself. The origins lay in the recession which led to a fall in its infrastructure revenues.

The Guangdong International Trust and Investment Corporation (GITIC) was the flagship of China's market reforms. These 240 odd local government-owned ITICs made investment in highways, hotels and energy projects and also property. GITIC, owned by the government of Guangdong, was the pioneer of the ITICs just as Guangdong was the pioneer among China's provinces in market reforms. At end 1996, GITIC was reported to have assets of $21.4 billion against liabilities of $18.7 billion.

Then the Asian crisis struck. East Asian countries had speedily opened their economies to foreign direct investment. Western MNCs had invested in establishing new manufacturing facilities in these countries such as General Motors establishing a car manufacturing plant in Thailand. The produce of these factories was to be exported back to their home countries such as the U.S. The Western MNCs were interested in making use of cheap labour in these countries. They established, so to say, outposts or islands in the host economies. They brought in the machinery. Produced goods with the cheap labour available there. Then exported the goods back to their home country. The linkage with the domestic economy was mainly in the supply of cheap labour.

The euphoria caused by these huge inflows spread to the domestic economy. Real estate and stock prices hit the roof. Domestic and foreign portfolio investors brought in huge amounts to make profit from this boom. The base of this boom was the demand from the Western countries like the U.S. for goods.

That changed as the U.S. economy went into a slowdown towards 1996-97. The demand for imports from the East Asian countries declined. The MNCs were no longer inclined to make more investments. Suddenly the flow of funds in the forex markets of East Asian countries reversed. Instead of more demand of Thai Baht for putting up factories, there was now more demand for the dollar for repatriation of profits and for remittance of the shares and property sold. This led to a run on the currencies of the East Asian countries and led to steep devaluations beginning with the Thai Baht in 1997.

Late in 2000, the Asian crisis started hurting exports deeply, economy slowed and business turned bad, the value of these assets eroded, income from infrastructure projects declined and GITIC did not have the income to repay its debts.

The problems of UTI followed the same pattern. The Unit Scheme-64 was the first mutual fund to be launched by UTI way back in 1964. Unit Scheme-64 had an enviable record of steady dividends and bonus and rights. It had made investments in bonds and equities. Among equities it had invested substantially in the infrastructure sectors–Oil and Natural Gas Commission, Indian Oil Corporation, State Bank of India and Steel Authority of India.

This was an important reason for its troubles. In 1999-2000, its top eight PSU holdings depreciated by 39 percent compared with a 24 percent drop in the Sensex. The value of its equity portfolio depreciated and led to massive redemptions. Once again the problem started with the decline in PSU-infrastructure shares. In this case no property investment was involved.

Whether it is LTCM, Renong, GITIC or Unit Scheme-64, the basic features of all these banking crises were identical. The problem started with a general economic slowdown. There is idle infrastructure capacity due to absence of demand–in toll roads or railways or in steel manufacture. The calculations of high rates of return from these investments go awry. Thence begins the slide.

The basic problem is that world demand is not stable. Thus value of investments can decline. All that 'regulation' can do is to soften the downslide. There is no way that regulation will increase in the revenues from toll roads in Malaysia or Guangdong, or improved performance of Indian infrastructure PSU stocks. Unless the underlying demand picks up, such collapses will continue to occur.

The developing countries should not build their growth strategies on the assumption that demand from developed countries will always provide markets. They should embrace protectionism and make efforts to develop their own internal markets and increase consumption of their people.

Sale of Gold Indicates Weakness of Economies

There is race to sell gold among central banks. Australia, Europe and the IMF have sold their gold reserves. To keep one's wealth in the form of 'unproductive' gold is considered 'foolish'. But it real reason for these sale is that the fundamentals of these economies are weak. Historical precedents help us understand the matter.

Historian AL Basham tells us that silver and copper coins were in use during the period of Buddha in India. They carried the punch marks of the issuing kings. Literary evidence establishes the use of gold coins at that time. In the Kushan period gold dinars and silver and copper coins were in vogue.

Economic Historian Joseph Schumpeter tells us that the bank notes were fully convertible in gold in England in the seventeenth and eighteenth centuries. Any person could claim gold from the Bank of England against notes of Pound Sterling held by him. The Bank maintained adequate reserves of gold to redeem the notes that it had issued. During the Napoleonic wars of early nineteenth century, however, England had to suspend the convertibility of notes into gold. The drain on government finances to finance the war destabilized the economy hence the Bank of England could not redeem the notes issued. The bank restored this convertibility after the war of Waterloo in 1816 i.e. after the economy normalised. The implication is that adequate gold reserves are an indication of normalcy.

In the nineteenth century it was generally believed that Gold Standard was the right policy. It helped foreign trade by establishing a clear benchmark of exchange rates. By 1900 most countries had adopted the Gold Standard. This situation, save a few exceptions, prevailed till the Great Depression of 1929. But immediately thereafter between 1931 most countries abandoned the gold Standard. They wanted to increase their exports despite the depression in the U.S. They wanted to devalue their currencies for this purpose. But devaluation is only possible when convertibility of the currency into gold is abandoned. Most central banks maintained adequate gold reserves until normal conditions prevailed till 1929.

After the Second World War the U.S. dollar was again made convertible into gold. The U.S. was committed to maintain a fixed exchange rate of 1/35 ounce gold to a dollar. Most other currencies of the world were freely convertible into the dollar. As such they could be exchanged for gold through that route. There existed, so to say, an all pervasive Gold Standard. But after 1960 investors became wary of the dollar and pressure for its devaluation mounted. But it could not be devalued because the U.S. was committed to maintain a fixed price of 1/35 ounce worth of gold from 1958 to 1971.

The situation deteriorated sharply in 1971 and President Nixon had to suspend the convertibility of dollar into gold. The implication is that as long as the U.S. economy was strong, the U.S. could maintain its gold reserves. As the U.S. economy weakened it has to sell its gold.

The common strand in the four examples above is that as long as the economy is strong, it can hold adequate gold reserves and make its currency convertible into gold. Whenever economies have weakened countries have been forced to sell gold.

Economic historian Schumpeter says that governments do not like the Gold Standard because it limits their ability to incur ever-increasing expenditures. Under the Gold Standard a government can print only so many notes as it is able to back with its gold reserves. It places an in-built restriction on government expenditures. If the economy is strong and the catalyst of government expenditures is not required then Gold Standard is quite suitable.

When the economy falters and government expenditures have to be increased, countries have to choose between (1) printing notes which leads to inflation; (2) impose taxes which further debilitates businesses; (3) borrowing; or (4) sell its gold reserves.

Gold sale, therefore, means two things. One that the economy of the seller country is weakening. Two, other routes to government intervention have been exhausted. Gold sale is the option of last resort. The spate of gold sales by developed countries implies, therefore, that soft options are getting exhausted. Thus, developing countries should focus on the development of their own internal markets by embracing, if necessary, protectionist policies.

Bubbles do burst

The scenario drawn by this author above is pessimistic. This flies in the face of the robust growth of the world economy seen in the first few years of the new millennium. But such episodes of growth are often deceptive. The growth of the world economy towards the beginning of this century is build upon a huge trade deficit incurred by the U.S. and purchase of U.S. Treasury Bonds by foreign governments. This is not sustainable in the long run. Of course, it is not possible to predict how and when the crisis may strike. Yet a review of the dotcom bubble of 1999-2000 gives us an indication how such growth can be deceptive.

The U.S. led the global economy in 1999. But the situation was precarious because the entire edifice rested on investor confidence in the U.S. dotcom revolution. Global investors were putting huge amounts in these companies. The flow of global capital was taking place towards the U.S. The net flow of capital from Europe to the U.S. was negligible in 1997. It had reached an astronomical $100 billion in 1999 according to UNCTAD data. European money flows changed direction to dotcom-driven America.

This money was largely pouring into new public issues of dotcom companies. The share prices of these companies were buoyant and this had placed considerable wealth in the hands of the U.S. consumer, who was buying imported goods on the strength of this paper wealth. They were borrowing from the market using their share certificates as collateral. This consumer spending had converted the U.S. into a buyer of last resort. The U.S. was virtually willing to buy anything that the world wanted to sell. Exports from Europe, Japan and the developing world were increasing and the world economy was booming.

It never dawned upon those investing in the U.S. that they were, in fact, exporting their goods to themselves. A Japanese investor sent his yen to the U.S. to buy dotcom stocks. Those same yen were used by the U.S. consumer to import electronic goods from Japan. It was like a shopkeeper giving a loan to a buyer to purchase his goods.

A virtuous cycle of global growth was established. Share prices of dotcom companies were the pivot of this fortunate circumstance. High share prices pulled world capital towards the U.S., which led to more wealth in the hand of U.S. stockholder, the demand for consumer goods in the U.S. increased, leading to a rise in world exports and a buoyant global economy.

There was a problem, though. The U.S. was importing goods in huge quantities but its exports were weak. It was paying for these imports not from export earnings but from foreign capital inflow. This could last only as long as the boom in dotcom companies persisted. The edifice of the global economy, therefore, rested on the dotcom boom. This boom attracted world capital. As the dotcom boom ended, factors which had led to the East Asian crisis came back into play once again. The East Asian crisis was precipitated by falling U.S. demand which translated into lower profits for Western MNCs operating in East Asia. That led decline in capital inflows into those countries. A decline both in export earnings and capital inflows had led to a collapse of their currencies.

At the height of the Asian crisis in the late 1990s, writers as me had put forth the opinion that the world economy was poised for a collapse. It indeed was. But the unexpected boom in dotcom had warded it off.

The question is whether such troublesome scenario, as the decline of the US economy in the late 2000's may again not be warded off by yet another unexpected boom elsewhere. The answer to such a question would lie in the advances in technology that may or may not take place. If, for example, another "revolution" would emerge in say genetic technology or space exploration, the crisis will certainly be pushed back again. The profits in these emerging sectors would once again fuel yet another consumption boom.

On the other hand there have also been occasions when such a saviour technology had not emerged. The U.S. was placed in similar position in the 1960s. At that time the U.S. Government was running huge budget deficits to meet the bill of its huge overseas military spending such as in Viet Nam. It was purchasing goods from across the world to meet its military requirements and paying with dollar denominated U.S. Treasury Bonds. The value of those bonds was dependent on the value of the dollar in terms of gold. The declining value of the dollar had led to the abandonment of the gold standard in 1971. Technological boom did not occur in time to save the situation.

In the 1980s, similarly, there was a boom in U.S. real estate prices which was fuelled by excessive borrowing. The bursting of that bubble had led to the stock market crash and "hard landing" of the dollar in 1986-87. The stock market crash of 1929 which led to the Great Depression was similarly caused by an unwarranted boom in the stock markets. We have, therefore, more than one instance when it had not been possible to ward off an economic imbalance by newer technological advances.

It is difficult to say when such a slippage may occur. But it can be asserted that the buoyancy of the global economy built on new technological inventions is not likely to be stable. The developing countries should make efforts to develop their internal markets.

U.S.' Growth Model is Not Replicable

The world economy in the early 2000s was being pulled by increased consumer spending in the U.S. The buoyant stock market had created a sense of euphoria among the American people. This buoyancy of the stock market was, in part, a result of inflow of global capital into the U.S. economy. Normally, such inflow of foreign capital should overheat the U.S. economy and lead to inflation. But this did not happen because price of imports were declining. The stable prices have enabled the U.S. Federal Reserve to maintain low interest rates and this had further reinforced consumption and investment in the U.S. economy.

The buoyancy of the U.S. economy towards the beginning of this century, therefore, is based on three factors: (1) the willingness of U.S. Consumers to incur debt; (2) inflow of global capital into the U.S. and (3) declining terms of trade against the developing countries.

Can this formula be replicated by other countries? The answer is no.

First, it seems that Japanese and Europeans are not as inclined to borrow for consumption. In Europe consumer expenditure continues to be restrained while government expenditure is restricted by European Monetary Union requirements.

Second, a buoyant stock market in Japan and Europe will require an inflow of global capital. If that were to take place, Japan's gain would be America's loss. If stock prices and consumption increase in Japan, they will fall in the U.S. There will then be no 'global' revival.

The developing countries cannot help either. An important reason for the recession in their economies is that terms of trade are becoming adverse. If these were to be reserved and the prices of their exports were to rise, there could be a revival in their economies. But in the same breath, the terms of trade for U.S. will become adverse and growth will suffer there. The developing countries' gain will be America's loss.

The conclusion is that the U.S. economy is buoyant precisely because Japan and Europe are depressed as a result of capital outflows to the U.S. Developing countries are similarly placed due to their terms of trade. It follows that the developing countries cannot follow the U.S. model. They should not assume that free trade will always provide new markets for their exports.

Why Capitalism and Inequity are Stable

Many socialists believe that capitalism will fall under its own weight because it has no way to increase demand in the long run. But there are reasons to believe that capitalism may indeed be able to solve the crisis that Marx had thought to be inevitable.

Marx had pointed out that capitalism unleashed two opposing forces. On the one hand, the pursuit of profit led to increased production while, on the other, it led to a reduction in the wages. The reduced wages led to a declining demand for the goods whose production had increased. There were too many goods chasing too little demand. Thus "breaks out an epidemic," he wrote in *The Communist Manifesto*, which, "in all earlier epochs, would have seemed as an absurdity—the epidemic of overproduction."

Never did Marx dream that the labourer would be able to rise within capitalism. He wrote: "The serf, in the period of serfdom, raised himself to membership in the commune. The petty bourgeois, under feudal absolutism, managed to develop into a bourgeois. The modern labourer, on the contrary, instead of rising with the progress of industry, sinks deeper and deeper below the conditions of existence of his own class. He becomes a pauper."

Theoretically Marx is correct. The demand *from wages* cannot increase in capitalism. But what about demand from the ruling class itself? Can the ruling class—the capitalists, bureaucracy, labour aristocracy and stockholders—not provide the demand?

In Marx's thinking the contradiction arose from the inability of capitalism to create demand. If the profits, instead of being used for reinvestment were to be used for consumption, then there would be no problem.

There are reasons to believe that events during Marx's own lifetime pointed out to capitalism adopting this solution. Marx and Engels, however, failed to take it to its logical conclusion. They could see that the British workers, instead of becoming paupers, were raising themselves to share in the profits of capitalism. A year before Marx's death in 1883, Engels wrote to Kautsky: "You ask me what the English workers think about colonial policy. Well there is no workers' party here, you see, there are only Conservatives and Liberal-Radicals, and *the workers gaily share the feast of England's monopoly of the world markets* and the colonies."

Marx and Engels did not quite appreciate the import of this observation of theirs. If the capitalists of England could share the feast with their workers, that could provide the demand to consume the goods that were being produced in increasing quantities. The so-called 'crisis of capitalism' was solved permanently. The capitalist could make profits in the colonies, and use that money to throw increase consumption of privileged workers such as those of England. This class of 'imperial' workers would provide the demand for the goods produced by the impoverished 'colonial' workers.

As we enter this century, the same demand can be provided by distribution of dividends by Joint Stock companies.

An article in *Newsweek* of August 17, 1998 says that the Asian tragedy has been largely positive for the U.S.—serving it with 'a big platter of cheap goods and money.' Asian flight capital has been pumping the U.S. markets: "There is no reason for the East Asia crisis to depress the growth rate of the U.S. economy. All that changes is where the profits are going to come from. Companies involved in foreign sales will be pinched. Domestic firms will do better."

The inflow of money from Asia by flight capital or dividends from U.S. operations abroad is 'pumping' the demand by the U.S. economy. The workers of East Asia are reduced to supplying cheap goods to meet this demand. Just as the feudal lord would employ the serfs to produce goods to be consumed by the nobility; and colonial England employed Indian natives to produce goods for the workers of Manchester, so the U.S. corporations can employ the workers of Thailand to produce goods to be consumed by the U.S. stockholder.

The U.S. corporations can invest abroad, use cheap labour to produce cheap goods, repatriate their profits to the U.S. which are distributed among the stockholders. This creates demand in the U.S. economy which consumes those cheap goods..

The essence of the 'crisis of capitalism' was the contradiction between wages and profits. Marx had correctly said that there is little possibility of an increase in wages providing the demand for the goods. But he had thought that the capitalist would not 'consume'. The capitalist's single concern was the pursuit of unending profits. He would invest and invest and produce more and more. The Joint Stock Company has changed the meaning of the capitalist. If the stockholder is the capitalist, then he may well consume rather than invest his dividends. Just as the feudal lords shared their wealth with their manorial staff, England shared colonial loot with her workers, so the modern corporation can share its profits with its stockholders.

This means that the 'workers' will be reduced to paupers across the world. The world economy will collapse in so far as it is based on worker's incomes. However, the recessionary tendency created by the declining wages could be compensated by the increased consumption from dividend incomes.

The question that remains is whether the people of the developing countries will accept lower wages? This is a social issue. The feudal lords could persuade the serfs to live a life of frugality amidst their extravagance. The spin masters of the developed countries can similarly persuade the workers of the developing countries to accept low wages. The leaders of the developing countries often are happy in this situation just like Indian Princes saved their skin by mortgaging the country to the British. The challenge before intellectuals is to counter the spin that low wages are destiny of developing countries.

This Chapter is adapted from the following articles:
"Why a global recession is unavoidable," *Japan Times,* July 4, 1998.

"The limits of U.S.-led economic growth," *Japan Times,* November 11, 1999.

"Whither globe.com," *The Pioneer,* October 3, 2000.

"Why are banks collapsing," *News Time,* October 23, 1998.

"Fall in gold price," *The Daily,* July 22, 1999.

"At last, Marx's crisis of capitalism solved," *Japan Times,* August 31, 1998.

2

The Roots of Inequity

The developing countries hold about 80 percent of the global natural resources but have only 20 percent share of global income. This anomaly arises because the developed countries have dominant control over world's capital and technology. They have acquired control of world capital substantially due to colonial exploitation. They created new technologies by investing monies obtained from this route.

The developing countries will have to redress this anomaly by acquiring greater share of world capital and technology. The starting point, however, will be to use their control over natural resources to extract higher prices for their products like OPEC has done for oil.

The developed countries, however, try to distract our attention from this aspect. They are keen that developing countries accept small improvements in their income within this iniquitous world economic order. The developing countries must resist free trade in commodities and instead make cartels. Of course, this prescription is applicable to countries still struggling to stand in the global economy i.e. those who cannot face free trade. The situation of countries like India in the new century is different. They can possibly win competition in the global economy and make a win upon the economies of the developed countries. This prescription does not apply to them.

The Roots of Inequality

The imbalances in the global economy towards the beginning of this century are caused by the flow of wealth of developing countries to the West through accumulation of large reserves by India and China and investment of oil income in the West by the Arab countries.

Globalization was expected to lead to flow of Western capital to the developing countries. That would be a win-win situation for both parties. Western countries would get higher profits while developing countries would get factories, employment and income. But exactly the opposite is happening. Governments of developing countries are sending large amounts of their wealth to the Western countries to accumulate large forex reserves. The flow of investment from the West is, on the other hand, turning out to be meagre. The net result is outflow of our wealth to the developed countries.

Initially it appears the Western countries are responsible for this imbalance. They could make more investment in the developing countries and rectify this imbalance. But the same holds good for our government. Our government is voluntarily sending its income to the Western countries to accumulate forex reserves far in excess of the requirements equal to six month's imports. Our government has also encouraged Indian citizens to make investments in foreign countries by liberalizing rules for making remittances and is steadily moving towards making the rupee fully convertible. This is beneficial in our world in the 21st century. But the same policy was not beneficial in the 1990s for us and is not beneficial for other developing countries in the 21st century.

The developing countries should bring back their excess forex reserves. They must sell U.S. Government Treasury Bonds and break the U.S. dollar. Weakening of the dollar will encourage private investors to bring back their money. This will prevent outflow of our wealth.

We should encourage FDI only in areas where we get advanced technologies and which have a positive indirect impact on employment. A technology- and employment impact assessment must be made mandatory for all FDI proposals. These assessments must be made public and objections invited before sanctioning the proposals. Then FDI will not come in unnecessary areas, MNCs will not send huge amounts as profit repatriations and outflow of our wealth will not take place.

The Western countries are earning huge amounts from investments made in the developing countries and using this income to import our goods. Say, Lever Brothers made investments in India. Hindustan Lever repatriated 100 Pounds to England out of profits earned in India. Lever Brothers imported Basmati rice with these 100 Pounds. The net result is that India's exports are more than imports by 100 Pounds. India will have a surplus of 100 Pounds on the trade account and a deficit of 100 Pounds on capital account. This is opposite to the logic of globalization which called for more imports of machinery and technology from the West into the developing countries. But this outflow occurs in the long run when profit repatriation starts. In the short run there is inflow of foreign capital when Lever Brothers sends foreign investment for establishing its factories.

The second imbalance is that many developing countries are exporting more and importing less. (India's position in the early part of the 21st century is different. India is receiving huge remittances by expatriates thus her imports are higher than exports. But the situation of most developing countries is not so fortunate.) But we are ourselves to blame for exporting our resources. Economists have spread the misinformation that exports are the route to prosperity. Various organizations like APEDA and CAPEXIL are working to increase our exports. These economists did not ask the country to import more at lower price and export more at higher price. Instead they said we should export more, even if the price is low. The imbalance in our current account is a result of this export orientation promoted by our government.

We should reckon development by measuring increase in imports instead of exports. The British laid a huge network of railways in the country, expanded our exports and destroyed our economy.

Leaders of poor developing countries are doing this favourite work of the Western countries with gusto. They should encourage imports. Exports in necessary amounts will take place automatically.

The third imbalance is that Western countries are providing huge agricultural subsidies that are depriving our farmers of the benefits from world trade. But we should ask, wherefrom did the Western countries get the money to pay these huge subsidies? Our government too could give huge subsidies if that could lead to development. Truth is that the Western countries are earning huge amounts from their monopoly over advanced technologies. For example, Bill Gates has become the richest person in the world because patents protection has been provided to the Windows software. The Western countries are making huge profits from their monopolistic control of technologies and are using part of that income to pay agricultural subsidies to their farmers. The solution is to demand loosening of the patents laws in the WTO.

The fourth imbalance in the global economy arises from increasing prices of oil. Oil exporting countries like Saudi Arabia and Kuwait are depositing a big part of the oil incomes in the Western countries. The money paid by India for the import of oil thus reaches the Western countries. Prima facie the oil exporting countries are responsible for this imbalance. But the question is this: why do we not make cartels like OPEC for commodities being exported by us? We could join with Malaysia to make a cartel for the export of rubber, with Bangladesh for jute, Sri Lanka for tea and Brazil for coffee. Then the loss incurred by us due to the high price of oil would be neutralized by the higher income from the exports of rubber, jute, tea and coffee.

The spin managers of the West seem to do a wonderful job of persuading leaders of developing countries to send their wealth to the developed countries. The developing countries should prevent this. However, this prescription is not applicable to the emerging economies like India and China. They are generating enough wealth that they can afford to give away monies to the West. This outflow creates a noose around the economies of the West that can later be used to turn the tables. But the poor developing countries should avoid taking this route since outflow of their wealth will make a strong negative impact on their situation immediately.

80/20 Misdistribution of Resources

The conditions of the workers are deteriorating across the globe. The situation is particularly bad in the developing countries where 80 percent of the global population survives on 20 percent of global resources. Previously man relied on wood or charcoal for fuel. The availability of biomass was greater in the developing countries hence there was greater concentration of population in these areas. At that time the developed countries may have had 20 percent people consuming about 20 percent of the world's known resources.

Then steam engine was invented in England. It made it possible to mine coal lying deep in the earth. The steam engine gave advantage to the developed countries by making a huge addition to the exploitable resources in those countries. This led to an increase in global inequity. Colonial loot perpetuated this inequity. In this way 20 percent people living in developed nations began to consume 80 percent of the world's resources.

Such imbalances have arisen many times in the history of mankind. Most of the people of the Indian subcontinent lived in the Indus basin before 10th century BC. Most of the known natural resources such as grasslands were located in the area around the Indus and the five rivers of Punjab. Eighty percent people of the subcontinent lived in the Indus basin and probably consumed about 80 percent of the known resources. Conversely, 20 percent forest-dwellers of the Ganges basin consumed about 20 percent of the known resources.

The invention of iron tools made a decisive difference. It became possible to clear the dense jungles of the Ganges basin. As a result, the resources at the command of the forest-dwellers of the Ganges basin multiplied manifold and these 20 percent people now commanded much more than 20, say 80 percent of the known natural resources. At the same time, some of the rivers such as the Jamuna flowing westward changed their course and began to flow eastward through the Ganges basin. The share of natural resources of the Indus basin reduced while those of the Ganges basin increased.

An 80/20 misdistribution like that prevailing between the developed and developing countries obtaining presently was created. But this misdistribution was soon rectified. Migration of people took place from the Indus to the Ganges basin. The population in the Ganges basin increased while that in the Indus basin declined. The higher per capita resource endowment of the Ganges basin was neutralized by immigration and a new equality between population and resource endowment was established.

The steam engine and other technologies have led to a similar misdistribution in the twentieth century and after. The resources available to the people residing in the developed countries have increased while those available to the people of the developing countries have declined. The straightforward solution to this is to allow migration of people from the developing countries to the developed countries. But the developed countries have prevented such migration. It is like the forest dwellers of the Ganges basin preventing immigration of the people from the Indus valley.

There are two ways of solving this problem. One is to ignore the 80/20 misdistribution and to make minor improvements in the conditions of the developing nations within this iniquitous situation. The second approach is to remove the 80/20 misdistribution and establish global equality.

To explain, the problem of misdistribution of resources in a village can be seen in two ways. One, the landlord can be asked to meet the basic needs of the workers while they remain bonded labourers. Two, land reforms can be implemented and land given to the tiller. The former approach leads to "amelioration" of poverty while the latter leads to its "removal."

The ILO had constituted a World Commission on the Social Dimension of Globalisation. The report of the Commission acknowledges: "From the perspective of developing countries the absence of a multilateral framework for the cross-border movement of people reflects yet another gap in the rules governing the global economy. Many of them maintain that freer migration to the industrialized world would be a swift and powerful means of increasing the benefits they receive from globalisation. From a labour perspective, the lack of a multilateral framework on migration is a clear illustration of the imbalance in the current rules of the game. While the rights of foreign investment have been increasingly strengthened in the rules set for the global economy, those of migrant workers have received far less attention."

But instead of taking the issue to its logical conclusion and asking for free movement of labour, the Commission back-tracks and gives an apology; "We have already referred to the significant potential benefits, both for the migrants themselves, and for the countries of origin and destination. But this needs to be tempered by the recognition of the potential costs such as the displacement of local workers, the disruption of labour market institutions and social protection systems, and the weakening of social cohesion."

This is like the people of the Ganges basin saying after the discovery of iron tools that they would not allow immigration from the Indus valley because it may lead to displacement of their forest habitats and disruption of their forest-based lifestyles. This exposes the true imperialist character of the United Nations' agencies like the ILO. If the world is becoming a village then why the fruits of the global orchard should be eaten mainly by the industrial nations?

The objective of ILO is not to remove the 80/20 misdistribution at its very roots. Rather, the objective is to ensure that the basic needs of the workers of the developing countries are met so that they do not revolt and the 80/20 misdistribution is maintained safe and secure for the industrial nations.

The developing countries should realise that economic policies pursued by them towards the beginning of this century will not rectify the misdistribution of world incomes. However, a different circumstance now prevails for emerging economies like India and

China. They can possibly beat the developed countries in their own game and must apply their mind to the conversion of the existing model in their favour instead of opposing the model in totality.

Wages Race to Bottom

Globalization assumes that the demand from developed countries will continue to pull the global economy forward indefinitely. But the economic leadership of the developed countries is slowly but inexorably being eroded. They may not provide demand for the goods of the developing countries indefinitely.

There is a deep relationship between technology and economy. A major technological advance like that of the steam engine ushers in an era of rapid investment. New opportunities for investment are suddenly opened up. Mines can go deeper because steam engines can easily haul up the coal. Steam-powered looms can produce more cloth. Ships can be made bigger if they are powered by steam engines.

Such technological innovation confers a special advantage upon the pioneer. It can charge high prices for its goods because other competitors need time to catch up. Until then, it can pay its workers higher wages and the cost can be passed on to the market. These "pioneer" wages also increase the demand in their market. Further demand is generated by new investments in the new technologies, for example in the manufacturing of steam engines for sale across the globe. This leads to an increase in their income and consumption.

Soon, however, competition catches up. Steam engines begin to be built in other countries. There is global competition. The price of steam engine in the global market declines. It is no longer possible for the pioneer to pass on the high wages paid to its workers to the market. The pioneer wage comes under pressure. The demand for consumption and investment declines. Thus there arises a fundamental imbalance. Production increases because of new investments but demand declines due to global equalization of prices and wages.

The ultimate cause of the Asian crisis of the nineties was that income of workers worldwide—the ultimate source of consumption demand—was declining. A global market means that wages will stabilize at the level paid by the lowest player (plus transportation costs). The result is that the real wages of U.S. workers are falling, the welfare state is crumbling in Europe and production is constantly seeking ever-lower-wage economies within East-Asia.

This decline is not immediately visible because of the pioneer effect. The pioneering countries, the U.S., in particular, that spearheaded the latest technological change, can pay high wages and pass on the consequences to the global market until others have caught up. Thus U.S. IT companies could pay high wages and charge higher prices for their wares in the nineties. Other competitors had not yet caught up. When they did—aided, in part, by globalization—these wages could only fall.

True, there was an increase in wages in the East Asian economies as well. But such an increase did not stand alone. These wages rose on the coattails of foreign investments and exports which, in turn, were contingent on even increasing wages in the developed countries.

U.S. imports have to decline in the same proportion as U.S. workers are deprived of their presently high wages because of global competition. Thus the world economy faces a basic contradiction between increasing investments by- and reduced demand from the developed countries. The developing countries must embrace protectionism and develop their own internal markets. The situation of emerging economies is different. India is making huge outward foreign investments. India can possibly turn the tables on the developed countries within the present model of globalization. But India has reached this fortunate position by rejecting free-for-all globalization recommended by the developed countries. Thus developing countries should resist all-encompassing globalization and first improve their situation by adopting protectionism, rejecting foreign investment, etc.

Globalization cannot Work by Compensation

Most economists hold that globalization is beneficial for all stakeholders just as trade between two persons is beneficial for both. The argument is correct if globalization is all encompassing and permits free movement of labour from one country to another. In that case a person living in an area bereft of any comparative advantage can migrate to another area and make a living. But this argument fails when free movement of labour is prohibited. It is possible that some countries may not have comparative advantage in *any* sector. In that case globalization becomes a loss proposition for them. They can get cheap imported products produced at lower cost from other countries but they do not have income to buy those goods. All the farms and factories in Timbuktu can be closed because the cost of production is high according to global standards and the people of that country are then left to rot within their borders.

Gandhiji promoted the production of Khadi even though the cost of production was higher than machine-made cloth imported from Manchester. Gandhiji rejected cheap goods because they came with British control of our economy. It was better, he said, for India to produce expensive Khadi than buy cheap imported cloth. Similarly free trade is harmful for the village potter. Availability of cheap aluminium and plastic pots has taken away his livelihood. The women indeed have to carry lesser load but the potter has no sales anymore. It is better for the potter that women continue to buy his earthen pots so that he can make a living. Thus free trade or globalization is not beneficial for every stakeholder. Some stand to loose.

The same holds for countries. Timbuktu may not have the capacity to compete with Indian software and Chinese textiles. Their software companies and textile factories will close down if they embrace globalization. They may also not be able to compete with cheap Australian wheat, Indian tea and Brazilian sugar. It is possible they may not have competitive advantage in *any* commodity. Globalization for them means that their factories and farms would close down since their cost of production is high. Their people will have to accept lower wages to reduce their cost of production and to compete with cheap imported goods. They would be better off remaining a protected economy where high-cost production of wheat and textiles can go on behind protectionist barriers.

This problem does not arise if free movement of natural persons is allowed. In that case the people of Timbuktu would migrate to India or China and work in the efficient factories in these countries. But globalization does not permit this. The people of Timbuktu are hemmed-in within their national borders while cheap imported goods are allowed free entry. The result is lower wages and starvation since they have no means available to make their livelihoods.

Professor Joseph Stiglitz of Columbia University accepts that globalization need not be a win-win situation for all the players. He acknowledges that there will be some losers. But he says that globalization can still be beneficial for all if those benefiting from globalization are willing to compensate the losers. The situation is similar to the people living in the submergence areas of dams. They loose their lands. But the same dam becomes beneficial for them if they are given adequate compensation.

This theory would be applied by Gandhiji as follows: Free trade in textiles would be beneficial for India if the textile mills of Manchester were willing to compensate the weavers of India for the loss of their livelihoods.

The problem is that globalization will have to be resisted in order to get such compensation. Experience suggests that people in submergence areas get compensation only when they oppose the dams. Gandhiji could have asked the textile mills of Manchester to provide compensation to the Indian weavers. But in order to demand such compensation he would have to first organize Indian weavers and oppose imports of machine-made cloth. Gandhiji could not demand such compensation if he had agreed to free trade. The present model of globalization prohibits such resistance to imports. Thus the very basis of organizing the losers is eliminated. Globalization has to be first negated for compensatory globalization to work.

Second, the continuity of such compensation is difficult to ensure. Suppose Gandhiji was successful in securing compensation for Indian weavers from the textile mills of Manchester. In a few years their looms would become unworkable because of disuse. The new generation will not learn weaving. The ability of India to make her own cloth will be reduced. In that situation it would make little sense for Manchester to continue to provide compensation to Indian weavers. Farmers in the U.S. are provided compensation for not cultivating their lands. But this compensation is paid only if they keep their lands in cultivable condition. Similarly, the losers would have to keep their inefficient industries in working condition to claim such compensation perpetually. That is contrary to the concept of efficiency on which globalization rests. The cost incurred in maintaining inefficient looms will be a net loss for the global economy.

Third, a global government is required to calculate the level of compensation that people of 200-odd countries have to receive or pay. This government should have the power to enforce its decision on all countries. Presently the Security Council of the United Nations is discharging this role. But that is not a representative institution. Many countries such as North Korea and Israel are not willing party to the decisions of the Security Council. This approach is dangerous because the capture of the world government by the rich and powerful countries can debilitate the poor countries. Thus compensatory globalization requires that first a global democratic government be installed. Until this is done it would be better for the weaker countries to opt out of globalization and to protect their high-cost economies from cheap imports.

Globalization is harmful for a large number of countries that do not have a clear competitive advantage in some sector. These countries would do well to erect protectionist barriers. This is what Gandhi had advised. The people of India would get at least high-cost Khadi to wear in a protected economy. They would run naked in a global economy.

It may be mentioned for avoiding confusion that this author does not support the idea of a global government. The point regarding the necessity of global government is made above to make the limited point that the philosophy of compensation cannot work without this precondition being fulfilled. It is an altogether different issue whether a global government should be made or not. This author's perception is that the dangers of manipulation of a global government are much greater than the benefits from increased efficiency etc. A multipolar world with governments in friction is better likely to lead to good global governance.

Mischievous Raising of the Issue of Domestic Inequality

Developing countries have to fight inequity on two fronts simultaneously—domestic and global. The common man is affected directly by the distribution of income within his country thus there is need to remove domestic inequity. At the same time, 20 percent of the people living in the developed countries consume 80 percent of the world's resources. This global inequity too has to be removed.

Which of these should be tackled first? Should the people of the developing countries first cooperate with their leaders, however iniquitous, and redress global inequity; or, they should first seek domestic equity and deal with the global issue later?

Mainstream economists give higher priority to domestic inequity. Prof. Amartya Sen has raised this issue in a novel way. He is a strong advocate of global redistribution from the rich to poor countries in order to establish fairness in the world economy. But he says that the donor countries should also peer into the recipient developing countries and examine the equity of the recipient country's domestic governance. In other words global redistribution is made contingent on domestic redistribution taking place simultaneously. He argues that if aid is given to developing countries having elitist governance then the aid strengthens the elite versus the common man. Aid then, becomes a tool in the hands of repressive regimes. In other words, the nature of domestic governance takes precedence over global redistribution. Global equity is put on the backburner till domestic equity is ensured.

Following the same logic, Professor John Connor of Purdue University says that the developing countries should not be encouraged to make OPEC-like cartels to raise the prices of their commodity exports because the incomes from these cartels can be misused to strengthen the domestic elite at the expense of the people. OPEC is a case in point. The incomes received by the oil-exporting countries have strengthened their ability to either 'buy out' the allegiance of local leaders or to repress them. The final beneficiary of the cartel has often been the ruling elite rather than the common man.

Professor Connor says that the free market would deprive such rulers and forced them to reform their domestic governance. They would not have the money to buy out petty leaders and stifle the demand for better governance from the people. They would have had to institute deeper economic reforms leading to better conditions for the people.

Gandhiji thought differently on this issue. He had a long and interesting exchange with Rabindranath Tagore who had opposed his slogan of Swadeshi. In 1921 Tagore had written; "Alien government in India is a veritable chameleon. Today it comes in the guise of the Englishman; tomorrow perhaps as some other foreigner; the next day, without abating a jot of its own virulence, it may take the shape of our own countrymen... The boycott of Manchester had raised the profits of the Bombay mill-owners to a super-foreign degree. And I had then to say: 'This will not do, either; for it is also of the outside...'" Here Tagore, like Amartya Sen, placed domestic good governance before global good governance. Independence could wait till we were able to ensure that the Indian Government that takes over would be just.

Gandhiji had replied that there is a difference between the profits of the English- and Indian businessmen. The fruits of the profits of Indian businessmen fell on the soil of this country while the fruits of profits of English businessmen fell on foreign soil. Thus, while recognizing the need to control the 'super-profits', it is urgent to stop extraction of our resources to the West even if it involved domestic inequity. Gandhiji had built a grand alliance including Indian businessmen and prices to throw the British out of India. He ignored the iniquitous behaviour of these allies in order to first expel the

British from Indian soil. Gandhiji said that the global issue had to be settled first. He did not first settle scores with Indian businessmen and princes.

Gandhiji thought that the transfer of India's resources to England would prevent relief for the people because there would remain little wealth in the country for redistribution. Thus, Gandhiji took up the question of global equity first while being ever alert about the domestic issues. It may be possible to redress domestic inequity after the British were expelled. But it would be very difficult to expel the British after domestic businesses had been made accountable. The Indian economy would become weak in the process and not be able to stand up to the British. The path shown by Gandhiji was the correct one.

We must see increasing inequity in our country in this context. It is true that the common man has got little relief. But this is our domestic problem. We should not discredit the improving stature of India in the world for this reason. This is the teaching of Mahatma Gandhi. The developing countries must not get distracted by the Western harangue about their domestic situation. The first target must be to beat the developed countries. Domestic inequality can be managed later.

Millennium Development Goals Distract from Redressing Inequality

The United Nations launched the Millennium Development Goals (MDG) in eight areas: poverty, primary education, women's equality, child mortality, maternal health, disease, environment and a global partnership for development in the nineties. There has been improvement in parameters such as that of poverty. It has to be examined, however, whether this improvement comes along with a basic solution of that problem. The cancer patient certainly gets relief by taking analgesic. But his true treatment lies in radiotherapy. Administering analgesics without radiotherapy can lull him into believing that treatment is afoot, dissuade him from taking the right treatment and worsen his situation in the long run.

The developing countries hold 80 percent of the world's natural resources but their share in the world income is only 20 percent. The prices of goods produced by them are declining due to competition among them. On the other hand the prices of the goods produced by the developed countries are increasing behind the protective wall of patents laws. The price of coffee, tea, rubber and cotton are declining but Bill Gates is selling his Windows software at high prices.

Former UN General Secretary Kofi Annan recognized the problem. In his report on MDGs he said, "The long term downward trend and volatility in non-fuel commodity prices continue to pose a major challenge to the exporting countries," and asked that the "international community should renew its efforts to alleviate these problems by improving existing mechanism and considering new approaches." But Annan was spectacularly silent on what these 'new approaches' may be. The result is that this crucial problem is relegated to cold storage. Clearly, the United Nations is disinterested in the solution of the basic problem of poverty of the developing countries and busy in administering analgesics.

Truly, the basic problems are getting worse. Proof of the same is available in Annan's report on the attainment of the Millennium Development Goals. There has been an increase in unemployment in all developing regions except for a marginal improvement in Africa since the MDGs were accepted. The unemployment rate of young people aged 15-24 years in Latin American increased from 12.4 percent in 1993 to 16.6 percent in 2003. The same story is repeated in Eastern Asia, Southern Asia, South-eastern Asia, Western Asia, Oceania and Commonwealth of independent states. Interestingly the situation in developed countries shows improvement with unemployment down from 16.7 percent to 14.6 percent. Another indicator is that the percentage of goods admitted free of duty by the developed countries from developing countries has declined from 62 percent in 2000 to 57 percent in 2002.

Annan does not discuss in his report why inequality among the developing and developed countries is increasing. He repeatedly stresses that there has been improvement in the Millennium Goals in the areas of poverty, education etc. Grahame Thompson of the Open University explains the politics of this approach thus: "The emphasis on 'poverty' allows the issue of 'inequality' to be backgrounded. There has been a desperate flurry of activity to bolster the 'we have all benefited from globalisation' thesis with a display of evidence that absolute poverty has been reduced internationally (or not got worse). But international inequalities are a somewhat different matter and here the evidence is much less sure footed. Indeed, it looks as though the trend in international inequalities has worsened during this period of globalization."

Developing countries should consider throwing out all UN agencies which distract us from measures to solve our basic problem of poverty. This applies equally to developing and emerging economies. If we listen to The UN we shall remain in servitude through the next millennium.

This Chapter is adapted from the following articles:

"The wrong rights," *The Pioneer,* July 11, 2000.
"Which comes first, domestic or global inequity?" *Businessline,* March 17, 2004.
"Fruits of labour," *Statesman,* July 13, 2004.
"Kofi Annan's tears on poverty but silence on growing inequality," *Dalit Voice,* February 16-28, 2005.
"Globalization cannot work by compensation," 2006. Publication details unavailable.

3

The Politics of Inequity

The world order prevailing towards the beginning of this century is unjust. The dominant countries will not let go of their dominance without a war. The quest for peace within this world order indirectly becomes endorsement of the existing injustice. Thus, war is a necessary part of establishment of a just world order.

The choice before India is to join the rich and powerful, promote 'peace' and try to snatch more within the unjust world order; or to lead the developing countries in establishing a just world order.

Some leaders of the developing countries have resisted the present iniquitous world order and challenged the might of the U.S. in particular. Small mistakes of these leaders are blown up by the spin masters of the West and such leaders are maligned and thrown out. The challenge before India is to resist such temptations and stick to the more difficult and tortuous route of establishing global dharma.

'Peace' is the Smokescreen for Perpetuating Injustice

Everyone wants peace. But peace can also be the cover for sustaining existing injustices. Mahatma Gandhi gave the slogan of non-violence as a tool for removing injustice. Many modern peace-seekers, however, give the slogan of peace without addressing the basic inequity of the global economy. The declaration of peace then becomes a declaration of injustice.

Let us understand why wars take place. Everyone seeks happiness. It seems that peace is the clear-cut route to achieving this. But many people find happiness in the acquisition of power and make wars in order to be happy. The warrior seeks war for his happiness while the common man seeks peace for his happiness. There arises a contradiction between the happiness of the warriors, who get happiness from war, and happiness of the non-warriors, who get happiness from peace.

The solution to this contradiction was found in our scriptures in the promotion of just war. The apostle of non-violence, Mahatma Gandhi, gave sanction to the Indian forces joining the British in their war against Nazi Germany. Not having joined that war would have meant that India becomes an accomplice to the injustices perpetuated by Hitler on the Jews.

The difficulty with the modern-day advocacy of peace is that it ignores the blatant injustices prevailing in the present world order. The five permanent members of the Security Council have unjustified veto over the affairs of the world. They have abrogated to themselves the right to intervene in the affairs of other nations in the guise of human rights violations. They use this right, however, only where their economic interests are at stake such as in Iraq and Kosovo, but abstain from a similar intervention when no economic benefits are to be had such as in Somalia and Rwanda.

The people of Tibet sought independence from China but the UN did not find it necessary to intervene there. When the people of Kashmir sought a similar right, the UN passed a resolution seeking plebiscite. The Red Indians of America sought the return of lands taken forcibly from them in violation of treaties from the European colonizers. The "boat people" of Haiti wanted to enter the U.S. They were prohibited. But the Jews were forcibly settled in Palestine against the wishes of the local people. The Jewish "boat people" were encouraged to enter Palestine.

Ethnic injustice to the people of Fiji was ignored while a similar injustice in Kosovo was sought to be remedied by armed intervention. A regional conflict between Iraq and Kuwait was sought to be remedied by armed intervention but a similar conflict between Somalia and Ethiopia was ignored. Blatant religious discrimination in the oil-rich Islamic countries of West Asia is routinely tolerated while isolated incidents in India are condemned. The list of such discriminatory treatments is endless. This is the true face of the "peace" that mankind has been able to secure in the last fifty years.

These fifty years have also seen little improvement in poverty in the poor countries. The Big Five sell their goods expensive and buy the goods of the poor countries cheap in the name of free trade. The Intellectual Property Rights regime was introduced in the WTO to serve the interests of the technology-rich North against those of the resource-rich South. "Peace," as it exists today, is an instrument of injustice.

The UN has declared 2001-10 as the decade of peace and non-violence. The Declaration speaks of peaceful resolution of conflicts through dialogue and cooperation. Let us say, the Red Indians engage in a dialogue with the European colonisers of America. If dialogue does not yield result, then what? The UN Declaration is silent. Presumably, those seeking redressal would be advised to live perpetually with the injustice and continue with dialogue.

The Declaration similarly speaks about "advancing understanding, tolerance and solidarity among all civilisation, peoples and cultures..." Fine indeed. But to what avail will be an understanding between the Pharmaceutical MNCs and the sick and the poor in the developing countries?

The Declaration says that peace is integrally linked to the "eradication of poverty and illiteracy and reducing inequalities within and among nations." But it does not say a single word about the terms of trade against the developing countries which are the source of the inequality among nations. The implication is that present inequality should be made a bit mellow to prevent any violent reaction from the deprived lest it lead to reaction such as the people of Haiti invading the coasts of the U.S. in big numbers.

The Declaration speaks of promotion "ways of life conducive to the promotion of peace among individuals, groups and nations." We know that most wars are fought over the control of scarce natural resources. The Western countries are today consuming resources far in excess of their reserves. They have to extract copper from Zimbabwe, rubber from Malaysia and tea from India. The 'way of life' which would promote peace would be to reduce the consumption of the West. But the UN Declaration does not recognize the linkage. What it means by a peaceful 'way of life' is that the people of the South should continue to transfer their resources to the North and live in their poverty peacefully. Only the severest of deprivations in areas close to those of the West would be "sanitised" in the name of poverty alleviation.

The people of the South, therefore, would be entirely justified in waging war for securing their equitable share in the world's resources and technologies that are under the control of the North.

In the same breath it must be recognized that the ultimate solution will come by introspection from within the West. The Western societies have become empty inside. There is an eerie discomfort. Indian philosophy of Yoga and thoughts on righteous management by Gurus such as Deepak Chopra are helping develop this consciousness. That is the correct approach in the long term. In the short term, however, the developing countries are justified in taking a more aggressive stance.

The other dimension is of rules of war. Megasthenes, the Greek ambassador to the court of Pataliputra, reports that in those days two kings would be fighting with each other while, within their eyesight, farmers would be tilling their fields. There existed a social consensus that "war" was a matter confined to the warriors. The common people should be left untouched by both sides. This social consensus was *dharma*.

A caveat is required here. The war mentioned by Megasthenes was between two kings who were both at the same level of technology etc. and sought to rule a country as their own abode. There was no transfer of resources or exploitation involved here. In such case, the local people have no moral responsibility in the war. They are not party to the exploitation of any foreign people. The wars of the present period, on the other hand, involve exploitation of one people by another. Thus the villagers on the side of the battlefield that Megasthenes saw are not a party to that war; but the persons who inhabited the World Trade Centre were morally responsible for the acts of the U.S. and stand on a qualitatively different footing.

What is required, therefore, is not peace but just war. There is no case for absolute peace. Peace implies perpetuation of the existing injustices. The developing and emerging economies should arm themselves and be ready for a global war.

Politics of Oil

Oil is the most accessible and inexpensive source of energy at the present. Sixty-five percent of the world reserves of oil are found in West Asia while 78 percent is consumed in OECD countries comprising mainly of U.S. and West European countries. It is necessary for the OECD countries to secure supply of oil. India too wants to increase our consumption of energy. Our domestic production of oil is limited and we have to increasingly depend on imported oil. The share of imported oil in our consumption has increased from 37 percent in 1990 to 70 percent in 2001 and is slated to increase further.

The oil supplying countries of West Asia can be broadly clubbed into two groups that have quite different views of the world economy. One group is led by Saudi Arabia, which is content with hitching its wagon to the powerhouse of the American economy. The Saudis have invested much of their incomes from oil in the U.S. The dollars received as payments for oil were used to buy shares in the New York Stock Exchange, properties in Manhattan or U.S. Treasury Bonds. The money paid by the U.S. for oil imports actually never left the shores of that country. The American purchasers deposited the money in Saudi bank accounts say with Bank of America. Saudis used that money to buy U.S. Treasury Bonds. In this exchange the U.S. got oil while the Saudis got ownership of U.S. assets. The U.S. paid for the imported oil by issuing paper money in the form of Treasury Bonds.

These investments have created an interest in the Saudis of maintaining stability of the U.S. economy. A higher price of oil is not necessarily beneficial for them. Higher price gets them more money from the sale of oil. But it can also derail the U.S. economy, lead to collapse of the dollar and to huge losses on their investments. Higher price of oil is no longer a win-win situation for the Saudis. Their situation is like that of the cottage soap manufacturer who has invested in shares of Hindustan Lever. He is happy if Hindustan Lever makes more profits and the price of its shares goes up. He forgets that increased sale of Lux soap kills his business. But he does not see the link of higher price of shares of Hindustan Lever with his livelihood and rejoices when the company makes more profits. Similarly, the Saudis are happy if the U.S. economy is buoyant and price of dollar goes up. They forget that increased price of dollar will get them less dinars for their exports of oil. They rejoice when the dollar rises and U.S. economy grows. The Saudis have no problem with the 20 percent of the people in OECD countries consuming 80 percent of the world's resources. They are happy if they can get a larger share of the 80 percent income of the OECD countries.

The other group of West Asian countries is led by Iraq and Iran. Saddam Hussein often asked at international forums why 20 percent of the people of the OECD countries were consuming 80 percent of the world's resources. He used Iraqi petrodollars for the improvement of education in his country, for which he was awarded by UN agencies, and for building armaments instead of investing in U.S. Treasury Bonds. One of the reasons for Iraq's attack on Kuwait was that the latter was obstructing Iraqi efforts to increase the price of oil in OPEC. Prime Minister Ahmedinijad of Iran shares the same worldview in asking why Israel should be carved out in West Asia instead of Germany or America. This group has nothing to loose and all to gain if the U.S. economy collapses under the weight of high price of oil.

India has a difficult choice to make. It has to embrace one of the groups to secure its supplies of West Asian oil. Prime Minister Man Mohan Singh appears to be closer to the Saudi camp. The Saudi King was made Chief Guest at the Republic Day ceremonies. India voted for referring Iran to the Security Council at the International Atomic Energy Agency. Man Mohan Singh has not reacted to U.S. objections on the proposed Iran-Pakistan-India pipeline. On the other hand, former Petroleum Minister Mani Shankar Aiyar appears to have embraced the Iraq-Iran group. He actively promoted the idea of Iran-Pakistan-India pipeline. He also entered into exploration and production contracts with Russia, Vietnam, Iran, Myanmar and Cuba. The External Affairs Ministry often disparaged his efforts to build bridges with Iran.

Then there is a China angle to the issue. The U.S. sees China as a threat and aims to encircle it. Man Mohan Singh seems to concur. He is willing to join the U.S.-led alliance against China. Aiyar, on the other hand, saw China as a friend. He proposed the extension of the Iran-Pakistan-India pipeline to China. Under his leadership India and China made a joint bid for oil assets in Syria. The U.S did obviously not like this. Iftikhar Gilani wrote in *Daily Times*, "Aiyar's removal from the oil ministry is widely seen as a result of intense pressure from domestic private lobbies and the Americans, who were not happy with his left-oriented view of the global economy." Aiyar has now been replaced with Murli Deora, who, says Gilani, "is known to be pro-U.S. and often throws parties for visiting U.S. legislators." It appears, therefore, that Man Mohan Singh has followed the U.S. diktat in removing Aiyar from the Petroleum Ministry.

The need for developing and emerging countries is to develop cartels and tilt the distribution of global resources in their favour.

Military Technology Cannot be Monopolized

Iran has restarted its nuclear enrichment programme. This follows the nuclear explosions made by India, Pakistan and North Korea. These steps have been taken by Iran, India, Pakistan and North Korea within the confines of international law. India and Pakistan had not signed the Nuclear Non-proliferation Treaty (NPT). North Korea had legally pulled out of the same in 2003. Iran has signed the NPT but has the right to develop nuclear energy sources within it. Yet prominent world powers have imposed sanctions against India, Pakistan, and North Korea after their nuclear explosions and against Iran for enriching uranium for possible use in nuclear weapons.

The sanctions imposed against India failed. Rather they had the salutary effect of prompting India to make even more efforts at indigenous development of technologies such as the supercomputer. Sanctions were in place against North Korea for more than a decade yet that country managed to make a nuclear explosion. The proposed sanctions against Iran are likely to have a similar ending because the nature of technology is like the water of the sea. Technology spreads across all lands given time just as water spreads evenly across all oceans. The Big Five do not appear to understand this reality and are trying to artificially restrict the spread of technology and to keep their exclusive control intact.

President Kalam, in reply to a question on the impact of economic sanctions, says, "I believe that Indians have always been able to successfully combat such challenges. Earlier, the West had imposed sanctions on us in the fields of nuclear and missile technology. That taught us to become self-reliant in these areas and today we do not need their help at all."

In his book *Vision 2020*, he writes: "Just as there has been a racial element in human history, it would appear that this element is entering into the technological arena too. Developed nations feel that only they are capable of developing certain types of aerospace, missile and nuclear technology. But we should ignore this and go ahead with our technology development." Kalam goes on to explain that Indian space and defence technology is substantially indigenous and quite up to the world standards. In some areas it is better than the West. Our missile Prithvi, he says, "is comparable to any world class missile system, and probably is the best of its class in payload capability." This *Vision* applies equally to Pakistan, North Korea and Iran. In the result it is unlikely that sanctions will prevent the spread of nuclear technology.

The impact of sanctions depends upon the mental makeup of the target country. The child who gets beaten up by colleagues at school can respond by sitting glum at home or by joining a wrestling school. Likewise, the impact of sanctions depends upon the mental makeup of the leaders of the targeted country. A 1992 document of the U.S. Government's General Accounting Office titled *Economic Sanctions: Effectiveness as Tools of Foreign Policy* explains this succinctly: "Cultural characteristics of the target nation and international publicity can either enhance or weaken the effect of the measures. If the target nation has a strong shame and honour code, that is, if 'saving face' is important—or if sanctions receive substantial publicity, sanctions may create a backlash in the target nation, particularly if harsh, comprehensive measures are used from the onset of sanctions." The document goes on to point out that sanctions do not ruin the target nation's economy. Over time, the targeted country can develop new suppliers and markets, although at increased cost. For example, South Africa's apartheid regime, the target of multilateral boycotts, replaced most lost exports in 2 years, but incurred losses from discounts on the prices of its products and the added transportation costs required to develop alternative markets.

The U.S. Government report states that sanctions can also raise costs for the sanctioning nation such as lost profits of forgone exports and financial transactions and additional expenses from purchasing more expensive imports from alternative suppliers. This last point is important in the context of India. The U.S. needs Indian software programmers and outsourcing outfits to remain competitive in the global economy.

The upshot is that the sanctions against North Korea and Iran are likely to fail just as they did against India. The problem is likely to become more difficult in the coming times. S Nihal Singh reports that according to the International Atomic Energy Agency, 49 countries, other than the present nine, have the capacity to make the bomb. Brazil, South Africa and Japan have declared intention of reviving their nuclear programmes. The logical result of the tendency of technology to spread spontaneously and the ineffectiveness of sanctions is that nuclear technology will spread inevitably.

The nuclear powers had promised to work towards comprehensive nuclear disarmament while making the NPT. There has been little progress in that direction. That is to be expected because global disarmament would require the establishment of a world government in some form and that would dilute the powers of the five permanent members of the Security Council. The Big Five will thus want to perpetuate the present arrangement to hold on to their status notwithstanding its failure to prevent non-proliferation.

The present world political and economic structure rests on the police authority of the Security Council dominated by the U.S. It suits these powers that the present unjust economic structure wherein twenty percent of the people of the Western countries consume eighty percent of the world resources is perpetuated. The consumption of world resources by the Western countries rests, in large measure, on their control of advanced economic and military technologies. This control will weaken as demonstrated by the explosions made by India, Pakistan and North Korea. Thus the present unjust world economic order will not sustain. We must think of establishing a new world order.

India has two paths open to her. She can try to join the Big Five as envisaged under the nuclear agreement made with the U.S. It can join in perpetuating the injustice perpetrated by the Big Five by becoming the sixth member of this unholy alliance. The alternative is to challenge the present unjust world order. India can call a meeting of the nuclear powers and aspirants excluding the Big Five. This group should propose new rules for the control and management of nuclear technologies and negotiate with Big Five as a group. The success of nuclear non-proliferation will rest ultimately on convincing the aspirants that one is more secure by not making the bomb. Every household does not keep a gun for its safety because the costs of keeping a gun are more than the cost of obtaining security from the police. Likewise, we have to provide the nuclear aspirants security and access to technologies and make it beneficial for them not to make the bomb.

Developing countries should make efforts to acquire advanced technologies by adopting various measures like those adopted by

China, India, Iran, Pakistan and North Korea. They should not depend on the existing economic order to make available these technologies lets they pay for that which is soon likely to be available free.

Protectionism did not Fail North Korea

Free trade is beneficial for the upper classes. They get the opportunity to buyout companies in foreign countries and to export their goods. But this is not necessarily beneficial for the common man because economic growth has opposite effects on capital and labour. The availability of capital increases and its cost declines as seen in low rates of interest. However, the costs of labour increases as workers want to buy TVs and refrigerators. The logical result of low cost of capital and high cost of labour is that businessmen prefer to use more capital and less labour. That results in unemployment and low wages for the workers. Thus it is seen that the number of persons employed in the organized sectors in India is declining since 1997. The way to provide relief to the workers in this situation is to provide protection to selected labour-intensive goods from cheap machine-made imports. Protectionism, not free trade, is the correct strategy to raise wages of our people.

An argument against this view is that the wages in developed countries are high. If free trade should lead to lower wages then the wages of their workers should be low. My submission is that high wages in the developed countries are due to incomes extracted from the developing countries through TRIPS, technology cartels and other stratagems. Their high incomes are not due to adoption of free trade.

Another argument is that countries which have embraced protectionism are in dire straits. One example is that of North Korea. The conditions of the workers of this country remain difficult despite it having followed the policy of protectionism as suggested above.

The economic condition of North Korea was much better at the time of partition of that country in the late forties. Northern part of Korea is mountainous but has most minerals and water resources while southern part was mostly agricultural at that time. Korea was under Japanese occupation from 1910 to 1947. The Japanese built railways, mines and industries in the northern part with the objective of extracting these resources for use in Japan. At that time the northern part was 'developed' while the southern part was 'backward'. According to a document of the U.S. Library of Congress the rate of growth of North Korea was higher than that of South Korea till the sixties but it slipped thereafter and in early nineties the per capita income of North was meagre $1,038 dollar per capita against $5,569 for the South. The gap has since increased. It is estimated that the income of North Korea has actually shrunk by 1/3 during the last decade. The policy of protectionism has not delivered in North Korea.

In order to determine the efficacy of this policy, however, we have to examine other factors at play. One was excessive interference of the Government of North Korea in the economy. All industries, banks, transport, telecommunication and land were nationalized in 1958. Farm families were provided a small plot of no more than 160 square meters for their personal cultivation. This centralization failed to deliver as in Russia.

The second factor is that of government corruption. Bradley Martin says in his book *The Kim's North Korea* that strongman Kim Il Sung promoted those officers who supported accession of his son Kim Jong Il to power. Distant relatives of the Kim family were appointed to key positions. By the 1970s, "the Kim family and its allies had come to resemble the nobility (yangban) of Korea in the Middle Ages, living a life of secluded luxury in an otherwise poor country," says he. The country was not being run to create wealth for its people; rather it was being run to provide luxuries to small elite.

The benefits of protectionism were squandered away by the losses from excessive interference of the government in the economy and corruption of the ruling elite. That country now needs technology, capital and food from rest of the world and has exploded a nuclear device to enhance its bargaining power.

What lesson does this have for the developing countries? They are caught between the devil and the deep blue sea. Adoption of free markets does not help because businesses deploy more capital and less labour leading to unemployment and low wages for the masses. On the other hand, protectionism becomes a screen behind which domestic corruption can flourish as in North Korea. The only solution to this predicament is to adopt the policy of external protectionism along with domestic good governance. That is the lesson from North Korea. Of course, emerging countries like India can play the game differently. They can adopt the strategies of the developed countries and beat them in their own game.

War-readiness is an Indicator of Self-esteem

The consensus in the world community is that although CTBT legitimizes inequality between nations and leads to loss of self-esteem of the developing nations, these are facts of life. It is more important to get of with the tasks of economic development and poverty alleviation than to worry about such intangibles.

The underlying premise is that economic development is a matter of resources. Defence expenditures, including those on nuclear weapons, are squandering of scarce resources. Such waste must be avoided. The argument made is that CTBT helps in doing so. Thus, let us sign it and get on with economic tasks.

If this were true, countries with low-defence expenditures should have done better in economic growth. A comparison of countries with different levels of defence expenditures gives us an altogether different result, however. It turns out those countries with high defence expenditures have done better than those having low expenditures. More interestingly, they have done well in poverty alleviation as well.

Mr. Serageldin, vice-president of the World Bank, had given a list of countries incurring, low- and high defence expenditures in his book *Nurturing Development*. The low-defence expenditure countries mentioned by him were Brazil, Costa Rica, Zambia, Ghana, Mexico and Niger. According to World Bank data, their average defence expenditures were mere 2.7 percent of total government spending in 1993. The high-defence expenditure countries mentioned by him were China, Egypt, Ethiopia, Korea, Malaysia, Oman, Pakistan,

Peru, Sri Lanka and Zimbabwe. Their average defence expenditure was high at 21.3 percent.

We can compare the growth rates of the two groups of countries to ascertain whether those countries that have not squandered their resources have actually achieved higher rates of growth. It turns out that the low-defence expenditure countries had an average negative growth rate of (-) 0.6 percent against (+) 3.2 percent of the high-defence expenditure countries. The conclusion is that countries that have high-defence expenditure also have higher rates of growth.

The high-defence expenditure countries have also had more equitable distribution of incomes. The share of income of the poorest 20 percent population in low-defence expenditure countries was 4.3 percent. In the high-defence expenditure countries it was 6.7 percent. In other words, high-defence expenditures turn out to be equitous as well.

How could these results be explained? If the same money were to be invested in power generation or health facilities, certainly the growth should have been higher. But that is not the case.

To unravel this result we have to examine the link between defence expenditures and economy. Let us think of defence expenditure as a proxy for national self-esteem. A people having greater self-esteem are likely to spend more on defence. They would abhor the idea of depending on another for their own security. They are likely to have fewer resources left over for economic growth. But the same self-esteem also leads to a greater zest for life, a willingness to invest and grow. They are, therefore, likely to make better use of the limited resources that are left over.

Compare two farmers. Mr. Self Esteem invests in a fence around his field. He has less money left for fertilizers. But he uses that less money much more efficiently. He applies his own mind to decide what crop to grow, what fertilizer to apply, when and how. Mr. Dependence, on the other hand, relies upon his neighbours for his security. He depends upon others for deciding what crops to grow etcetera. He does have more money left over, but he uses it as dictated by others. The result is that Mr. Self Esteem grows a better crop although he had fewer resources.

There are two opposite effects of defence expenditures on economic growth. Directly, they lay claim on scarce resources and lead to reduced investment. Indirectly, however, they increase self-esteem and lead to better utilization of the limited resources.

The increase in growth from self-esteem is greater than the decrease due to lower availability of resources. It is for this reason the high-defence expenditure countries obtain higher growth as well as more poverty alleviation.

We have to examine how CTBT affects self-esteem. The Treaty provides that no nation would henceforth undertake nuclear tests. That means that the five nuclear-powers would be allowed to sit on their nuclear arsenals while other late comers, or those who have exercised self-restraint until now, will be permanently deprived of that option. The developing countries would accept that they remain perpetually inferior to the five nuclear powers. It is a direct attack on their self-esteem, and thereby on their growth potential. It is for this reason that the developing countries must not accept the CTBT.

Unfortunately, the debate on CTBT is being carried out in terms of security. Whether, nuclear weapons do indeed enhance security is indeed doubtful. But it is clear that accepting CTBT leads to loss of self-esteem.

The developing- and emerging countries should reject CTBT, NPT and other unequal treaties that affect their self-esteem. They should focus on better use of their fewer resources. That will lead to higher growth.

This is not to advocate every country building the nuclear bomb. That is a question of military strategy. It is possible for a small country to collapse under economic sanctions imposed by the powerful countries as has happened to Cuba. The trick lies in biting as much as one can chew. The point here is that one should not be swayed by the harangue that defence expenditures are 'bad' for the economy.

PIOs Against their Motherland

India has named the weather forecasting satellite Metsat after Kalpana Chawla who died in the Columbia disaster. Certainly a person who contributes to the advancement of science should be honoured. But it is also the responsibility of the scientist to find out the purposes for which her knowledge is used. The police do not exonerate the driver because he did not know about the criminal activity being undertaken by his employer. Similarly, an assessment of Kalpana Chawla should rest on the objectives of the U.S. space programme of which she was a part.

A joint vision statement issued by the U.S. military command clearly states that the objective of the U.S. is 'full spectrum dominance'. Tina Bell of *Women's International League for Peace and Freedom* pointed out in a discussion at the United Nations in 1998 that the U.S. was publicly committed to the peaceful uses of outer space. In a U.S. space command brochure, it is mentioned how the U.S. is going to 'dominate outer space'.

A Treaty was signed in 1967 prohibiting militarization of space. But the Treaty is weak. It only prohibits placement of nuclear or weapons of mass destruction in space. Pierce Cordon of the *U.S. Arms Control and Disarmament Agency* admitted, "It would be fair to say that it is not prohibited to put a rifle in orbit. I suppose it would not be prohibited to put some kind of missile up there that wouldn't have an ABM capability. If you think of anti-satellite weapons, it is not prohibited to put a launcher on the surface of the earth that could launch an anti-satellite warhead to knock down a satellite, or notionally to orbit such a system. That's not prohibited."

Bill Sulzman of *Global Network Against Weapons And Nuclear Power In Space* pointed out that the U.S. had bragged that the 1990-91 war against Iraq was the first space war: "They understand that when you collect information, select targets through the use of space, and then direct weapons to targets using space, you have the equivalent of a piece of the weapon being in space. A gun sight is a part of the gun. A spotter, who in the old days targeted artillery, was using a weapon and shared responsibility for the deaths that were caused. And so space already, in current military jargon and practice, has an important piece in the weaponised part of warfare, getting people killed and getting explosives sent to targets."

Karl Grossman, author of *The Wrong Stuff* said in a discussion: "The U.S. is clearly trying to dominate space. In the next two decades, new technologies will allow the fielding of space-based weapons; space-borne lasers with reasonable mass to affect many kills. It is a problem putting lasers in space, getting power for them. So a natural technology to enable high power is nuclear power in space. The TRW Corporation had been granted a $10 million contract to develop a pilot programme for a space-based laser."

The space has already been militarised. The U.S. is developing weapons to dominate the world through its control of space. Many countries, therefore, want to review the 1967 treaty to make it tighter and prevent such militarization of space. Marc Vidricaire, Counsellor at the Mission of Canada to the *Conference on Disarmament* said during the Disarmament Week 2000 at the UN, "In January 1998, Canada formally proposed negotiation in the Conference on Disarmament of a legally binding instrument for preventing an arms race in outer space. A review of the industry literature confirms that over a dozen states are at the present capable of placing an object in outer space. Many more have direct experience working with orbiting satellites. These states come from all regions. Obviously, the U.S.A. is the most advanced in this field, but the Russian Federation has a long and remarkable history in outer space, European nations also have this capability, as do China, India, Brazil and Japan. If it is possible to put an object in outer space, then it is also possible to put a weapon in outer space. The 1967 Outer Space Treaty prohibits the orbiting of weapons of mass destruction and the stationing of such weapons on the moon or any other celestial body. The continuing advance of technology, however, makes it possible to orbit conventional missile interceptors, or exotic weapons based on other physical principles (such as space-based lasers) capable of harming both space-based and land, sea or air-based targets. This fact was first noticed by a Canadian Prime Minister speaking at UNSSOD II when he called the 1967 Outer Space Treaty 'evidently inadequate' a mere fifteen years after its entry into force." Canada wants to open the discussion for making the 1967 Treaty stronger.

However, Pierce Corden of U.S. stated "The U.S. has not been persuaded that the multilateral arms control regime as it impacts on outer space should be augmented in order to maintain the strategic stability." The reasoning is clear. The U.S. is the most advanced in space warfare technologies and it is unwilling to accept any restrictions on its effort to gain global military supremacy through militarization of space. The Columbia was part of this large military strategy of the U.S. The experiments would enhance the military capability of the U.S. Kalpana Chawla, not only had she taken a U.S. citizenship and married an American, she had willingly participated furthering in these hegemonic ambitions of the U.S. She was part of the American space militarization and world conquest programme. God Bless her soul but the people of the developing countries should be aware of the consequences of such participation in the activities of the developed countries.

The developing countries should know that future wars will be fought in space and they should make efforts to acquire the relevant technologies.

Sunita William's Contribution to U.S.' Unilateral Control of Space

Following Kalpana Chawla, Sunita Williams went on a six-month journey in space abroad the International Space Station in late 2006. The Station is made with the joint efforts of U.S., Europe, Japan, Russia and Canada. Space efforts such as this have provided mankind with many benefits. The technologies of MRI and Cat Scan, for example, used so widely in the world of medicine, were developed out of efforts to enhance the pictures of moon taken during the Apollo space mission. Global Positioning System also evolved out of space research. One must give kudos to brave persons like Williams for these great advances.

The other aspect of such efforts is that of defence activities. Christopher Petras writes in *Air Force Law Review* of 2002 that only two platforms are currently available to make a manual assessment of space weapons—the Space Station and the U.S. Space Shuttle. Sunita Williams is U.S. Navy Commander hence it is safe to presume she is involved in the expansion of U.S. capabilities in the deployment of space weapons. Such expansion of military activities in space can be beneficial for mankind like the establishment of a police outpost on the deserted road crossing. But an outpost can also be used by the thief to watch the activities of police. We have to look at the objectives of establishing the post to determine whether it is beneficial or harmful for mankind. A bamboo bridge may be built on the stream by the dacoits to loot the village; or it can be built by a NGO to help village folk in reaching the market. The utility of the bridge has to be assessed in the context of its purpose. Likewise the value of the Space Station has to be assessed in relation to the objectives of its promoters.

In his remarks on the National Space Policy delivered at the George C. Marshall Institute, Washington, DC on December 13, 2006, Robert G. Joseph, Under Secretary for Arms Control and International Security of the U.S. Government elaborated on this. He said that the U.S. was more dependent on space-based technologies than other countries since it uses technologies like the Global Positioning System extensively. Many countries were making efforts to acquire the capability of destroying U.S. satellites in space. Thus, the U.S. should have the capability of defending its satellites. This statement should be read along with President George W Bush's doctrine that the U.S. has a natural right to make pre-emptive strikes against any country which threatens its interests. Mr. Joseph's comments indicate that the same doctrine is to be applied in space. The U.S. seeks to put weapons in space in order to gain the upper hand vis-à-vis its opponents in securing the safety of its satellites. It also seeks to develop the capacity to destroy satellites that threaten its interests. Navy Commander Sunita Williams is part of that effort.

This vision of militarization of space has been criticized by many observers. The argument is that one-sided militarization of space by the U.S. will fuel efforts by the opponents to acquire similar capabilities. This will lead to a race to nowhere and one that threatens the welfare of all humanity. Particular apprehension is that the debris from broken satellites can create a permanent threat to all future use of space.

In 1985 the U.S. had destroyed a spent satellite during a test effort. The target satellite broke into more than 200 pieces some of which fell into the ocean about 17 years later. A satellite war in which countries destroy each others' satellites can contaminate the space beyond use. The suggestion is that the U.S. enters into a multilateral agreement barring militarization of space instead of developing weapons to destroy opponent's satellites.

Peter N. Spotts, Staff writer of *The Christian Science Monitor* quotes Larry Wortzel, chairman of the U.S.-China Commission to the effect that space-empowered countries could agree on rules for behaviour in space. During the cold war, he notes, the U.S. and the Soviet Union agreed to keep hands off each other's reconnaissance and early-warning satellites. The Chinese have approached the State Department on this issue with no success so far. The U.S. is stonewalling efforts to make such an international agreement and is determined to pursue a unilateral militarization of space. Undersecretary Joseph confirmed this in his Marshal Institute lecture. He said the U.S. did not see the need for a new international treaty for demilitarization of space when no such threat was to be seen. The objectives of the U.S., he said, are to make available free use of space to all countries for peaceful purposes. The U.S. has thus appointed itself as the policeman of space. This assurance is not credible given the track record of that country in Vietnam, Afghanistan and Iraq. It is likely, therefore, that the militarization of space being undertaken by the U.S. will continue irrespective of what other nations may suggest.

This perspective of the U.S. is justified, however. A treaty is reliable only if there is a credible mechanism to punish the violator. A rouge country can develop and deploy space weapons behind the smokescreen of such a treaty in absence of military deterrence. It follows that militarization of space is inevitable and the U.S. is justified in proceeding in that direction unilaterally.

That is the U.S.' perspective. We in India must assess these activities, and the role of the likes of Sunita Williams, from our standpoint. Williams has dared Indians to dream as her. In other words, she wants every Indian to cooperate in the U.S.' efforts to develop its unilateral control over space—including U.S.' superiority over India's use of space just as ICS officers caught and put freedom fighters behind bars or just as the Maharaja of Jaipur attacked Shivaji at the behest of the Mughal Emperor.

I have no quibbles with the U.S.' space programme. But peace-loving Indians can either support the U.S. in developing its unilateral control over space; or they can support India in developing her space capabilities and developing a multi-polar space order. Williams, of course, wants to strengthen the U.S.' control over space. Kudos to Williams for her great achievement. It would be better, though, if it was tempered with a pro-developing country perspective.

Professional Dharma of PIOs

The Indian Government annually honours Persons of Indian Origin (PIO) from developing countries like Zimbabwe, Fiji and Guyana. Honouring PIOs from developing countries is a step in the sight direction since they are natural allies among countries oppressed by the economic and military supremacy of the West. The role of PIOs from developed countries stands on a different footing. They are living in the stronghold of global injustice. Twenty percent people living in the developed countries, including them, are consuming 80 percent of the world's resources. PIOs in these countries have a moral responsibility to oppose those policies of their countries which are responsible for this unjust world order.

These PIOs have a choice of following Vibhisana or Kumbhakarana. The former opposed the policies of unjust Ravana while the latter supported his evil ways. We should not make the mistake of honouring Kumbhakarana even though he was much honoured in Ravana's Lanka. We examine the roles of four honoured PIOs from this perspective. Consider the roles of four PIOs.

Case 1: Conditions of the Indian farmers are deteriorating day by day. Farmers of Gujarat are not getting good price for their cotton because the world price is low due to the subsidies given by the developed countries such as the U.S. to their cotton growers. There is consensus among economists that the removal of these subsidies will be beneficial for the developing countries though the depth of this impact is debatable. It becomes the moral responsibility of Indian PIOs living in the U.S. to oppose these subsidies.

Many Indian PIOs are working in the American Media and Government. They often remain silent on this issue but give out huge donations to Indian NGOs to alleviate poverty etc. This is not acceptable. The cause of poverty of Indian farmers should be removed along with provision of relief. To remain silent on these harmful policies means the PIOs are a part of the exploitative machinery and they are only giving back a small part of that wicked income as charity to alleviate the suffering that their silence has perpetrated. In this context, honoured PIO, *Newsweek* columnist and India's candidate for the job of General Secretary of the United Nations, Shashi Tharoor should be asked whether he has been opposing the American policies.

Case 2: The handloom weavers of India are facing difficult conditions. In the free market he will win who makes cloth cheap. The market does not take into account how many jobs have been created and how many families are earning their livelihood from that production. World prosperity is leading to ever lowering of interest rates which are near zero in countries like Japan. It is becoming profitable for businessmen to use more machines and less labour. Cloth made in big textile mills is selling cheap in the market while weavers lose their livelihood.

Some jobs are indeed created in the developed countries in the manufacture of the looms but the overall impact is to displace labour. Many PIOs are involved in the making of economic policies of multilateral organizations like IMF, World Bank and UNDP which have espoused this model of the free market-led development. These PIOs have a moral responsibility to highlight this dimension of the free market and help create better policies. In this context, honoured PIO and advisor to organizations like UNDP Meghnad Desai should be asked whether he has been opposing these free-market policies in his advice.

Case 3: India is emerging as a knowledge-based power. The problem faced by Indian software programmers is that companies like IBM and Microsoft have got patents on certain basic technologies such as the Windows software. The unavailability of these codes prevents us from making new products. These companies are selling expensive software in India and paying huge salaries to PIOs. The PIO gets his salary, in part, from this monopolistic pricing and sale of high-priced products in India. The moral responsibility of the PIO is to pry open the code for Windows platform so that this loss to India can be mitigated. In this context, honoured PIO and consultant to IBM and U.S. Robotics Dipak C Jain should be asked whether he has been trying to break this stranglehold of the U.S. companies.

Case 4: Many scientist of Indian origin have been working in NASA which leads the U.S. Government's space programme. The explicit objective of this programme is to establish U.S.' control over space. The U.S. is developing weapons, which can destroy Indian satellites in space. The PIOs working for NASA become part of the machinery which aims to disable Indian defence establishment.

The moral responsibility of these PIOs is to prevent the U.S. from acquiring such powers and to pass on those technologies to other developing countries including India. Mr. Schindler of the *Schindler's List* did precisely this. He changed the specifications of German armaments so that they would not work. In this context the PIOs like Sunita Williams should be asked about their efforts to prevent U.S. hegemony on space.

Other examples can be given. The main point is the first responsibility of the PIOs is to conduct themselves morally in their professional life. To promote adharma in their professional life and then give charity to lessen the ill-effects they have created is not acceptable. It is like the dacoit going to the temple before looting the village.

PIOs are often eager to give charity to India. I often receive email from PIOs saying they want to contribute some money for the development of villages. But they do not want to talk about the impact of their professional work upon India. I asked one American PIO as to what, in his view, was the impact of America's policies in the WTO upon India. He replied that he had no interest in these issues. He was not willing to examine the morality of his income obtained under the protection of WTO though he gave lacs every year in charity to Indian NGOs. Such a charity should be declared morally bankrupt.

We must certainly honour our PIOs. It is a matter of satisfaction that our brothers have reached high positions in the West. But our mantra is *Vasudev Kutumbakam*. Thus, before honouring the PIOs we should examine whether they are discharging their moral responsibility in their professional lives.

The Western countries have a history of honouring Jai Chands from the developing countries. We should not honour a PIO merely because he or she has been honoured in the West just as we would not honour Kumbhakarana merely because he was honoured in Ravana's Lanka. The developing countries should beware that developed countries co-opt the bright individuals from the developing countries and turn them against their motherland much as ICS officers actively jailed freedom fighters.

Relooking World War II

The common perception is that Hitler was a tyrant who was killed by the democratic British. Unquestionably, Hitler perpetrated atrocities on the Jews. But the British did the same in the colonies. There is a need to make a dispassionate reassessment of the Second World War. This is important because in the early part of this century, Hitler was ranked third after Mahatma Gandhi and Atal Bihari Vajpayee in the type of leader that our young want to see. Subhas Chandra Bose, Abraham Lincoln and Nelson Mandela have been left behind. Something about Hitler is clearly striking the chords of our young people's hearts. Might it be that Britain may be the villain of the Second World War and Hitler the failed hero? After all, the devtas often lost to the prowess of the asuras.

The point of difference between the two contending parties of the Second World War was that while England was enriching herself by looting the colonies, Hitler wanted to acquire new lands for habitation by the Germans, which he thought rightfully belonged to them. In his autobiography *Mein Kampf*, he writes that the population of Germany was growing by 0.9 million persons every year. It was necessary to find "ways and means to forestall the danger of misery and hunger." He continues, "It certainly cannot be part of the dispensation of Divine Providence to give 50 times larger share of the soil of this world to one nation than to another... If this earth has sufficient room for all, then we ought to have that share of the soil, which is absolutely necessary for our existence... Colonies cannot suit this purpose as long as they are not suited for settlement by Europeans on a large scale."

Hitler's case for war was based on a particular view of justice—equal European land per European person. Both England and Germany were pursuing their self-interests. Britain wanted to extract the wealth of the colonies while eschewing expansion within Europe while Hitler wanted Germany's share in Europe's land. The difference was this: Britain wanted to enrich her people by exploiting those of other continents while Germany wanted to do the same by throwing out others from European lands.

Notionally, Britain wanted to maintain peace. 'Peace' meant that exploitation of the colonies should continue; and Germans should remain confined to the lands held by them. Hitler rejected this idea. He wrote, "The chatter about the peaceful conquest of the world by commercial means was probably the most completely nonsensical stuff... No nation prepared the way for its commercial conquests more brutally than England did by the means of the sword, and no other nation has defended such conquests more ruthlessly."

The choice before Germany was to wage war within Europe or against the people's of other continents. England chose the path of waging war on colonies, while Hitler chose that of expanding into Russia. Hitler was not a warmonger and Britain an apostle of peace as is often portrayed. Both were equally warmongers in keeping with the mood of the times. British historian A.J.P. Taylor writes in *The Origins of the Second World War*. "In international affairs, there was nothing wrong with Hitler except that he was a German."

Another difference was that Britain had conquered the world by deceit and fraud. Hitler, on the other hand, wanted to wage an honest war. Hitler writes, "Our far greater honesty and our freedom from that specifically English 'perfidy' would be assets on our side." Hitler's version was that Britain was dishonest and brutal in exploiting the colonies. Germany would not stoop to that level. War was the accepted mode of political discourse at that time. But Britain indulged in deceitful war while Hitler wanted to wage an honest war.

Yet another difference was that Britain killed and victimized hapless people of the colonies who had done no harm to that country. Britain was brutally exploiting the colonies and using military might to kill them, as in the Jalianwala Bag firing, to extract their wealth. The hapless people of the colonies had done no harm to England. It was a one-sided aggression upon the weak. Hitler, on the other hand, killed the Jews who, in his view at least, had exploited the people of Germany.

Hitler explained the working of the Jews as follows: the Jew would enter a country as merchant. He was never a producer. He only worked as the middleman. He was cunning while the native German was clumsy. Soon the Jew established his monopoly over commerce. He began to lend money at usurious rates of interest. He made vulgar display of his wealth, giving rise to popular envy. He bought land but never tilled it; rather he exploited the poor peasant. He secured privileges from the kings in return for payments and then extracted twice the money from the people. He provided the kings with money to 'squander on their pleasures'. It mattered little to the Jew that in due time, this led to the downfall of the kings themselves. Their position was undermined 'by their continued failure to guard the interests of their subjects'. Hitler compared the Jew to a leech who clings to the body of his unfortunate victims surreptitiously and cannot be detected, let alone removed.

Hitler accused the Jews of infecting the people with moral pestilence, distributing 'smutty' literature, financing theatre that was 'trivial and often pornographic', financing prostitution and white slave traffic, completely lacking 'the most essential pre-requisite of a cultured people, namely the idealist spirit,' being a 'parasite thriving on the substance of other nations' and not being concerned with 'moral problems.' Thus, said Hitler, Christ "drove those enemies of the human race out of the temple of God because then, as always, they used religion as a means of advancing their commercial interest." Surely these abuses are exaggerations, but they must surely contain a grain of truth.

Hitler over-reacted by seeking to exterminate the Jewish race. But the Jews also failed to discharge their *dharma* towards the people amidst whom they resided. Their single point focus was to use the weakness of the host people to extract their wealth by whatever means they could. The result was that the German people revolted against the Jews. While Britain killed the hapless natives of the colonies who had done no wrong to the British, Germany killed the Jews who were behaving immorally towards their hosts.

Britain might really be the villain of the Second World War. Britain specialized in looting, while Germany sought land for habitation. Britain was the apostle of unjust war upon colonies while Germany wanted its 'just' share of the Europe's soil. Britain used deceit and fraud, while Germany sought to wage an honest war. Britain killed innocent habitants of the colonies, while Germany exterminates Jews who had wronged those people. No wonder so many of our youth emulate Hitler.

The present 20/80 misdistribution of world's resources has its roots in European conquest of the colonies. The foundations of present unequal distribution of wealth lie in the British policies before the Second World War. The wealth extracted by Britain at that time enabled it to develop London as the world's financial hub. Thus, instead of emulating the nominal support to peace by the British, we must peer behind the political economy of status quo that was being preserved.

The developing countries are today enthralled by the free trade regime of the WTO. This is much like the enthralment with British pursuit of peace during the Second World War. Just as that peace was the cover under which British exploited the colonies, so also free trade along with patents protection is the cover under which developed countries are exploiting the developing counties.

A caveat is that countries like India and China, that have resisted the indiscriminate opening of their markets to imports and FDI, have successfully emerged and are now challenging the might of the developed countries. They now need a different set of policies than enumerated above. They need to work out a strategy to directly challenge the might of the developed countries as outlined in Part 2 of this book.

The Principle of 'Collective Responsibility'

The mainstream understanding of terror is that innocent citizens should not be made victims in a dispute with the government. By implication, the British citizen is absolved of responsibility of the acts undertaken by the British government. It is forgotten, however, that the British government has held innocent citizens of other countries collectively responsible for the acts done by their governments.

In an article titled 'Dresden' on *Winds of Change* website, it is told that towards the end of the Second World War the British bombed the German city of Dresden holding the German people collectively responsible for the atrocities committed by Hitler: "British strategic bombers used a combination of high explosives–to create kindling and phosphorus to ignite it–to create fire storm that killed half a million German civilians... The direct military role of Dresden (and Cologne and Hamburg, which were equally treated) was limited."

Many citizens of Germany hold that they were not responsible for the atrocities committed by Hitler. They deny the principle of collective responsibility. This denial is rejected by the mainstream politicians of the West, once again upholding the concept of collective responsibility. Jodie Hemerda writes in an article titled *Collective Responsibility*: "The majority of residents of Germany during the late 1930s and 1940s resoundingly cry foul at the notion of collective responsibility. They claim ignorance of Hitler's atrocities even in the midst of numerous concentration camps scattered throughout their country, the slave labour used extensively in the German industry and farming, and German propaganda and mass media bragging about the burning of synagogues. According to Alexander Kimel, a holocaust survivor, 'they chose to deny the knowledge and remain silent'. That choice sealed their responsibility to their society." The victors–U.S. and U.K.–held every German citizen responsible for the atrocities committed by Hitler by choosing not to oppose the Nazi regime.

In a provocative article *Targeting Civilians*, Professor Thomas J DiLorenzo of Loyola College, Maryland, explains how Abraham Lincoln held the people of the Confederate states responsible for the acts of their government: "Lincoln intentionally targeted civilians from the very beginning of the war... In 1862 Sherman was having difficulty subduing Confederate sharpshooters who were harassing federal gunboats on the Mississippi River near Memphis. He then adopted the theory of 'collective responsibility' to justify attacking innocent civilians in retaliation for such attacks. He burned the entire town of Randolph, Tennessee, to the ground... Jackson and Meridian, Mississippi, were also burned to the ground by Sherman's troops even though there was no Confederate army there to oppose them. After the destruction of Meridian Sherman boasted that 'for five days, ten thousand of our men worked hard and with a will, in that work of destruction, with axes, sledges, crowbars, claw bars, and with fire... Meridian no longer exists'." DiLorenzo concludes: "Had the Confederates somehow won, they would have found themselves justified...in stringing up President Lincoln and the entire Union high command for waging war against non-combatants." Truly Lincoln waged war to liberate the slaves. But then he held the people of the Confederate States collectively responsible for slavery.

In an article in *The Revisionist* ("On Terror and Its Other Names," Codoh Series, No. 2, 2002), Ernest Sommers writes, "Collective responsibility is one of the oldest forms of social control and social manipulation known to mankind. The situation in which an entire community, or some randomly chosen segment thereof, is destroyed for the sins of a few is a very common theme throughout history. Communities and tribes, even in the Bible, were decimated or destroyed to the last man out of blood lust. There was a calculated message being sent: the slightest infraction of one will lead to the destruction of all, or at least an arbitrary portion." The same idea of collective responsibility lay at the root of the American bombings of Hiroshima and Nagasaki. The purpose was to impose collective responsibility.

The principle of collective responsibility finds place in our law as well. Some time ago a District Magistrate in Bihar had imposed a collective fine on some villages.

The people of Dresden, Meridien and Hiroshima were held responsible for their complicity in their government's policies. Likewise the residents of the World Trade Tower are held responsible for the policies of the British and American Governments.

The main issue is that 20 percent of the people of the U.S.-EU-Japan alliance are consuming 80 percent of the world's resources. The U.S. attacks on Iraq and Afghanistan were made to protect the supply of oil. Many are demanding that the U.S.-U.K. withdraw from Saudi Arabia, Iraq and Afghanistan. In the process they are holding the innocent citizens of London and New York responsible for the acts of their governments just as the British and Americans held the people of Dresden, Meridien and Hiroshima responsible for the policies of their governments. The result is that talk of containing terror without removing the basic injustices of the global economy will not be successful. The developing countries must take a balanced view of the global war on terror and demand that it be conjoined with a global war for economic justice.

This Chapter is adapted from the following articles:

"Unjust peace," *The Pioneer,* August 14, 2001.
"Oil politics," 2006. Publication details unavailable.
"As you sow, so you reap," *Gomantak Times,* July 20, 2005.
"What Kalpana stood for," *Newstime,* February 22, 2003.
"Country first," *The Pioneer,* January 27, 2004.
"Relooking World War II," *Eurasia Times,* April 2003.
"The economics of CTBT," *Daily News,* Colombo, September 2, 1996.
"Did protectionism fail North Korea?" *New Indian Express,* November 1, 2006.

4

TRIPS and the Importance of Technology

One important dimension of globalization is the prevalence of continued inequality. Twenty percent of the people of the Western countries continue to consume eighty percent of the natural resources of the world. Globalization was expected to provide immense benefits to the developing countries leading to some equality but that has not happened. The main culprit is the TRIPS agreement under the WTO which enables the developed countries to preserve their monopoly over frontier technology. While developing countries pursue free trade and compete with each other to supply their resources at ever declining prices; the developed countries bask in the income earned from monopolistic control of technologies. The march toward equality will have to dismantle the TRIPS structure.

This is the correct strategy for India of the nineties and other developing countries towards the beginning of this century since they have little to gain from TRIPS agreement. The situation for India in the 21st century is qualitatively different. R&D activities are being outsourced to India in a big way although the control over patents remains with the dominant Western MNCs nevertheless the knowledge percolates in the Indian economy. In due time it may be possible for Indians to beat their Western principals in the game of patenting. The number of patent applications emanating from India is increasing. It is conceivable, therefore, that India may emerge as the global hub of generation of new technologies. Simultaneously, India's dependence on income from exports of low-value commodities like onion and rice is declining in same proportion as the share of services exports is rising. Thus declining prices of these commodities will not impact India much. It may even provide political dividends by creating dependence of the Western countries on agricultural supplies from India. Thus the strategy of an emerging economy like India will be different than that followed by her in the nineties. There is a need to take a balanced view of the benefits and costs in the new situation.

At a yet higher level, it needs to be examined whether India would be justified in capturing benefits from the patents regime. No country can exist peacefully in the long run unless it behaves justly towards its neighbours. India can join developed countries in exploiting other developing countries. This is against the principle of Vasudev Kutumbakam. Thus, India's adoption of the patents regime should only be a strategic action to cause a collapse of the unholy Western view of extracting huge technology rents from the developing countries. The final objective should be to dismantle the TRIPS regime and allow free flow of technology for human welfare.

The attitude to TRIPS must be seen in a dynamic way:

- Creation of WTO, 1995: Support TRIPS as a quid pro quo for access to markets of developed countries.
- Loss from trade, 2000: Oppose TRIPS since market access is a loss proposition due to competition among developing countries.
- India, 2007: Support TRIPS with caution because we can possibly gain from becoming the global R&D hub.
- India 2015-plus: Oppose TRIPS because it is against the principle of *Vasudev Kutumbakam*

The articles in this section most relate to the second level above—Oppose TRIPS because it is a loss-loss proposition. This must be borne in mind while reading this section.

Importance of Technology in the Progress of America

The cutting edge of American economic strength lies in technological innovation. The consequent buoyancy in the share markets pulls world's wealth into the American economy. This results in an increased demand of dollars which leads to more purchases of dollars for holding forex reserves. The inflow of this money gives America the ability to buy goods from across the world. That gives it a further political tool to twist those who may disagree. The weak point in this scheme is that foreign dollars are financing the imports of foreign goods into America. Chinese people are investing their money in America and Americans are buying Chinese goods with that Chinese money. The U.S. economy may crash if China, and India, stop purchase of dollars.

At the time of signing the WTO agreement it was known that we would be hit by the new patents regime. But this loss was setoff against the gains that were expected to take place from free trade. It was thought that the loss from the patents regime would last for say 20 years while the gain from free trade would accrue for hundreds of years. But it has since become clear that the patents regime is more restrictive than thought. The control of the West on technologies continues beyond 20 years. Small improvements in the earlier technologies get patented and prevent commercial use of the technologies even after the expiry of the patents.

Gains from free trade have also been less than expected. Free trade has created a global competition in the markets. Vietnam is competing with India and Brazil in the coffee market leading to lowering of prices. Thus WTO has become a loss-loss proposition for us. We loose twice—in the payment of technology premiums and in the lowering of price of our produce.

The developing countries should, therefore, make a fresh study of the short-and long run gains and losses from the WTO. Serious consideration should be given to withdrawing from the WTO. That would enable us to copy the technologies of the West and produce goods of same quality at cheaper prices.

This may be a beneficial proposition. The reason is that loss to the developing countries from imposition of retaliatory tariffs will hurt the developed countries equally. Their consumer will not get cheap goods produced by the developing countries. This will push up the cost of production in the developed economies. At the same time the developing countries will have to hit at the Western leadership in technological innovation.

The innovativeness of the American people comes from the pressure to perform. American universities employ their professors on five year contracts. They are shown the door if they do not innovate. Scientists of Indian origin do much of the innovation in America because they get proper incentives for producing results. We must, therefore, place all scientists in the CSIR and ICAR laboratories and in universities and colleges on five year contracts with specific targets of innovation in their respective fields.

America has a system of intensive collaboration between the universities and defence research establishments and private corporations. This makes it possible of them to quickly commercialise their technologies like that of global positioning system and satellite imagery which were first developed for defence purposes.

The expenses incurred by the American government in this research are an indirect subsidy to the corporations which commercialise those technologies. CSIR laboratories, on the other hand, treat private corporations as *kamadhenu* to be milked. Government scientists are more interested in preserving the secrecy of their knowledge than sharing it with private users. We should instead create partnerships with businessmen. We should make a scheme to subsidise commercialisation of new technologies. We had a scheme to provide capital subsidy to industries set up in backward areas. A similar scheme can be made for new technologies.

Much technological innovation in America is being undertaken by Indian expatriates. We held a NRI mela last year to encourage our expatriates to invest in India. Instead we must ask them to transfer the frontier technologies. A ministry must be established to track down persons of India origin in the developed countries, assess their technological expertise, locate user or buyer of those technologies and then provide subsidy for transfer of the same.

False Arguments in Favour of TRIPS

Mainstream economists often hold the view that acceptance of the Intellectual Property Rights regime under the WTO is beneficial of India. A deeper scrutiny reveals that the arguments did not hold at least till the beginning of this decade. However, as mentioned in the introduction to this chapter, some of these arguments diluted as we enter the second decade of this century in view of India's emergence as a R&D hub. Yet they remain valid for other developing countries today.

Argument 1: A weak IPR regime would discourage the MNCs from bringing into India the recent life-saving technologies: "If I cannot afford heart surgery, I should not prevent others from benefiting from the same."

Here the question is not merely of heart surgery or not. The technology of heart surgery comes along with higher prices of the drugs used by the common man. The question then becomes that of weighing the benefits to a few thousand heart patients from access to advance heart surgery against the costs to our billions of ordinary folks from payment of high price of drugs. Moreover, we can innovate our own heart surgery technologies in due time. The U.S. had refused to give us supercomputer technology. We made our own supercomputer. Similarly we can create frontline health technologies. In that case we only loose some time. We have to examine the loss is only to heart patients in, say, the ten years, against gains to heart patients for a long time thereafter due to the availability of cheaper surgery procedures.

Argument 2: A patent granted in the U.S. or another country does not become automatically valid in India. It has to be granted by our patents authority. Hence the reins of the patents machine remains in our hands. There is no fear of surrendering our economic sovereignty.

The catch is that the patents law which is implemented by our Government has to be WTO consistent. The Indian Government becomes merely the executor of the rules laid by the WTO. And these are appealable in the WTO. For example, the Indian Government will not be able to grant process patents even if it wanted to.

Argument 3: There are substantial gains to be made in knowledge-based exports in other software-type areas such as genetics, biotechnology, etc. In order to protect these potential benefits in foreign countries we need a global patents regime. Our exports of films and music too will be hit in a weak IPR regime.

Here we have to weigh the benefits from knowledge-based industries and loss from patented products. The role of these products in our export basket, though increasing, is still small. Against the benefit in these exports, we would lose by paying higher prices of imports of various patented products. These costs can be much greater than the benefits from the former. Our civilisational strength lies in trade, not technology. The number of patents registered by us is small. Therefore we lose more and gain less. Moreover, the benefits from the export of knowledge-based products and films will accrue to the rich while many of the costs will be borne by the poor. Hence the question of equity should also be studied.

Nevertheless, this aspect is important in the light of outsourcing of research activities to India. Our scientists are getting much access to frontline technologies. They can possibly turn around and use this knowledge against their erstwhile employers. However, this has to overcome the hurdle of patent laws. Indian scientists will be able to use their knowledge only if permitted by the patent holders. This aspect becomes beneficial if we break out of the patent laws. Then indeed our scientists will become free to use their knowledge. This is less important as long as we remain bound by patent laws.

Argument 4: IPRs are consistent with our own tradition of protecting IPRs.

Our tradition was of the gharana system. Knowledge was handed over from generation to persons considered suitable for handling it. If a suitable person was not found then it was thought better to let the knowledge to die rather than it fall into evil hands. The focus was proper use of knowledge for social good rather than preservation of knowledge *per se*. The present IPR regime, on the other hand, focuses on preservation of knowledge for profit rather than social good and violates the basic principle of our civilisation of lok kalyana.

Another difference is that the gharana system relied on secrecy like practiced by Coca Cola. It did not rely on protection of knowledge by the government. The IPR regime is based on use of state power to preserve profits. The two are entirely different both in content and form.

Augment 5: There is some evidence that FDI flows may increase with a stronger IPR regime.

The evidence is mixed. The MNCs have a track record of investing heavily in China in the 1980s with a poor IPR regime. It is likely that MNCs will invest even with a weak patents regime. In any case most FDI is not coming with frontline technologies.

Argument 6: Our industries like Ayurveda have been languishing because of a weak IPR regime. There is no investment in research in these areas.

There is a basic philosophic difference between Ayurveda and allopathy. Ayurveda holds that the cure of a disease is to be found in the area where the disease occurs. The vaidya was encouraged to look of herbs in his area and devise his own treatments. The stress was on experiential rather than experimental knowledge. The vaidya was accountable to the people. The pharmaceutical MNCs fulfil none these criteria. The stress is on letting the underlying psycho-somatic causes of the diseases remain untreated and treating the symptoms with ever increasing doses. Ayurveda will be decimated if we abandon the principle of localization. Thus, instead of trying to develop for-profit Ayurveda by strengthening patents regime, we should encourage philanthropic research in Ayurveda.

Argument 7: We should concentrate on grabbing the benefits of exports rather than crying about the loss from patents.

This argument has considerable merit. There indeed exists a massive potential in exports that we can grab. But this argument only establishes that the IPR regime is loss. It is necessary to weigh the benefits from trade and costs from IPR regime. We know that China is not a member of the WTO yet it has been able to export huge quantities. Thus we should examine the possibility of benefiting from exports sans patents.

Argument 8: We have been able to get the patent on neem withdrawn due to the multilateral framework of TRIPS agreement.

The withdrawal of neem patent, though a good achievement, is like reducing the level of poison in the system. Why was the patent granted in the first place? Would it not be better to break up the wrong system itself rather than aiming at preventing its bad effects?

In conclusion, the IPR regime is basically harmful of us. Yet there may be a case of accepting it strategically in order (1) to secure outsourced technologies that can be turned around; and (2) capture the benefits of trade. In order to arrive at a correct assessment of these costs and benefits it is necessary of us to undertake a dispassionate study. In the meanwhile the overwhelming evidence is that IPR regime was harmful for India till recently and continues to be harmful for most developing countries.

How Leaders Mislead on TRIPS

The Director General of the Council of Scientific and Industrial Research, Dr Raghunath Anant Mashelkar, has led a valiant and commendable drive to get India to patent her traditional knowledge and acquire patents on many innovations. That, however, does not remove the fundamentally iniquitous nature of the TRIPS agreement.

In an interview posted on the net with the title, *Knowledge and Its Protection*, Dr Mashelkar acknowledges this fact: "This globe of 6 billion is growing and producing huge asymmetries in terms of production and distribution of knowledge. For example, General Motors' R&D budget is 8 billion dollars while entire India's R&D budget is less than 3 billion dollars.... Knowledge asymmetries are where very few are spending large sums, when new knowledge is not getting generated for the poor, and that is a challenge that we have to meet."

In another article, "Intellectual Property Rights and the Third World," Dr Mashelkar says, "The battle today is between those that are not equal—economically and institutionally. TRIPS, like other World Trade Organisation agreements, is a legal framework. Its implications will be decided by the resolution of disputes. That makes case law of great importance. The Third World has a clear disadvantage here."

Dr Mashelkar clearly recognises that the TRIPS regime is heavily loaded against the developing countries. Our first effort, therefore, should be to seek the removal of TRIPS from the WTO. Unfortunately, Dr Mashelkar cedes the game to the Western countries by assuming that this is not possible. The Report of the Commission on Intellectual Property Right set up by the British Government in September 2002 with Dr Mashelkar as one of the members simply states, "TRIPS is likely to remain an integral part of the WTO framework. While we have reservations about the extension of TRIPS standards to all developing countries, we recognize that it is most unlikely that any WTO members would be keen to renegotiate the agreement." Dr Mashelkar has here ceded walkover to the rich countries in the first over of the cricket match by assuming that the match cannot be won!

The situation of large countries like China and India is, however, qualitatively different than other developing countries. In an article, "RA Mashelkar: India needs patents on medicines," James Love quotes Mashelkar: "With the 21st century of knowledge and mind, Indians must learn to create wealth from patents." Here the thrust is on gaining what we can from patents in a basically unfavourable environment.

Mashelkar was perhaps echoing the words of Gita Piramal of Indian drug company, Nicholas Piramal who said in the same conference that Intellectual Property Rights can become a boon for India: "IPR will give rise to 'virtual monopoly' which India will lead because of its knowledge power. Indians must learn to create wealth from patents." It is reasonable for a company like Nicholas Piramal to harp on the benefits of patents because it may stand to gain. But the government has to take a larger view. Will it be fair to put higher burden on millions for obtaining small benefits for a few?

Elaborating on the theme further, Dr Mashelkar says in the same article: "Countries like India and China, which are endowed with a large intellectual infrastructure, can gain in the long term by stronger IPR protection. However, least developed countries, where innovation is minimal, are likely to face higher costs without the offsetting benefits... There are concrete examples to show that technology transfers to the Third World have not taken place when they were needed most."

Dr Mashelkar argument is changing in a subtle way here. Earlier, he said that the Third World has a disadvantage due to inadequate budgets and asymmetry in the field of technological innovation. Here he has changed tune and is saying that India and China do not suffer from such asymmetry in the long run if they play their cards well.

The efficacy of this line of argument is doubtful. For India and China to emerge as knowledge powerhouses we will have to increase our research budgets many fold. That will not be possible as long as TRIPS is in place because the rich countries will be able to suck our wealth by selling us patented products at exorbitant prices. In fact, we have greater chance of becoming a knowledge power by dismantling TRIPS, increasing our national income by reducing the level of technology rents charged by the rich countries and investing the same in research.

Moreover, even if India and China can benefit from TRIPS in the long run, other developing countries will continue to face higher costs without getting the offsetting benefits. We would be joining the unjust world technology order established by the rich countries.

One would have expected Dr Mashelkar to argue of taking TRIPS out of the WTO. We should work within TRIPS to strengthen ourselves only as a second-order strategy in the event that TRIPS cannot be dismantled. But Dr Mashelkar ignores the fundamentally unjust nature of TRIPS and presents TRIPS as an opportunity that India must grab. In "Economics of knowledge," he says, "Tomorrow's societies will be knowledge societies. Tomorrow's markets will be knowledge markets. Tomorrow's wars will be fought not be the conventional weapons, guns, missiles and so on, but they will be fought in the knowledge markets with the new thermonuclear weapons called information and knowledge... Finally, for cash starved but intellectual-capital-rich country like India, emergence of knowledge industry is good news."

This line of argument is problematic. It is possible that the TRIPS agreement may lead to permanent disablement of our research efforts due to budget constraints, refusal to license existing technologies, etc. Second, assuming that India can match the might of the Western countries and beat them in their game of patenting, that still does not remove the fundamental inequity of TRIPS vis-à-vis the other developing countries.

Dr Mashelkar should not mislead India into supporting TRIPS. India's aim should be to remove TRIPS from the WTO.

Legal Framework of TRIPS

The judiciary was established to ensure that the executive and legislative do not vitiate the constitutional mandate. Often, a conflict arises between different parts of the Constitution. In such cases, the judiciary has spelled out the need to give priority to the basic structure of the Constitution. In an article, 'The Basic Structure of the Indian Constitution' Mr. Venkatesh Nayak tells that in the Minerva Mills case then chief Justice YV Chandrachud, delivering the majority judgment (4:1), held that "the harmony and balance between fundamental rights and directive principles was a basic feature of our Constitution. It follows that the judiciary should uphold TRIPS only if it furthered fundamental rights and directive principles.

Article 38 of the Constitution says the state should make efforts to reduce social and economic inequality and secure people's welfare. Article 51 asks the state to make efforts to secure just and honourable relations between nations. We should examine whether IPR regime would help in attaining these objectives that are fundamental to our Constitution.

The impact of the IPR laws on the welfare of the people is a mater of debate. Mainstream economists hold that stronger IPR regime will beget us more foreign investments and access to frontline technologies. Many social activists, on the other hand, hold that the IPR laws have had a strong negative impact on the people, especially by increasing the prices of life-saving drugs. The WTO agreement in Doha explicitly says the IPR regime will be lessened where pubic health of the developing countries is affected. This proves that the IPR regime does have a negative impact on the people of the developing countries.

The report of the Commission on Intellectual Property Rights set up by the British Government was headed by Professor John Barton of Stanford University, California, and had among others Mr. R A Mashelkar, as one of its members. The report says: "Developing countries, taken as a whole, are net importers of technology, most of which is supplied by the developed countries. Organisations in developed countries own the overwhelming proportion of patent rights worldwide. Econometric models have been constructed to estimate what would be the global impact of applying the TRIPS agreement. The latest estimate, by the World Bank, suggests that most developed countries would be the major beneficiaries of TRIPS in terms of the enhanced value of their patents, with the benefit to the U.S. estimated at an annual $19 billion. Developing countries, and a few developed ones, would be the net losers. The crucial question from our point of view is to what extent IPRs promote growth. The evidence we have reviewed does not suggest strong direct effects on economic growth in developing countries."

The primary duty of the judiciary is to preserve and promote the basic mandate of the Constitution, which consists of the fundamental rights and directive principles. The directive principles mandate the state to secure people welfare and just and honourable relations between nations. The impact of the IPR laws, however, is exactly in the opposite direction as evinced by above report. It follows that there is a strong possibility that IPR laws are against the basic spirit of the Constitution.

TRIPS Hurts Transfer of Technology to Developing Countries

Mainstream economists hold that acceptance of TRIPS by developing countries will create confidence among the developed countries that their technologies will not be surreptitiously duplicated. That will act as an incentive for them to transfer frontline technologies to countries like India.

IAS officer Dr Veena Jha has edited a collection of papers on the theme of transfer of technology, environmental non-tariff barriers to trade and related issues (*Trade and Environment: Issues and Options for India,* published by the United Nations, 2003). She should be commended of putting together detailed grass root studies of problems of technology transfer in the age of globalisation.

The case for adopting the IPR regime rested on the assumption that the IPR regime would encourage MNCs to transfer their technologies to India through foreign direct investment or joint ventures. The papers in this volume, however, paint a different picture.

HFC134a is an agent that is an eco-friendly replacement of the ozone layer damaging CFCs. It is reported that Indian firms who were interested in importing the technology of the production of this material found that most of the HFC134a producers contacted "showed no interest in transferring technology." A few said they would consider doing so if they had a majority stake in the Indian venture and even then quoted very high technical fees. In the case of genetically modified seeds the joint ventures between Monsanto and Mahyco of Bt Cotton and between PGS and Proagro of pest-resistant tomatoes contain only marketing agreements and did not include transfer of technology. It is clear that the IPR regime has not encouraged MNCs to transfer technologies to India.

The provision in the WTO, that countries can impose their own environment standards as long as they provide national treatment to foreign players has allowed European importers to require ISO 14000 certification, the costs of which are prohibitive.

Of course there are exceptions, like BHEL not having faced much difficulty in importing the technology of Circulating Fluidise Bed Combustion Boilers. But here too BHEL has "found that access to foreign technology has become difficult and costly in the 1990s... The technology owners... are now able to supply plants directly to India due to economic liberalisation." While TRIPS provides an incentive for the transfer of frontline technologies; free trade provides a disincentive. The patent holder has two options to benefit from markets in a developing country. He can transfer the technology and obtain royalty etc. for the same. Alternatively, he can export the high-technology goods under the free trade regime. The developing countries do not get access to the frontline technologies if the patent holders exercise the second option. The experience of BHEL indicates that patent holders are more inclined to rely on foreign trade. Hence TRIPS, in conjunction with free trade, has a negative impact on transfer of technology.

The facts given in the book make it necessary of us to reassess the benefits and costs from the WTO. The combination of the patents regime and free trade has become and obstruction in transfer of technologies. The MNCs are now free to export their product directly to the Indian market. They have less incentive to transfer technology. In the case of HFC134a, it is reported that the holding firms feel that technology transfer will conflict with (their) business. They would prefer to export HFC134a, which is now possible. The result is that the IPR regime, instead of enabling us to acquire technology and building upon it to improve our export advantage, has hit at our ability to acquire technologies and made us more dependent on imports.

The situation is likely to become worse after the provision of product patents in the chemical industry are put in place: "New substitutes of Ozone Depleting Substances are likely be patented by foreign firms in India. This will certainly limit India's ability to develop technology and to produce these substitutes and will increase dependence on imports." Similarly it is apprehended that adoption of ISO 14000 would hinder innovation.

This is the situation in respect of clean technologies which the developed countries are morally obliged to provide to the developing countries at concessional terms as per the provisions of Article 7 of the Rio Declaration. The situation with respect to other technologies is much worse.

Isolated examples have been reported of Indian firms having been able to develop those technologies themselves. Manali Petrochemicals, of example, has been able to develop HFC134b-based systems in-house. The Multilateral Fund established under the Montreal Protocol has helped Indian firms to adopt clean technologies of foam production.

These examples indicate that two different routes that are open to us. We can take an incrementalist view and try to scrape what little we can within the IPR regime by introducing incentives for innovation by the private sector, providing information, increasing public investment in R&D, preventing bio-piracy, etc. The alternative is to come out of the WTO regime and develop new technologies unencumbered with the IPR regime. Unfortunately the second alternative is not considered by mainstream economlsts.

Agriculture Versus Patents

Developing countries are demanding reduction of domestic subsidies on agricultural products being given by the developed countries to their farmers. The belief is that reduction of these subsidies will raise the domestic price of agricultural commodities in the developed countries and make it possible for the developing countries to export their produce.

This line of argument is problematic for two reasons. One, the loss from patents may be much more than the gain from agriculture. Two, the developing countries may stand to loose and developed countries may stand to gain from reduction of these subsidies.

The Commission on Intellectual Property Rights, referred to above, pointed out that 20-year patents as provided under the present TRIPS agreement are hindering the development of new technologies. The experience of countries with shorter patents is better. To quote; "An approach common to Germany and the East Asian countries was the introduction of easily obtained utility models (or petty patents), which combined a lower standard of inventiveness with registration rather than examination, and a shorter protection period. When introduced in Germany, in 1891, these provided for three years of protection (renewable of a further three years) and by the 1930s, twice as many utility patents as examined patents were granted. Studies of Japan's patent system in the period 1960-1993 have suggested that utility models were more important than patents in stimulating productivity growth. There is also some evidence relating innovation in particular sectors in Brazil and the Philippines to such utility models. In Japan, the evidence suggests that systems of 'weak' protection based on utility models and industrial designs facilitated incremental innovation by small enterprises, and the absorption and diffusion of technology. This was associated, as in Taiwan and Korea, with an absence of patent protection of chemical and pharmaceutical products."

The report gives many other data to show the negative effect of the present TRIPS agreement on new inventions. It is not encouraging research and it enables developed countries to sell their inventions such as Windows software at monopolistic prices. At the same time the free trade regime is leading to lower prices for the exports from the developing countries.

Reduction of Agricultural Subsidies by Developed Countries is a Loss for the Developing Counties

Farmers of the developing countries are unable to sell their produce in the developed countries because the latter are giving huge subsidies to their farmers which depress domestic prices. The developing countries are demanding that these subsidies be substantially reduced. This will ensure their farmers get access to the markets of the developed countries. But the truth is that developed countries stand to gain more by the reduction of domestic subsidies. In a 2006 study titled "The Impact of the Doha Round on Developing Countries," Sandra Polaski of Washington-based Carnegie Endowment for International Peace has estimated that the benefit of the cut in domestic subsidies by the industrial countries will accrue wholly to the developed countries. Polaski estimated that the developed countries will benefit to the tune of $5.5 billion while the developing countries as a group will *loose* to the extent of $63 million by a reduction of 36 percent in subsidies. Among the developing counties those from South America and East Asia will stand to gain somewhat while Bangladesh, India, African countries, China and about one-half of the developing countries will stand to loose. Of these India will loose by $42 million.

Why should rich countries gain by reduction of domestic agricultural subsidies? Polaski explains that developed countries stand to gain by better resource allocation. They are paying subsidies to the extent of about $600 billion to their farmers. This money will be saved and used for development of manufacturing and services sectors. The world trade in agricultural commodities is worth $783 billion whereas in manufactured commodities and services it is much larger at $6.57 trillion. The redeployment of $600 billion agricultural subsidies in the manufacturing and services sectors will get them much larger benefits—like the use of urea in irrigated fields gives more benefits in comparison to its application on dry lands.

Why should developing countries stand to loose by reduction of domestic agricultural subsidies by the developed countries? The reason is that this reduction comes with a combined package requiring developing countries to open their markets for free trade in agricultural commodities. While they stand to make some gains by more agricultural exports to the developed countries, they stand to loose more from opening their markets to agricultural imports from other developing countries. Many developing countries are producing agricultural goods at prices above those prevailing in the world markets. The farmers of these countries will not be able to compete with imports from more efficient developing countries. For example, Indonesia produces rice cheaper than India. Opening markets to imports will enable cheap rice from Indonesia to enter or country and Indian farmer will stand to loose. Polaski estimates that the gain to Indonesia will be small in comparison to the loss to India. Hence the developing countries as a group stand to loose from reduction of subsidies by the developed countries.

Polaski has made these estimates on the basis of 36 percent reduction in domestic subsidies by the developed countries. Developing countries, however, are asking for deeper cuts. I have not seen any study of the impact of deeper cuts but my estimate is that the loss to India will then be larger. If few bitter gourds make the mouth bitter, more of the same is not likely to make it sweet.

This negative effect is not fully compensated by the incorporation of special provisions enabling developing countries to protect their domestic agricultural markets from cheap imports in selected commodities on which large number of their people depend for their livelihood. Say, India's farmer produces rice at Rs 12 per kilo while Indonesian farmer produces it at Rs 8 per kilo. Economic theory suggests that free trade will benefit both countries. Indonesian farmers will produce more rice and Indian farmers will produce more tea and coffee where they have comparative advantage. But it is not necessary that every Indian farmer has a global comparative advantage in some commodity. Possibly the land and climate of Tanjore and Orissa is not suitable for least-cost production of another commodity. Those farmers will be in trouble then. Thus developing countries should be entitled to special provisions to prevent free trade in selected agricultural commodities.

But this too will lead to loss for the developing countries from foregoing cheaper imports. About 70 percent people in our country buy food grains. They would have to purchase rice produced by Indian farmers at Rs 12 per kilo and forego Indonesian rice that was available at Rs 8 per kilo. India therefore stands to loose.

Clearly reduction of subsidies by the developed countries will lead to loss for developing countries. The wise men of the developed countries have cleverly misled us. They are pretending as if reduction of domestic subsidies is a loss proposition for them. Actually, this is beneficial for them. By getting the developing countries to focus on this demand, they will get us to open our markets of manufactured goods and services. The developed countries will benefit twice—(1) from the reduction of domestic agricultural subsidies and (2) from access to our markets of manufactured goods and services. The developing countries should, therefore, focus on dismantling the TRIPS structure in WTO instead of removal of subsidies being given by developed countries.

This Chapter is adapted from the following articles:
"American Hegemony," *The Pioneer,* June 2, 2003.
"Patently False Arguments," *The Pioneer,* January 2, 2001.
"Knowledge Industry," *The Statesman,* October 14, 2005.
"Priority to National Harm," *The Pioneer,* December 28, 2005.
"The other side of WTO regime," *Business Standard,* June 20, 2003.
"Remove TRIPS from WTO," *The New Indian Express,* December 28, 2005.
"Will developing nations trip on TRIPS?" *Businessline,* August 31, 2005.
"Double Harm, Courtesy Kamal Nath." 14.7.2006

5

Theory of Foreign Investment

Institutions like the World Bank propagate the view that FDI will bring capital and technology to the developing countries. The reality is quite different. FDI brings capital and leads to growth in the short run but debilitates domestic industries in the long run and leads to lower rates of growth.

The resistance to FDI by Swadeshi economists led to low rates of FDI coming into India in the nineties and gave enough breathing space to Indian industries to rise to meet the MNC challenge. Indian industries are no longer threatened by MNCs. However, this issue remains important for other developing countries. Hence it is necessary to understand the dynamics of FDI.

India was Enslaved due to Reliance on Foreign Capital

Percival Spear describes how the British enslaved India due to her leaders' ineptitude (*A History of India,* Vol. 2, Penguin). Europe's trade with India was in the hands of the Portuguese at the beginning of the 17th century. They controlled the Arabian Sea then. In 1670, Captain Hawkins of England sought but failed to secure trading privileges for the English despite his having become a companion of the Mughal Emperor, Jehangir.

Then the East India Company defeated the Portuguese in the Swally Estuary off Surat. Thereafter Sir Thomas Roe was able to secure these privileges in "return for the protection of the commercial and pilgrim's traffic." The Mughal emperor, instead of building his own navy and trying to become a maritime power, preferred the easy way out and collaborated with the English. The Company, writes Spear, "Tacitly became the maritime auxiliary of the empire." Thus was laid the foundation of the British Raj in India.

History repeated itself in Bengal. The East India Company had set up factory at Calcutta. It launched a military expedition to Chittagong which ended in a failure. The British retreated. But the Nawabs allowed them to fortify the area of their residence. This fortification led to later undoing of the Nawabs. It was the Nawab's desire to absolve him from the task of maintaining law and order that enabled the East India Company to harbour political ambitions.

Spear says that Indian leaders of those times were afflicted with "neglect, ineptitude, divided counsels and treachery." There was "an inner malaise, a kind of general loss of nerve" on the part of the Muslim community and Mughal rulers. It is this loss of inner self that enabled the East India Company to make inroads in the garb of European trade.

When a government, instead of setting right its own internal disorders, seeks the easy way out by inviting foreigners to solve its domestic problems, it is the beginning of a collapse.

Instead of taking the hard way of removing the roadblock to domestic investment, the World Bank and other multilateral institutions suggest that developing countries take the easy way out of inviting foreign investors. The Mughal Empire could have built its own navy. Instead it chose to depend on the British. Similarly, instead of aggressively acquiring foreign technologies themselves, the World Bank is keen that the developing countries should get the same from foreign investors.

We are trying to cover up our domestic bad governance in the same way that the Mughal emperors had done by inviting the East India Company. It is not, therefore, the quantum of foreign investment that matters but the underlying moral bankruptcy of our Government that is the issue.

Negative Impact of Foreign Investment due toDiminishing Returns

The application of the theory of diminishing returns to foreign investment leads to the conclusion that foreign investment leads to high growth rates only as long as it continues to flow in. Once the inflow ceases, the growth rate is reduced. In the long term it actually shrinks.

Let us think of the total investment in terms of two pies–those of the foreign and domestic investors. The foreign investor may decide to shift from reinvestment to repatriation and day. This is the short run pie. The domestic investor's pie, on the other hand, goes on ever increasing. Restrictions on capital convertibility or preferences of domicile ensure that their profits continue to be reinvested in the domestic economy.

As foreign investment flow in, the total availability of capital in the host economy increases. The law of diminishing returns tells us that the rate of return on capital would decline correspondingly. Thus, the domestic pie grows at a slower pace than it would have grown without foreign investment.

Once the foreign investors start repatriating their profits, the additional investment comes only from the domestic pie. This pie is now smaller than it would be had foreign investment not come in. The rate of growth of domestic investment pie was lowered because entry of foreign investment increased the supply of capital and lowered the rates of profits on all investments in the economy. The long term investment pie is, therefore, smaller than it would be in absence of foreign investment. Foreign capital flows did lead to a short run gain but caused loss of investment and growth in long run.

This is not a hypothetical scenario. As of now, there is no major country in the world that has been able to maintain its growth rates after foreign investors have withdrawn. The experience of countries that had attracted high foreign investment in the seventies shows this. Colombia, Guatemala, Ecuador and Mexico are four countries which had received foreign investment in excess of 1 percent of their GDP in the seventies but failed to attract more of the same in the eighties. The growth rates of all four were negative in the eighties—between (–) 3.3 percent and (–) 4.3 percent

Countries which continued to attract high levels investment in the eighties, Sri Lanka, Argentina and Brazil, had negligible or negative growth rates at 0.2 percent, (-) 2.4 percent and (–) 4.8 percent respectively. Only Chile, Thailand and Malaysia continued to attract high levels of foreign investment and were able to maintain positive growth rates. The real test of these countries too is yet to come. We have to wait and watch what happens after the foreign investors withdraw.

The conclusion is that by attracting foreign investment the developing countries may be impairing their growth rates in the long run.

Short-sighted Arguments by Indian Businessmen

One argument given in the favour of foreign investment is that once an economy is opened, the government is forced to reform. If it does not, then its domestic capital flees while foreign capital does not come. North Korea, for example, is able to maintain inefficient government because it is closed. The argument is correct. The flip side, however, is that these same foreign inflows provide easy money for government profligacy. Inflow of foreign money increases the liquidity in the domestic money market and enables the domestic government to borrow heavily at low rates of interest. The record of East Asia and China points out that foreign investment leads to bad governance.

The second argument is that Indian MNCs can bring in as much or more profits than foreign MNCs take out of India. Many Indian companies like Ranbaxy have foreign operations. They can bring in profits just as Hindustan Lever takes home from India. This is a strong argument. But the problem of justice remains unaddressed. If we are exploited by others, it does not follow that we should do the same down the line?

The third argument is that of technology. The track record of MNCs, however, is that they come more on the strength of their brand values rather than technology. There is growing evidence that MNCs often kill research in the domestic companies that they may acquire. Moreover, most so-called 'world class' technologies are available in the market. The TVs produced by Videocon have nearly all the features provided by Samsung. It is not necessary to get FDI in order to access technology.

The fourth argument is that it is better for India to ask MNCs to produce goods in India instead of importing them. Production would lead to additional wealth generation and employment in the country. This argument is not correct. High imports necessarily imply high exports in another sector. For example, India is exporting carpets for importing TVs. Domestic production increases in both cases.

Truly, the impact of FDI on the domestic governance can be negative. The RBI does not sell all the dollars brought by MNCs in the market. It retains some of them to argument its forex reserves. It prints rupees and provides them to the MNCs against these dollars. These rupees lead to an increase in liquidity in the Indian money market. This makes it easier for the government to borrow large amounts of money. This connection has been acknowledged by the RBI in more than one of its annual reports. Thus, foreign investment is a source of easy money for the government. It enables the government to continue with its profligate ways.

Another negative impact is through profit repatriations. Many UN organisations have noted the disastrous impact of profit repatriations on developing countries. In such event, foreign investment works as a catheter on the host economy siphoning off its wealth to the MNCs' home countries.

Domestic Savings, not Foreign Investment, Explains Asian Growth

The mainstream argument is that foreign investment is required to bridge the investment gap. This line of argument fails to appreciate that foreign investment has worked only in such countries where domestic savings have also been very high such as in Asia. Therefore, one cannot say that their high growth rates owe themselves to foreign investment.

Take, for example, *World Development Report*, 1995. The World Bank had cited Malaysia as an example of a country that had been successful in attracting foreign investment and Ghana as one that failed to do so. True, Malaysia has grown much faster than Ghana in recent times. But can one attribute this growth to foreign investment? Let us consider the facts.

In 1970, Ghana had received foreign investment of $68 million against $94 million by Malaysia. In percentage terms this translates to 5.1 and 3.1 percent of GDP respectively. In other words, Ghana had received higher foreign investment in comparison to Malaysia in the seventies. At that time Ghana saved 13 percent of its GDP against 27 percent by Malaysia. It is clear that Ghana had higher foreign investment and lower saving. The result was that Ghana's growth rate in the seventies was (-) 0.1 percent against (+) 7.9 percent of Malaysia. Clearly, higher foreign investment did not lead to higher growth in Ghana. Other instances can be given. The present high growth rates of China are often attributed to high levels of FDI. The role of high domestic savings rate of about 45 percent is ignored.

Mainstream economists underplay the role of domestic investment. Actually, foreign investment may have a negative impact. The high rate of growth that could be attained from high domestic savings is somewhat lessened by the entry of foreign investment. Say China's growth rate is 10 percent. This is attributed to FDI. But it is possible that the growth rate may be 12 percent in absence of FDI. There may be a decline of 2 percent in growth rate due to FDI. But if we ignore domestic savings, we may conclude that FDI has a positive impact. Thus we should assess the role of FDI by simultaneously looking at the rate of domestic savings.

FII is Better than FDI

The mainstream view is that FDI is preferable to portfolio investments as it is 'productive' while the latter is 'speculative'.

There is different impact of FDI and FII on domestic industries. An example would help bring out the issues. Bajaj Auto Limited is India's largest producer of scooters and motorcycles. It was considering a tie-up with Ford to produce cars in the early nineties. The proposal fell through because Ford insisted upon having the casting vote in the 50-50 partnership. Ford found another partner in the Mahindras. At the same time the Bajaj script attracted FII heavily. That strengthened the Indian company. Its ability to raise funds on the bourse improved. It could put up yet more plants using this foreign money. It could compete with Ford itself. FII, therefore, strengthened the Indian company against the multinational.

The impact of FDI is altogether different. Another example makes this clear. Lever Brothers and Coca Cola have come to India with large amounts of FDI. Lever is the dominant player in the soaps and detergents market. Tatas, one of the largest domestic industrial houses, could not face the competition from Lever. They were virtually forced to sell their once prized company TOMCO to Lever. Similarly the largest domestic aerated water producer, Parle, was much afraid of the competition from Coca Cola. Parle sold off its soft drink business without giving a fight in the market. These domestic businesses collapsed in front of the FDI onslaught.

The conclusion is that FII, although fickle, strengthens domestic entrepreneurs while FDI, although relatively stable, marginalizes them.

FDI in Small Amounts is Good

The economic reforms initiated by Mr. Manmohan Singh in the 1990s had two components. One part was domestic reforms. Banks were given the freedom to fix interest rates. Industrial licensing was scrapped. The Tatas had been asking permission to make passenger cars of a long time which was denied to them. They have since produced Indica successfully. The Controller of Capital Issues was dismantled and companies given freedom to fix the price of the share offerings. These domestic reforms have certainly had a positive impact on the economy. Mr. Singh deserves credit of the same.

The second part of economic reforms was external, which too had two parts. The regime of fixed exchange rates was dismantled. The resulting devaluation of the rupee gave a big boost to our exports. The balance-of-payment crisis of the early 1990s was caused by the refusal of Finance Minister Yashwant Sinha to devalue the rupee despite increasing adverse trade balance. Such a crisis cannot take place now. The price of the dollar is determined by the supply and demand and the currencies find their own equilibrium.

The other part of the external reforms was the opening of the economy to foreign investment. Prime Minister Narasimha Rao had loudly proclaimed from the ramparts of the Red Fort that the country would use its savings of providing relief to the people while foreign investment will provide the capital for economic growth. Many sectors were opened for foreign investment. However, economists like me have long held that FDI was most harmful. The *World Investment Report* 2004 published by UNCTAD has now endorsed these fears.

UNCTAD says that much FDI is aimed at exploiting the domestic markets. Such FDI leads to increased remittances of profits, payment of interest on external loans and imports of equipment. Of these, "Profit remittances can be quite high, amounting to 35 percent of the total income of services foreign affiliates of U.S. MNCs in 2002 and 53 percent of the total income of services foreign affiliates of Japanese MNCs in 2001; the figures of manufacturing foreign affiliates were 50 percent 62 percent respectively. Such payments can quickly outweigh the benefits from initial capital inflows, and thus entail net foreign-exchange losses. In times of crisis, MNCs can accelerate transfers abroad and so exacerbate crisis." This is precisely what we have been saying since long.

UNCTAD has also listed the many harmful effects of the entry of MNCs on the host economy. More specifically, UNCTAD has listed the many dangers of the entry of foreign banks:

- Transnational Banks' (TNB) entry can affect the degree of concentration of the banking industry.

- TNBs may target the largest and most creditworthy clients and crowd out domestic banks from the most creditworthy customer base.

- If domestic banks are unable to compete effectively with TNBs, they may respond by taking on high-risk business, which could undermine their health and that of the domestic banking system.

- TNBs may ration credit to Small and Medium Enterprises making it difficult of the latter to obtain credit.

- TNBs may be less amenable to monetary policy via "moral suasion."

- TNBs may shift funds between markets, even in an abrupt manner, reflecting perceived risk-adjusted returns; this could cause relatively volatile credit patterns if risks and returns in different markets change quickly.

- Profit repatriation by TNBs may place pressure on the balance-of-payment of host countries.

- TNBs may reduce local operations or withdraw from a host country market because the parent bank may "cut and run" during a crisis in a host country, rather that act as a sources of stability.

- TNB entry may expose a host country's banking system and the host economy to contagion of crisis and wider economic and financial developments abroad.

- TNB entry might reduce the ability of national authorities to exercise control over international capital movements to and from the host country.

These are precisely the fears expressed by Swadeshi economists since the reforms were initiated.

FDI should be accepted in limited quantities. The entry of foreign investors heats up the competition in the domestic economy and forces domestic businesses to up-grade to global standards. This is welcome. However, the same FDI, when accepted in large scale, leads to huge profit remittances and kills domestic industries. FDI should be taken like chutney with roti.

Increased Prices is a Better Way of Getting Foreign Capital

The IMF view is that more foreign investment is required in the developed countries. That would lead to improvement in labour productivity and to better standards of living.

This advocacy is based on the premise that the productivity of labour, in the main, depends upon the capital intensity. However, this is really not so. There are two sources of labour productivity. One, the quantity of production, measured in physical terms; and two, the price of the goods produced. The quantity increases with capital investments but not the price.

The developed countries are obtaining high prices for their products. This is much responsible for the high standards of living in those countries. A readjustment of prices would lead to a decline in the productivity of their workers and a corresponding reduction in their standards of living. This is not acceptable to the IMF. Thus, the IMF ignores the effects of prices on productivity.

The productivity of labour is measured in terms of the value of production. Say, a baker produces a hundred breads valued at a-dollar-a-piece. The productivity of the baker, broadly speaking, would be 100 dollars per day. Now if the bread is sold at two-dollars-a-piece then the productivity of the baker increases to 200 dollars per day. On the other hand, if the baker acquires a cutting machine and is able to produce 200 breads per day then too his productivity increases to 200 dollars. The productivity of labour can be increased in two different ways—by increased capital investments or by increased prices.

The productivity of labour in the developed countries is much higher than that in the developing countries. According to World Bank data the per capita income in the U.S. was 24,740 dollars whereas it was 300 dollars in India. This difference arises for two reasons (1) higher capital investment per worker; and (2) higher prices of the same product in the U.S.

Take a petrol station attendant. An attendant in India and California would fill petrol in the same number of vehicles in a day. Their physical productivity would be equal. However, for the same work, an American attendant would get ten times the wages of his Indian counterpart. Thus the same physical productivity translates into vastly different levels of labour productivity. This difference is due to price differentials. This applies to all products. A loaf of bread of same quality is valued ten times as much in the U.S. because of the overall ability of the American economy to extract better prices for its products.

This would become clear by another example. A personal chauffeur is available at half the price of company chauffeur. The reason is that the organisational power of the company's trade union forces the management to raise wages. The two chauffeurs produce the same goods but their productivity and wages are different.

The price differentials between the industrial and developing countries are determined by a similar process. The bargaining power of the developed countries is higher than that of the developing countries. The result is that the incomes of their workers are high. This difference arises from two sources—higher capital investments and higher degree of organization. Following the same logic, there are two ways in which incomes of the developing countries may increase—by higher capital investment or by better organization.

It has been accepted in an essay by Jeffrey Madrick published in the *New York Times* that the productivity of the U.S. worker increased at the rate of 2.7 percent per year in the post-war period. However, after 1973 it increased only at the rate of 1 percent. Why the change In 1973? That was precisely the year that OPEC countries increased the prices of oil. The international prices underwent a distinct change. The money-measured productivity of the oil-producing countries increased and that of the oil-importing countries decreased. It should be noted that 1973 does not mark any decisive period from the point of view of technology or capital investment.

There are two ways in which the developing countries can improve their labour productivity—by increasing capital investments or securing better prices. The IMF focuses only on capital investment and ignores the impact of prices on productivity.

The focus of IMF and other multilateral agencies on capital flows distracts the attention of the developing countries from the existing (unnatural) price differentials. The developing countries run around seeking money by way of foreign investment rather than by an increase in prices since such increase would adversely affect the developed countries, something that the IMF wants to avoid.

This Chapter is adapted from the following articles:

"Problem with 'panacea', *The Pioneer,* September 12, 2000.
"Why foreign investment hurts," *Daily News,* Colombo, October 17, 1996.
"Foreign investment," *Newstime,* June 13, 2001.
"Virtues of portfolio investment," *Daily News,* Colombo, June 3, 1996.
"Take FDI like chutney with roti," *The Pioneer,* October 19, 2004.
"Why does the IMF ignore prices?" *Daily News,* Colombo, March 7, 1996.

6

The Case Against FDI

The experience of developing countries with large FDI has been negative. In this chapter we show FDI has not led to transfer of technologies, to good governance or to long term increase in growth rates.

This discussion does not have much relevance to the contemporary situation in India in the new century. Our companies are successful in facing the MNC onslaught and are becoming MNCs themselves. However, this discussion is relevant for two reasons. One, there is a recurrent harangue in the media about the need to attract high levels of FDI. This section shows the erroneous nature of this advocacy even if it is not very successful presently. Two, the issue remains important for other developing countries who are vying with each other to attract higher FDI. India has the moral responsibility to lead the developing countries out of FDI-fixation hence this discussion.

FDI is not Bringing Frontline Technologies

The common view is that we need foreign investment in order to secure the latest technologies. But the *World Investment Report*, 1999 of UNCTAD has pointed out that MNCs have failed to transfer frontline technologies and have hurt R&D efforts of domestic companies. Therefore we need to aggressively regulate MNCs to ensure that technology is transferred.

UNCTAD points put that the takeover of public utilities in Brazil by MNCs actually led to a reduction of investments in R&D. In the mid-nineties Brazilian auto component producers Metal Leve, Freios Varga and Cofap were acquired by MNCs. Subsequently, "the R&D activities of the local firms were downgraded, and their frontier research was relocated to parent firms' R&D centres in their home countries." Similarly two switching system manufactures Zetax and Batik, which were continuously upgrading their systems, became part of the MNC, Lucent Technologies. The later was "not interested in local R&D, preferring to rely on technologies developed n the parent company."

It was no different in other telecommunications MNC affiliates: "R&D activities geared to the development of new products were discontinued in a number of cases, and the effort shifted to the more simple adaptation of imported processes and products. In most cases, this has meant that highly qualified engineers engaged in R&D are transferred to other less-specialized functions, such as production, quality assurance, sales or marketing."

In Argentina, UNCTAD says, 'MNCs gave very little attention to R&D in affiliates. Of the privatized utilities, only one Telephone Company had an R&D unit. This unit dealt only with domestic operations, with no link with parent company R&D."

Only one telecommunications equipment manufacturer developed new products and was able to license its developments to the parent firm. In the automobile sector the main technological activity was to adapt products from parent companies to local requirements. FDI, therefore, does not automatically lead to transfer of technologies. In fact they can derail domestic R&D efforts.

According to UNCTAD, the two countries which have succeeded most in developing domestic technological capabilities–Korea and Taiwan–had relied on acquisitions of technologies by their domestic companies. But as they matured they found that they could not get state-of-art technologies externally. It was at this point they invested in their own R&D, took over innovative firms or established "listening posts" in developed countries.

MNCs can be cajoled to transfer technologies if conditions are imposed upon them. When Singer started operations in 1964, the Taiwanese authorities stipulated that it "procure 83 percent of parts and components locally within a year, provide local suppliers with standardized blueprints, send technological experts to improve productivity, prepare materials specifications and inspect final products." The result was the establishment of backward linkages and upgrading of competitive capabilities of the industry as a whole. Soon, other local firms also became major exporters. Similarly Singapore enticed MNCs to transfer technologies by providing better domestic skills, capabilities, supplier networks and infrastructure so that it becomes more profitable for the MNCs to use Singapore as their technology base. The conclusion is that we need to increase regulation of foreign investment to ensure that they transfer technologies.

A businessman would continue to churn out substandard products in a protected market. FDI provides a pressure to upgrade. Thus the argument is that FDI must be welcomed. But the problem arises from excessive opening. It is the character of the businessmen to seek profits. If he can make more profit by churning out substandard products then that is what he will do. In the case of automobiles, Indian companies were protected even from domestic competition. The government did not allow the Tatas and other businessmen to compete. The real culprit, therefore, is not the Indian businessman but the over-protection that he was given. It was the responsibility of the government to create domestic competitive environment in which he would be forced to upgrade technologically. FDI can provide incentive to upgrade when secured in small quantities that does not threaten the existence of domestic businesses.

FDI Comes to Exploit Our Bad Governance

There appears to be a consensus that India's failure to attract large amounts of foreign capital is due to domestic bad governance. Corruption, red tape, rigid labour laws and judicial delays deter foreign investors. But we are unable to put our own wealth to productive use precisely because of these problems. If we had good governance, we would not need foreign investment. If we had bad governance, foreign investment will not come. Either way it is a no-go situation.

According to the *Economic Survey*, the savings made by the Government of India stood at an average of Rs 209 billion-a-year in mid-1990s. In 2001, however, instead of saving, the Government was dissaving. The saving of the Government sector was negative at Rs 345 billion. Our Government would have been able to save and invest an additional Rs 554 billion if it had only kept to its previously attained levels of savings. Bad governance has led to a loss of this huge amount.

The World Bank has estimated that developing countries loose about 11 percent of their savings through illegal remittances such as *hawala*. According to this estimate, we have lost another Rs 537 billion from such outflow of our wealth. Furthermore, we import about Rs 480 billion worth of gold every year because people do not trust the banking sector and the stability of our currency. The loss of capital to the country due to this bad governance is about Rs 1,571 billion. Further sums are lost through leakages in various government programmes. Against this huge loss, we have succeeded in attracting a meagre Rs 208 billion as foreign investment at the close of the last century. We are losing about 7 times the money we are getting.

It is said that our inability to attract large foreign investment is due to bad governance. Of course, bad governance does dissuade foreign investors. But if good governance was obtained then we would have saved 7 times the money and there would have remained no compulsion to attract foreign investment.

It appears that foreign investor do not like good governance. India's record in honouring its international obligations is far superior to others like Indonesia, Argentina and Russia, who have attracted more foreign investment than us. Those who have defaulted on their obligations get more foreign investment. Unlike China, we have a vibrant democracy. It is precisely these elements of good governance that seem to discourage foreign investors.

We have received foreign investment only in sectors where there is bad governance. In telecom we have established and independent regulatory authority. We have also imposed stiff regulations. Our telecom companies pay nearly 40 percent of their revenues to the Government in one form or the other. Foreign telecom companies have made an exit from their Indian operations. They would rather invest in China where there is little regulation to be faced and taxes to be paid. One IAS officer who has dealt with these departments said in a seminar that foreign investors are more comfortable dealing with "closed" government departments rather than "transparent" regulatory regimes.

Enron is another example of bad governance attracting foreign investment. That company, it is now known, had indulged in accounting malpractices. It had paid huge amounts as bribes to secure profitable contracts in developing countries. The Government of Maharashtra agree to buy power at Rs 4.80 to Rs 8 per KwH when its own State Electricity Board was producing it of about Rs 2.20. Clearly, it is not competition or good governance that brought Enron to India.

The automobile industry is yet another example. Our Government has prevented the import of use cars by imposing about 200 percent import duty. We can easily make do with two to three-year-old used cars which conform to our environment and safety standards. We would have saved huge amounts of capital by importing used cars instead of investing in manufacture and purchase of new cars. It is a strange spectacle to see the Ford Motor Company–the epitome of free markets–opposing the import of used cars in India. It is time that we recognised that foreign investors come to our country not to complete with our businesses on a level playing field. They come to exploit our bad governance. Establishment of good governance would, if at all, deter more foreign investors as it has done in the telecom sector.

If we had good governance we would have invested our own money productively and there would have arisen no need to attract foreign investment. If we have bad governance then we will, if at all, receive foreign investment in sectors that provide monopoly profits to foreign investors. Either way foreign investment has little to contribute.

Lessons from the Argentina's Crisis

Large-scale foreign investment abets bad governance and leads the host country deeper into the crisis in the long run. The Argentine crisis of 2001 was attributed to that country's inability to service the debt of about $150 billion. The immediate reason was that Argentina was unable to devalue because it has pegged its currency to the dollar. But the real reason was that it had attracted large amounts of FDI. It had used these FDI inflows to service its debt. The party continued as long as FDI inflows were strong. But a reduction in FDI inflows led that country to default on its loans.

There exists a link between bad governance and foreign investment. Argentina's domestic savings rate had been continuously declining from 23 percent in 1980 to 16 percent in 1999. This was a clear indication of 'bad governance'. The disastrous consequences of this were, however, been 'covered up' by a huge increase in FDI from $2.6 bn in 1990 to $24 bn in 1999. The result was that the declining domestic investment was hidden.

The problem is not unique to Argentina. Most of the star performers on the FDI front have seen only small improvement in their growth rates despite huge increases in FDI inflows. A 342-percent increase in FDI brought 0.2 percent increase in Brazil's growth rate. The corresponding figures of China are 1,138 percent and 0.6 percent, and Malaysia 373 percent and 0.4 percent.

Clearly, large scale FDI is not bringing forth much increase in growth rates. As soon as FDI inflows decline, these countries are trapped into a crisis of having to attract yet more foreign investment.

Low FDI is our Victory

The low levels of FDI in India reflect its strength. It indicates that, unlike China, Indian businessmen are able to hold in the global marketplace without association with MNCs. India and China have both been growing at high rates but there is a great difference in their approach to FDI. China has emerged as a favourite destination of FDI receiving a record $53 billion in 2002. India, on the other hand, has been loosing its sheen. FDI flows have remained unchanged at about $5 billion between 1993 and 2004. The question is whether this indicates a failure or success?

There are three crucial points of difference between China and India–domestic savings, corruption and FDI. According to World Bank's *World Development Report* 2001, China's domestic savings rate increased from 38 percent in 1990 to 42 percent in 1999 while India's declined from 22 percent to 20 percent during the same period. China's rate of domestic savings is not only nearly double than that of India; it is increasing while India's is declining. There positive impact of domestic savings on growth is undisputed. This is one reason of China's higher rates of growth.

The second difference is regarding corruption. A deputy director of the government Religious Affairs Commission of China Hu was sentenced to death of taking bribes worth $658,000 and possession of nearly $195,000 worth of property from unidentified sources. Hu appealed his sentence, but the Jiangxi Higher Court rejected the appeal citing a Supreme Court's decision a saying that "as a senior government official, Hu should have acted as a model and strictly abided by state laws, instead of abusing his power to make illegal profits." Hu was made an example to warn other corrupt officials, the Communist Party's newspaper, *People's Daily*, said in a commentary.

The situation is dramatically different in India. The numbers of scams like those of fodder and urea continue. The Indian courts have dismissed the *hawala* case on the ground that the diaries cannot be held as admissible evidence. The courts have taken a narrow legalistic approach while dealing wlth corruption while Chinese courts have sought to set an example of others by meting out death penalties.

The third point of difference is regarding the flows of foreign investment. The figures for China are higher compared to India though the quantum of difference is suspect. According to one study, China's FDI inflows in 2000 were composed of $6 biilion of non-cash, $7 billion of round-tripping, $16 billion of reinvested earnings out of the total $38 billion received in that year. The net cash inflow was only $8 billion, which is not terribly higher than our net cash inflows of $5 billion.

The central question is to which of the above three factors should the difference in growth rate between the two giants be attributed?

The positive impact of domestic savings on growth rates is unquestioned. According to the *World Development Report* 2003, the average annual growth rate of China in 1990-2001 was 10.0 percent against 5.9 percent of India. The nearly double rates of domestic savings would explain this difference substantially, if not wholly. This is further augmented by China's efforts to remove corruption at high places. It appears that these two factors alone would much explain the high growth rates. It is strange, therefore, that mainstream economists focus on China's success in attracting FDI and not on her success in raising the level of domestic savings and stamping out corruption. The confirmed route to growth—of raising domestic savings and establishing good governance is being defocused while the uncertain route of FDI is being overplayed.

Asia's Growth is Propelled by High Savings, not FDI Inflows

Asia's economic miracle was forged by the high savings rates of its people. FDI played only a minor role. This analysis is supported by World Bank and UNCTAD data of the 13 years between 1980 and 1993.

One reason of the confusion is that countries with high levels of domestic savings have also had high levels of FDI. In order to analyze their relative roles, we have to look at the impact of FDI at similar rates of savings. Then alone we may come to any conclusion whether the growth can be attributed to FDI or to savings. Looked at from this point of view, it emerges that the growth of Asian countries is more influenced by savings and that FDI has played a marginal role.

Across Asia, countries that have saved little have experienced slow growth, which is hardly surprising. Nepal, Bangladesh and

Pakistan, of example, with savings of up to 10 percent of gross domestic product and per capita FDI of up to $1.4 have experienced only 2.4 percent per capita rate of growth. India, whose savings rates are slightly higher at 23 percent but which attracted levels of FDI as low as its South Asian neighbours, did somewhat better, seeing its economy grow 3 percent. The Indian experience compares well with countries that saw much more foreign money. Sri Lanka and the Philippines, for example, received up to $12 per capita in FDI and nonetheless grew slower than India. Sri Lanka's economy grew 2.7 percent during the 13 years in question, while the Philippines' economy actually contracted 0.6 percent. Significantly higher FDI resulted in slower growth rates.

The countries that did best were those that saved, irrespective of how much foreign money they attracted. Indonesia and China, which received FDI at around the same rates as the Philippines and Sri Lanka, but saved 25 percent and 35 percent of their GDP respectively, were faster growers. The Indonesian economy advanced at an average rate of 4.2 percent and China's at 8.2 percent during the years in question.

Inter-regional comparisons can be interesting for those who contend that mixing South Asia and East Asia is like mixing apples and oranges. In this sense, comparing Malaysia with fast growers Thailand, China and South Korea can be edifying. All were high savers, but Malaysia took in $97 per capita in FDI between 1980 and 1993, and yet its economy grew at a comparatively paltry rate of 3.5 percent. Thailand, China and South Korea, which took in only an average of $10.7 per capita in FDI, had their economies grow at an average of 7.6 percent.

Why should the real engine of growth be savings and not FDI? One possible explanation is that strong foreign capital inflows breeds complacency among domestic entrepreneurs or, worse, a kind of dependency. FDI profits may also be repatriated. The dependency might lead to lower re-investments by domestic businesses and pull down the overall rate of growth.

Short-sighted Arguments in Favour of FDI by Indian Businessmen

Indian industrialists plead the case for MNCs. This does not auger well for the country. A handful of Indian industrialists may indeed gain by FDI, but most others will be losers.

The first argument in favour of FDI from a senior industrialist was that FDI brings in capital: "All this talk of profit repatriations leading to drain of wealth is theoretical," he said. Not quite. According to RBI's annual report for 1998-99, the inward foreign investment in that year was $2,412 million. The outflow due to profit repatriation was $3,544 million. We sent out more money as profit repatriations than we received as FDI. This drain from profit repatriations is not theoretical.

Indian industrialists appear to like FDI because they can get a good price for their companies that are often making losses. The industrialist can realign his business keeping with his global strengths. Ramesh Chauhan, the erstwhile owner of Limca and other soft drink brands, for example, can benefit from FDI because it gives him cash for a not-so-profitable soft drink business. But the country loses. The wealth that is sucked out by the MNCs in profit repatriations is lost. Had the soft drink business stayed in Indian hands the repatriations would not take place.

The second argument was that it would make available goods of international quality to the Indian consumer. The face cream manufactured by Hindustan Lever is stable for three-four years. That technology is not available to Indian cosmetic manufacturers. If FDI is prohibited, then the Indian consumer will not get such superior products. But there is another dimension to such FDI. While making available a superior cream, Hindustan Lever has also thrown lacs of people involved in cottage soap industry out of employment. It has to be seen whether the benefits form such face cream are greater than the loss due to such eating away of employment.

Moreover, the same products could also be made available by an optimal opening of imports. The impact of FDI and imports are entirely different on the Indian consumer. An increase in imports of face cream would be possible only of there was a parallel increase in exports of some other products, say carpet. The soap maker in the cottage industry might lose his livelihood but he would have increased opportunity to make a living as a carpet maker. But FDI by Hindustan Lever killed the soap maker without providing another opening.

The third argument was that it creates competition in the country and forces Indian business to become globally competitive. Haldiram modernised on being threatened by the entry of Pepsi. That may indeed be the case. But the same upgradation could be obtained by implementing a domestic competition policy. To think such an improvement can come only from foreign competition is erroneous. The correct policy would be to first create domestic competition; second, create competition from optimal imports; third, allow small amounts of FDI selectively in those sectors which do not rev up.

This Chapter is adapted from the following articles:

"State of the art," *The Statesman,* November 11, 1999.
"Shortcut to prosperity," *The Pioneer,* June 18, 2002.
"FDI: Lessons to be learnt from Argentina," *The Financial Express,* December 29, 2001.
"Victory of Indian Businessmen," *South Asia Politics,* July 2003.
"Asia doesn't need Europe," *Asian Wall Street Journal,* April 8, 1996.
"Dollar divine," *The Pioneer,* May 16, 2000.

7

Aid Kills the Developing Countries

Western countries pretend to be well-wishers of the people of developing countries. They demand that developing country government protect the human rights of their people. They give aid for provision of health cure and spreading computer literacy. Their real agenda, however, is to extract the resources of the developing countries by manipulation of prices and repatriation of profits. They give aid to distract attention of the developing countries from these extractions.

This argument is perhaps no longer applicable to India which has no need of foreign aid. But India has reached this fortunate circumstance, in part, by refusing to accept aid. For example, the World Bank withdrew from the financing of the Sardar Sarovar project. Gujrati NRIs stepped in and provided the money. The lesson for other developing countries is to take foreign aid with care lest they be distracted and strangulated.

Political Economy of Human Rights

Agencies of the United Nations want to persuade the people of the developing countries to accept the suzerainty of global capital over their national governments. The sales strategy is that it is necessary for the "global community" to intervene in the domestic affairs to secure human rights of the developing people. The catch is that the "global community" is constituted by global capital. The result is that global capital has the right to intervene in the affairs of developing countries to secure its interests; but the people of the developing countries do not have any right to seek redressal from the global capital for the evils wrought by it.

At the root of the problem lies the Universal Declaration of Human Rights. Article 13 states that, "everyone has the freedom of movement and residence *within the borders of each state.*" Article 21 (2) says that "everyone has the right of equality to public services in *his country.*" Article 22 states that "everyone has the right to social security *in accordance with organisation and resources of each state.*" While the human rights themselves are allegedly universal their application–wherever a question of economic resources is involved–the rights become entirely national.

The strategy is that civil rights should be promoted aggressively because they give global capital a locus standi to intervene in the affairs of the developing countries. But where economic rights are concerned, the Declaration suddenly acquires a national ambience.

The UN Development Programme seeks to promote the interests of global capital with this philosophy. In *Human Development Report*, 2000, UNDP has suggested that international human rights machinery be set up and that international human rights norms are recognised as being supreme over domestic laws. This seemingly good suggestion has grave implications.

Consider what would have happened in Punjab in the 1980s under the above dispensation. Let us say the economy had disintegrated because of terrorist activities. India would not be able to enact a TADA and prevent such terrorism because the "global community" would have taken direct action against it. Now let us say that the economy of Punjab suffered. Vegetables could not be sent to Calcutta and people became poor. Their human rights of livelihood were violated. Yet, the people of Punjab would not have the right to demand unemployment compensation from the global community headquartered in New York and Brussels. They will have to stay put within the borders of India. Reason? Article 22 of the Universal Declaration states that right to social security is secured in accordance with the resources of each state. They would also not have the right to migrate to New York to secure their human rights of livelihood. Article 13 restricts the right of movement within the borders of a state. While the "global community" will have the right to intervene in the political affairs of India, they have no responsibility to mitigate the effects of that same interference.

The UNDP is favourably disposed towards the establishment of "core labour standards." Human rights should be linked to trade, it says, "so that the stronger enforcing mechanism of trade" can be applied. Let us examine how this will work. Say those working in the *agarbatti* export industry are able to make a living despite the wages being meagre. The enforcing mechanism of the "global community" now determines that core labour standards have been violated. India loses its agarbatti exports and those people are rendered unemployed. But they are not entitled to unemployment compensation and social security from the same "global community" because these are, according to the Declaration, to be provided such relief according to the resources of the country.

The Universal Declaration of Human Rights and the UNDP seek the subjugation of the developing countries. Lofty proclamations are made about the "universality" of human rights and the need for human development. But, when it comes to their application to economic rights, the universality disappears and "nationality" sneaks in.

It is in this sequence that the UNDP invokes Amartya Sen, who has argued that it is not necessary to fulfil all the human rights: "We need not jump from non-fulfilment of the rights to the denial of the rights themselves... If a particular government does not, right now, have the resources needed to bring about the fulfilment of specified rights for all, it is essential to encourage the government to work towards making their fulfilment feasible."

The implication is that while interference by the "global community" can take place immediately, the other rights can be left unfulfilled till an unspecified time. The "global community" can impose trade sanctions to secure political rights of the people (and economic rights of global capital) but the economic rights of the people can be left to be secured at a future unspecified time.

When a state is unable to protect human rights, the "global community" can act in a straightforward way. But if an MNC undertakes such violation then, says UNDP, incentives in the form of "profit" motives should be relied upon. If a state should violate human rights the UN forces should march in straightaway. But, if an MNC should do the same then "media campaigns," "consumer boycotts" and "labelling schemes" should be relied upon.

The real aim of the Universal Declaration of Human Rights is to persuade the developing countries to hand over sovereignty to the "global community" based in New York and Brussels so that they can secure the interests of global capital.

UNDP does not Want to Remove Poverty

The UNDP has pointed out in its *Human Development Report* that the developed countries had agreed to provide 0.7 percent of their income to the poor countries as development assistance but they have failed to meet their promise. In fact development assistance has declined from $52 billion in 1990 to $50 billion in 2000. This implies a steep reduction from 0.33 percent to 0.22 percent of their incomes.

The Report points out that the European Union gives hundred times the subsidy to a European cow than aid to a human being in Sub-Saharan Africa. The EU gave a subsidy of $913 per European cow every year while its aid to Sub-Saharan Africa was $8 per person per year. Japan does even better. It gives a subsidy of $2,700 per cow against aid of $1.5 to Sub-Saharan Africa. The poor countries are being doubly hit. On the one hand, they are prevented from accessing the markets of the developed countries by the huge subsidies they give to the domestic farmers. On the other, they are starved of money by little aid flowing in.

The objective of the developed countries is to extract the income of the developing countries. They are justified in upholding this self-interest in keeping with the geopolitical environment towards the beginning of this century. But it is inexcusable that developing country leaders also try to stabilize the transfer of the resources from developing countries to developed countries. Former Chairman of India's Planning Commission Mr. K C Pant was asked by this author during a release function of the *Human Development Report*: "Why do poor countries always keep demanding more aid instead of setting their own house in order?" Mr. Pant's reply was illuminating. He said," We are moving towards an equitable world order. If there are islands of prosperity amidst a sea of poverty then there will be global instability. Increased aid is required to maintain a stable world order." Mr. Pant is demanding increased assistance so that the poverty of India does not become a threat to the prosperity of the developed countries. His objective is not that India becomes equal to the developed countries.

Again Mr. Pant was asked, "What is the strategy for the poor countries to become equal to the rich?" Mr. Pant Said, "I agree in spirit with the point raised. It is through market access that equality can be established." Mr. Pant is living in a dream world. The experience after WTO is that free trade has increased competition among the poor countries and lowered the prices of their products leading to worsening of poverty. The *Human Development Report* says that heavily indebted poor countries "rely heavily on exports of primary commodities—which have suffered from declining prices." Mr. Pant is selling free trade—which is the problem—as the solution.

The challenge before us is to develop a strategy which can provide quick relief to the poor countries while taking them towards equality with the developed countries. This can be achieved with the following four-pronged strategy.

- Developing countries need to develop their own capacity to manufacture pharmaceutical and other technology products. The poor countries should come out of the WTO and start copying the high technology products of the developed countries. They should stop running after market access and focus on breaking the source of the income of developed countries which lies in the patents protection of their technologies. India must provide technologies to other poor countries. That will hit at the monopoly incomes of the developed countries and establish true equality.

- The poor countries are affected by declining prices of their produce. The developed countries are dependent on the resources of the poor countries–oil, minerals, water and labour. The poor countries can make cartels and jack up the prices of these commodities like OPEC has done successfully for oil. The Western countries are rich because they have monopoly over technologies. The countries of the South can become rich only by creating their own monopolies of natural resources. The poor countries should not be worried at the developed countries taking retaliatory measures and making cartels for their products. They have *already* made cartels as we see in drugs and aircraft industries. They have already priced their products optimally. They can go no further. The developing countries, however, have under priced their produce and can gain by raising their prices.

- India has a huge pool of human capital. We have been successful in maintaining high rates of growth and reducing poverty. India should create a programme of providing this knowledge to other poor countries so that they can get out of their mental dependence on the developed countries.

- The poor countries should make common markets among themselves. Let there be free trade so that the benefits of comparative advantage are obtained and the pitfalls of closed economy avoided. But, at the same time, let the poor countries stand as a bloc against the rich.

It is tragic that our leaders seek more assistance so that poverty can be kept at sustainable levels and the richness of the developed countries can be protected from poor people of India.

The Psychological Damage that Aid Causes

The *World Development Report* 2004 called for increased development aid so that basic services like water, sanitation, power, health and education reach the poor.

Two concepts are relevant in this context. First, charity is given without expecting any *material* gains. It is given so that the giver develops detachment towards his worldly possessions and rises spiritually. If charity is given for social, political or economic gains then it should be called 'trade' or investment. The Sethji who gives money to build a room in a temple and has his name plate put there is undertaking a trade. He buys social acclaim with money.

Second, charity is to be given to the destitute and the ascetics. Charity or aid is not to be given to a person who working hard to raise himself by his own efforts. Aid is meant for those who have lost everything and have nothing more to lose. If charity is given to a person who is rising, it kills his self-efforts, makes him dependent, orients his mind towards 'begging' for more instead of earning, and causes great damage to his psyche. Thus we find that many self-respecting poor people will not accept free food when offered. They do the right thing. The psychic loss is greater than the material gain from charity.

Charity has a negative effect when given to secure political gains. The World Bank has given instances of aid having such negative effect.

- *Aid influences the nature of domestic spending.* The donor may give aid for only capital expenses and expect the recipient to incur running expenditures from its own budget. A donor may make a huge hospital for AIDS, which is high its own agenda, and that may lead to the poor country spending its scarce revenues towards the recurring expenditures in AIDS prevention. The recipient country then spends less money on thc prevention of tuberculosis or malnutrition which is more important and spends more on AIDS prevention.

- *Aid may be given for projects in which the recipient is not interested in.* Some villages in Rajasthan dug up their well-functioning tanks and spoiled them under government-led famine relief works because they would get famine relief only if they undertook earth works like digging tanks. I once suggested to a foreign donor to finance research for locating tree species which the farmers would find profitable to plant. But the donor wanted immediate publicity and quick results. Thus it persisted with the programme of providing subsidy to the farmers for planting trees which were not useful for them.

- *Donors may insist that the recipient government spend their own money in specified sectors as conditionality for receiving aid.* The IMF has insisted that the poor countries seeking debt relief have to open up their economies and follow an 'open border' policy for Western exports and entry of MNCs. Aid then becomes a tool of arm-twisting nationalist or *Swadeshi* governments to fall in line.

- *The donor can bypass the existing slow-moving sustainable works and supplant them with fast-track works that are unsustainable.* A NGO was encouraging people to make their village tanks with their own efforts. Foreign donors stepped in to support the good work. The result was that the tanks began to be made with foreign money. These tanks were often not repaired when they broke. The result was that sustainable tanks were killed and unsustainable tanks were built instead.

A more dangerous aspect of aid is that it kills nationalist politics. The World Bank has given some indications of this happening.

- *Foreign donors often provide big salaries to their domestic employees.* A salary of Rs 50,000 per month or consultancy charges of Rs 5,000 per day is 'normal' for such appointments. One friend of mine was the State-level Secretary of a Left party. He got disillusioned by the internal politics of the Party. Instead of fighting within the Party, he became a highly-paid representative of a foreign donor. He was distracted from fighting against the bad politics of his Party.

- *Donors often provide the needed services directly.* If a donor builds schools in the village, it takes the pressure off the government system to perform. The result is that the government system becomes worse. This undermines the line departments of the recipient country in the long run. Many health and education services are being provided by the donor-NGO network in Bangladesh. This reduces the accountability of the political system for providing these services.

Despite these negative aspects aid provides immediate relief. But the recipient countries pay a heavy cost in the long run. Thus we see that countries that have received huge foreign aid have virtually never risen. Districts like Udaipur in India have remained in the economic backwaters partly because they received huge amounts of foreign aid.

These negative effects of aid explain why the World Bank yet seeks more of the same because the objective is to cut short the economic development of the poor countries.

There are other non-government donors like Oxfam, Amnesty International and Greenpeace which criticize their own governments while providing assistance. What do we say to them? The answer is that instead of providing us money they should put pressure on their own governments to follow dharmic economic policies. Developed countries have turned charity into a political tool to disempower the poor countries. These organizations should pressurize their governments to relax patents acts, ease visa restrictions for the entry of workers from the developing countries and provide access to their markets. These measures will genuinely empower the developing countries and provide them with more money than aid could ever provide. They would no longer need foreign aid either from the Western governments or these well-meaning organizations.

Bill Gates' Charitable Pretensions

Bill Gates is the richest man in the world. He is also the biggest philanthropist. He has established the Bill and Melinda Gates Foundation with a corpus of $60 billion—nearly equal to the total annual income of Karnataka and Andhra Pradesh combined. But true charity is made with honest income. In order to assess the nature of Gates' charity we have to examine the nature of his income.

Gates' main source of income is from the Windows software sold by his company Microsoft. Gates has got the right to sell this software at monopolistic prices across the world under the TRIPS agreement of the WTO. Maarten Vanheuverswyn tells on marxist.com website that 94 percent of the computers in the world use Windows software. The main competitor to Windows is the Linux software which is available free. Lila Rajiva tells on the CounterPunch website that President Kalam has suggested that free software is the way to go for India. But Gates has succeeded in persuading most consumers not to use Linux, which is available free, and to use Windows, from which he makes huge profits. Admittedly Linux has some problems. But one would have expected philanthropist Gates to help remove those problems. Instead, Gates highlights those very problems to increase sales of Windows software sold by him. He is like the hotelier who has persuaded the tourists to buy bottled water instead of drinking from the clear spring that flows nearby.

Andrew Colley of ZDNet Australia explains how Gates aggressively tries to kill the use of Linux. Commerce Minister John Della Bosca of NSW Territory had made his intention known to end the state government's reliance on Windows software. Immediately Gates flew into Australia and announced a charity of 40 million Australian dollars for the spread of computer literacy among the poorer people. Gates intention, says Colley, was to dissuade the government from using Linux. Similarly he says India's BJP Government had planned to encourage the use of Linux in 2002. Immediately Gates flew in and announced a charity of $500 million. Of this $100 million was to go for AIDS treatment and $400 million of computer literacy. Thereafter the Government went silent on the use of Linux.

Australian Democrat's IT spokesperson Brian Greig says Gates' charity is designed to create more addiction to Windows so that user becomes dependent on Microsoft for future requirements of software.

Sergio Amadeu, president of the Brazilian National Institute for Information Technology compared Microsoft's activities in giving software to developing governments for free to that of "drug dealers" who give free drug to the young to get them addicted. The Open Source Industry of Australia quotes Gates regarding software piracy in China as follows: "As long as they are going to steal it, we want them to steal ours. They'll get sort of addicted, and then we'll somehow figure out how to collect sometime in the next decade."

Marketing companies initially give away free items along with some purchase to get the customers hooked. Then in Round 2 they start charging for the same items. Similarly Gates provides free products with Windows or gives away money in computer literacy-linked charities to create future demand for Windows.

Further, Gates tries to kill his competitors. Maarten Vanheuverswyn gives the case of Microsoft's Internet Explorer. In the early nineties Netscape held around 90 percent market share. Microsoft saw Netscape's success as a threat to its dominant Windows operating system and in 1995 launched an aggressive campaign to establish control over the browser market. They launched Internet Explorer 1.0. Netscape may have had nearly 90 percent market share, but as a relatively small company it lacked financial backing. Microsoft Windows had a monopoly in the operating system marketplace that was used to push Internet Explorer to a dominant position. The trick was to provide Internet Explorer free with every copy of Windows. In this way Microsoft was able to enlarge its market and push Netscape out of business.

There are problems with Gates' charities in the field of health as well. Gates is concentrating on development of vaccines for the prevention of diseases such as malaria and AIDS. But various studies have pointed out that the main problem of sickness among the poor is that of malnutrition. Developed countries are selling Windows software, computer chips, mobile phones and drugs at high prices. This monopoly pricing of advanced technologies makes the developing countries poor, deprives their people of food and increases sickness. Big drug companies enter to provide vaccines from this sickness. Gates should have reduced the price of Windows for the developing countries, enriched them and helped solve their health problems. Gates' efforts become more suspect because Buzzle.com website reports that he has ploughed $76.9m into Merck shares, $37.3m into Pfizer and $29.7m into Johnson & Johnson. Perhaps Gates wants to pressurize these companies into doing research on these diseases. Even then, he is supporting the monopoly of these companies on life saving drugs while the developing countries are demanding loosening of those patents and expansion of generic drugs. The important victory of the developing countries at WTO Ministerial at Doha was to get the right to restrict the patents on public health concerns. Gates' approach is at crossroads with that of the developing countries in whose interests he claims to make charities.

Gates often ties up health charities with computer education. In India, for example, he gave $100 million for AIDS and $421 million as investment in new software development, including a Hindi version of Windows XP. This was duly applauded in the NY Times. During the visit, Chandrababu Naidu committed Andhra Pradesh state to use Microsoft products for all future computerization. Andrew Leonard says on Salon.com that the $200 million pledged by Gates for the development of libraries will go for 'Internet access', which will further promote the use of Microsoft products. Clearly Gates' charities are no different than the 'free' seed distributed by sugar mills to farmers in order to increase the sugar content of the cane produced.

Gates should do two things. One, he should open the code of Windows software and other Microsoft products. That will lead to much more broad-based development of the next generation of software. Two, he should buy the patents of live-saving drugs from pharmaceutical companies and provide them free to the developing countries to lower the cost of treatment of diseases.

Western Countries give Aid to Extract Resources

The developed countries give aid for the enabling the developing countries to trade in the world markets. But the expansion of every type of trade is not beneficial for them.

Vietnam has emerged as the No 1 supplier of pepper during the last few years. Previously, the quality of pepper produced by that country was poor. The International Trade Centre initiated a program of quality improvement with Swiss assistance. Contacts were established with spice importers associations in America and Europe. The weight, volatile oil content, moisture and other parameters were adjusted according to accepted global standards. This resulted in huge expansion of exports and that country has emerged as supplier No 1 of pepper today.

We should examine who was the final beneficiary of this expanded trade. The farmers of Vietnam are able to supply pepper at low prices in the world markets because the wages are low. In comparison the wages in Kerala are high hence pepper of the same quality produced in India is higher. The success of Vietnam has brought trouble for the farmers of Kerala. They have had to reduce the wages in order to remain competitive in the world markets. The main beneficiary of Vietnam's success has been the consumers in America and Europe who have got good quality pepper at lower prices.

It must be admitted that the farmers of Vietnam also have made some gains. They are able to obtain wages even if they are low. But the farmers of Kerala are net losers. The net impact on the two developing countries taken together is *reduction* of wages of their labour.

A similar model of trade-led development was imposed by the British rulers on colonial India. Our share in world income in 1700 was about 23 percent. It declined to about three percent by 1950. These 250 years also witnessed a huge expansion in our trade. Railways were built and telephone and telegraph lines were laid. Indian farmers produced indigo and sugar cane but they continued to starve. The reason was that the price of the commodities was set by London-based importers who had monopoly over the markets. Most benefits of this trade were obtained by the British consumers. The Indian farmer only got poorer.

The problem is explained well in the *Mahabharata*. It is asked, to whom does the cow belong—to the owner, to the sheppard, to the milkman, the shop keeper or to the consumer who buys the milk? The answer is given—the cow belongs to he who drinks the milk because the activity of all others is aimed at providing him with milk. Likewise the cultivation of pepper belongs to he who consumes it.

This does not mean that we must abandon trade. It only means that expansion of trade enables us to survive at subsistence incomes. The export of pepper enabled farmers of Vietnam to obtain subsistence wages. They got buttermilk. The question is how to get the butter?

The American consumers of pepper and British consumers of indigo and sugar gained from expansion of exports by Vietnam and India because they had a monopolistic control over the market. The American spice importer determines the price of Vietnamese pepper. Thus, expansion of trade in an environment of competition brings scant benefits to the producers. We should apply our minds to creating monopolies instead of blindly assuming that expansion of competitive trade will bring benefits. Instead of competing with Vietnam in the global markets and forcing a decline in prices; we should, therefore, join hands with that country to increase the price of pepper.

UNICEF does not Raise the Issue of Price of Exports

Mainstream economists suggest that developing countries should invest more of their own incomes in health and education. Higher capabilities will enable their people to grab opportunities in the global marketplace. But the record points in the opposite direction. If we compare the performance of countries that spent more and those which spent less on the social sectors in the 1980s, it transpires that those spending more on social sectors had lower growth rates.

Nations that spent the least on social sectors in 1982 are Pakistan, India, Cameroon, Sri Lanka and Indonesia. On average, they budgeted a measly 7.8 percent on health and education. At the other end of the scale are the big spenders Kenya, Zimbabwe, Papua and New Guinea, Togo and Costa Rica. On average, they poured more than one-third, or 33.8 percent, of their national budgets into social spending. And what happened? During the 1980s, the economies of the lowest social spenders grew by about 2.2 percent. The big spenders, meanwhile, managed to achieve a negative growth rate of 0.1 percent. Whatever else these figures tell us, they show that spending money on meeting the public's physical needs did not lead to better incomes for them.

Even more significant, perhaps, is the fact that low social-expenditure countries appear to have ended up with healthier populations than those of more generous governments elsewhere. The life expectancy among the countries that spent less increased by an average of 6.6 years. On the other hand, life expectancy increased by only 1.6 years in the high-expenditure group.

How is this possible? Why do social expenditures appear to be counterproductive? This riddle can be solved by understanding the intricate inter-relationships among the physical, economic and political faculties of the human animal. Some people, of course, need helping hand at the most basic and intimate levels of their life. A person, who is mentally retarded, for example, might require government assistance in looking after his physical needs. More sophisticated or indirect help, in the form of government efforts to create a good climate for business opportunities, is probably not as useful for him. For people with certain handicaps and disabilities, the provision of physical assistance is the best way of ensuring that they reach their highest potential.

The situation is quite different for a person who is capable of running, say, a petty shop. He can work. He can earn money. The correct area of assistance for him would be economic inputs. What he needs most is better security for his shop, less harassment by government officers, protection from competition from Wal-Mart and maybe some credit. If an atmosphere were created in which the shopkeeper is able to earn money, he would be able to obtain the physical facilities of health and education himself.

On the other hand, if such a person is simply handed everything he needs to survive, he may not be able to realize his highest potential. If the government gives nutritional supplements to his pregnant wife and mid-day meals to his children, he starts believing that he is himself incapable of obtaining those facilities for his family. Over time, his self-esteem plummets. The focus on his lower faculties, instead of empowering his higher faculties, actually kills them. It follows that creating income-earning opportunities for the poor, not aid or increased social spending, is the sure way to improve their conditions.

This leads to an advocacy of protectionism. But there is a catch. There are three stages that must be delineated:

- *Stage 1:* Provide protection to domestic businessmen from MNCs to enable them to face global competition.

- *Stage 2:* Dismantle protectionism and help domestic businesses to conquer the world.

- *Stage 3:* Provide protection in selected labour-intensive sectors to generate employment and incomes for the poor.

Debt Reduction is used as a Pincer to Extract Resources

Archbishop of Canterbury George Carey and World Bank President James D Wolfensohn jointly authored an article proclaiming that the Church, NGOs and World Bank share the same dream: "to eliminate poverty." The G-8 agreed to provide debt relief to the poorest 36 countries. There is a catch in the move though. The indebted countries will be entitled to relief only if they adhere to IMF reform and austerity package, which involves opening the domestic economy to foreign investment and imports. In the process these countries may land up in worse situation.

The problem of indebtedness arose because the governments borrowed but spent the money unwisely. Debt *per se* is not the culprit. It is the misuse of money–or bad governance–that is responsible for indebtedness.

The obvious solution is to write off the accumulated debt; provide more incomes and, if necessary, new debt to the now-reformed "good governments" and bring the country back to the path of progress. The Church and the World Bank should ask for better prices for the produce of the developing world. If it could secure an increase in the prices of copper and timber, Zimbabwe would be able to make the roads and power houses without having to ask for either foreign debt or aid.

But that is not what the Church asked for, nor what G-8 has done. They have made debt relief conditional on the countries following an 'IMF reform and austerity plan'. One essential ingredient of all IMF packages is that the borrowing country should open up to foreign investment and imports. Free entry to FDI allows MNCs to come in and smother domestic industries. If Hindustan Lever can gulp away TOMCO, and Coke can do the same to Parle, we can well imagine the plight of domestic industries in less developed countries like Maldives, Bhutan and Mozambique.

Foreign debt could also be used to build roads and power houses. ICICI, for example, takes debt abroad and lends down the line to domestic industries. Under the relief package, such 'friendly' debt will be replaced with 'unfriendly' foreign investment.

The second dimension of IMF packages is that the borrowing countries are required to dismantle import restrictions. Normally, free trade should beget benefits. A developing country would export what it can produce cheap and import what others can do so. But the same free trade becomes debilitating in conjunction with foreign investment or debt inflows.

These capital inflows increase the supply of dollars. The price of dollar declines in the same measure as that of the domestic currency, say rupee, increases. Cheap dollar leads to higher imports. Normally, this should have led to a deterioration of Balance of Payments. But this does not happen because the gap is covered by capital inflows. The situation is similar to a company which covers losses by increasing equity or taking fresh loans. The situation remains stable as long as these inflows continue. But once they stop the world comes crashing down.

The domestic industry is doubly hit. One, it has to face competition from MNCs which have access to cheap credit. Two, it has to face competition from imports. The result of IMF packages therefore is that domestic industry folds up. But it is not visible in the short run because construction of factories by foreign direct investors creates a short run demand and cheap imports contain inflation. But once FDI inflows stop, the country gets into yet deeper problems. Demand is no more created from the construction of FDI factories. No more can cheap imports be financed out of capital inflows.

The Church and the World Bank have joined to make sure that the domestic business of indebted countries is extinguished. Their interests are best served if the developing countries remain healthy, educated and poor. The World Bank can promote MNCs and the Church can harvest the impoverished souls.

Aid is only a Pain Reliever

Poor country governments often look to the developed countries for salvation instead of their own people. The first reason is corruption. The leaders of the Latin American countries bled their economies and stashed away that wealth in Swiss banks. That was labelled as 'capital flight'. The developed countries stopped giving loans and instead asked them to seek FDI so that such a bleeding would not take place. Allegations of similar bleeding have been levelled against Rajiv Gandhi in the Bofors case. The consequent loss of a nation's wealth is made up by foreign investment. Instead of encouraging and supporting their own businesses to create world-class facilities, the MNCs are given a red carpet welcome. Special facilities and tax concessions are granted. These corporations produce goods in the poor countries. In the process they compete with and kill whatever domestic entrepreneurship may exist. They repatriate profits and remit moneys to the developed countries by royalty payments, pricing and many other charges.

The bureaucracy joins the politicians in bleeding their countries. Corrupt governments pamper government servants because they are partners in corruption. This leads them to impose high tax burdens on their businesses rendering them globally uncompetitive. This killing of the domestic economy makes them more dependent on foreign investment and aid.

The people are partners in this unholy game. In my village in Rajasthan we offered to bear the losses for the first six months if any youth would start the business of food processing. Not one youth came forward. They all wanted safe and secure jobs. One can easily line the people up for free distribution of blankets but they do not want to undertake business. This makes the country dependent upon doles from foreign donors.

This serves the domestic governments too. The ministers can claim that the people are being looked after. The NGOs get fat grants from rich country governments to distribute these doles. They too become advocates of 'aid'.

There has come into being an unholy axis between the leaders of the rich and poor countries. The developed countries support corrupt government in poor countries so that they continue to export their wealth to Swiss banks and are ever dependent upon doles and investment from the developed countries.

This Chapter is adapted from the following articles:

"Rich and Poor," *Statesman,* September 8, 2003.
"Who needs Aid?" *Swadeshi Patrika,* August 2003.
"Bill Gates' charitable pretensions," 2006. Publication details unavailable.
"The salt and pepper of 'Aid for Trade," *Businessline,* January 3, 2006.
"The UNICEF Fallacy," *Asian Wall Street Journal,* February 8, 1996.
"In the name of debt reduction," *The Pioneer,* July 7, 1999.
"Dependence on aid," *Newstime,* September 19, 2002.

PART - 2

THE ASIAN CENTURY

8

India's March Towards World Conquest

The Indian is the longest surviving ancient civilisation. India has often turned the tables on its conquerors. In order to understand India today, it is helpful to understand how it has acted in the past.

The Importance of being a Mercantile Civilization

One of the accusations against India is that it is laggard in technology. But, it seems, India has always been so. The earliest masonry walls have been found in Jericho in Palestine. Iraq is supposed to have developed the first wheeled cart. Earliest gold was found in West Asia. Copper and bronze, too, were first smelted there. India appears to have contributed nothing to these great technological innovations of the past. Yet Indian towns of Mohenjodaro and Harappa by far excelled those of Egypt and Iraq.

India won on the strength of her acumen in trade. India specialized in exports of manufactured items in the Bronze Age. Apart from Mohenjodaro and Harappa, there were other commercial towns. Lothal, near Ahmedabad, was the centre of bead-making and had a man-made dockyard. Harappa, now in Pakistani Punjab, was a centre of metallurgy. Kalibangan near Hanumangarh in Rajasthan near was a market of agricultural produce and had a stone-working industry. Sind was an important shipping centre.

These cities produced partly for exports. Indian seals of that period have been found in many of the Bronze Age cities of West Asia. This shows that Indian traders had a presence there. Curiously, only rarely have seals of other countries been found in India. This might indicate that foreign traders rarely visited India and international trade was mainly in the hands of Indians. Sea-trade with West Asia was conducted partly through intermediaries at Bahrain. King Sargon of Iraq boasted that ships of Meluhha and Makan, as India was then known, were moored near his capital.

The items exported and imported make an interesting list. A bale of cloth has been discovered at the city of Lagash which bears the imprint of an Indus Valley seal. Inscriptions discovered at the ancient Iraq city of Ur establish that their traders imported copper from India. Ingots discovered in Iraq, Bahrain and the Indus Valley basin are of identical shapes and weight. Archaeological evidence suggests that this copper may have come either from the Khetri mines in Rajasthan or may have been imported from Persia by land, refined in India and exported to Iraq by the sea route! Other items of export from India were ceramic beads, statues, stone vessels, pearls (known as fish-eye), spices, perfumes, ivory items and onions. Items exported from India were either agricultural or industrial products. This manufacturing activity appears to have been the source of wealth of the cities of the Indus civilization.

Against this, it appears that India imported very little. Almost no products of West Asia have been discovered in the Indus cities. However, there is evidence to show that lead and tin–the two metals essential for alloying copper to make bronze–were imported. India imported lots of silver and gold. A large number of gold objects have been discovered in the Indus Valley cities. These include beads, pendants, amulets, brooches, needles and borlas. Since no deposits of gold are found in India, it is presumed that this gold was imported.

The pattern of external trade in ancient India consisted of exports of textiles, beads, copper and other manufactured items and imports of tin, lead, silver and gold. The country that made no technological innovations, and where no gold was found, came to be known as the 'golden bird'.

A similar pattern appears to have established itself in the Iron Age. Cotton textiles were manufactured at Mathura, Kalinga and Kasi, among other places. Some of these were exported to the Western world though Bharuch. The famous steel blades of Damascus were made from steel imported from India, which was known for its hardness and purity. Other items of exports ranged from spices and diamonds to ivory and dyestuffs. Ancient India also exported elephants, lions, tigers and buffaloes, apart from monkeys, parrots and peacocks to Rome. In return for this, it imported gold. Interestingly, gold from Siberia was acquired by Rome only to be sent to India for the procurement of various items of luxury. The trade was highly unfavourable to the West. In fact, some historians have held that the penchant for luxuries imported from India was an important factor behind the draining of the coffers of the Roman Empire and led to its ultimate downfall.

Strange as it may seem, the present buoyancy in India's exports appears to be following this historical pattern. Some of the items in which India has established an edge have been her historical items of exports. India is an important player in the world cotton textiles market. India dominates the international polished diamond trade. Rice and milk products are emerging as important items of export. Thus, India seems to be moving towards re-establishing its historical trade pattern based upon the exports of agricultural and manufactured commodities. An added dimension is the exports of services such as computer software and Business Process Outsourcing. And, imports of silver and gold have surged.

Ultimately it is trade that wins the day. Gains from technological innovations do not pay in the long run. After a technology has been standardized, those who excel in adapting it to trade, win. Egypt may have made the first blown glass objects, but India exported the beads. The Greeks may have made the first iron armaments, but India exported Wootz steel to make swords.

It would seem, therefore, that the U.S., with its technological edge, may wind up as loser with its focus on Intellectual Property Rights. She would certainly stand to gain where a few new products are concerned. But that may take the attention away from manufacturing competitiveness and she may not be able to compete in most markets.

Technologies are like water. They have an inherent tendency to find their own level. This flow can be restricted only for a short time and that too at considerable cost. Therefore, instead of concentrating on protecting intellectual property, the U.S. must look inward and examine how to make its manufacturing industry internationally competitive.

Collaborate and Kill

India is not facing a technological onslaught for the first time. Towards the beginning of the Iron Age, Alexander invaded India. Before that time wars were conducted with chariots–which were not easily manoeuvrable–and the infantry–which was slow. Alexander's father Philip combined the two. He put a spear-wielding warrior on the horse and invented the cavalry.

Based on this technological superiority, Alexander had conquered the entire civilised world of that time–Greece, Egypt, Babylon and Persia. Then he moved on to conquer India. Many Indian kingdoms tried to resist his attacks in vain. However, Chandragupta Maurya saw the technological advantage which Alexander had.

He sided with the Greeks. He gained their technology and soon deserted them. He returned to Pataliputra and established the Mauryan Empire from there. Later, when the Mauryan Empire was attacked, he was able to hold his own. The risk that Chandragupta had taken to join the Greeks and acquire foreign military technology enabled him to protect his empire's sovereignty in the long term.

Chandragupta's grandson, Ashoka, expanded the Mauryan Empire. After the war against Kalinga, the focus shifted to economic and social consolidation. Till that time, the primary source of state finances had been land revenue and loot. Ashoka changed that and made taxation of trade and manufacture the chief source of state finances. Political unification enabled trade to expand by leaps and bounds. This was sustained by the guilds which had the support of the government.

The establishment of a single political empire, a common administration and reliable communication system helped the economy grow. The guild and manufactories spread across the subcontinent. Taxila, Bharuch and Tamluk became important commercial towns in the period.

A consequence of this spread of the guilds was that the peripheral regions of the empire gradually became stronger. They absorbed the economic technologies of the guilds and were no loner dependent upon the centre at Pataliputra which soon weakened. And soon after Ashoka's death, the various local rulers became virtually independent. That was the eclipse of the Mauryan Empire.

A similar phenomenon occurred with Alexander's empire. Immediately after his death, a Greek general, Ptolemy, became the independent ruler of Egypt. His successors ruled Egypt for 300 years. Another general, Selucid Nikator, proclaimed himself as the king of Babylon. His descendants ruled that country for 250 years. These generals used that military technology of Alexander to break away from the Greek centre.

Technology, by its very nature, is information, not a product. It does not exhaust itself. The more it is used the more it grows. Taxila, Bharuch, Egypt and Babylon adopted the new technologies and were, consequently, able to stand on their own. The governments at the centres at Pataliputra and Greece were unable to prevent this empowerment of the periphery no matter how much protection they afforded to their guilds and their generals. Law was not able to prevent the spread of technology. Clearly, technology empowers its users. However, it the local people refuse to adopt it, and then obsolete technology condemns them to a longer period of subservience.

Of course, there is a risk. When Chandragupta had joined the Greeks he took a risk, but it was his vision that saw him through. When Taxila and Bharuch succumbed to Pataliputra, it was their defeat. But the fact that they went on to absorb the technologies of manufacturing and expanded their trade enabled them to stand up against Pataliputra in a short time.

Technology has an innate propensity to spread itself. No one has been able to hold it back. No government can maintain technological monopoly ad-infinitum merely on the basis of laws. Pataliputra could not sustain the monopoly of its guilds nor was Greece able to keep the technology of the cavalry secret. India should, therefore, make all efforts to absorb advanced technologies and then try to turn the tables on the innovators!

More Recent Evidence of Mercantile Civilisation

India turned the tables on her British conquerors in the nineteenth and twentieth centuries as it did in Bronze and Iron Age civilisations. Britain's political and economic power was unquestioned at that time. So was its technological advantage. Yet, Indian industry emerged with its own identity and businessmen supported the Congress in its struggle for Independence. How did they manage to do this?

The Oxford Economic History of India gives some interesting facts about the evolution of Indian industry. The cotton textiles industry was the first important one to be set up in India. Two Frenchmen had set up a spinning mill in Pondichery in 1830. C N Davar was the first Indian to set up a textile mill in 1854. He was a broker to two English commercial firms. Two Englishmen had bought a 13 percent stake in his venture. Soon many Indians established textile mills. By 1914, 95 mills had been established with 37 being promoted by Parsis. One group of Parsis had become the East India Company's shipbuilders. Among the Parsis was Jamshedji Tata who had promoted the Empress Mills at Nagpur. Indian businessmen who had initially accepted British superiority soon set up modern industries on their own.

The first iron and steel unit was established by an Englishman in South Arcot in 1820. This unit was supported by the East India Company and the government of Madras. But inefficiency led to its collapse. Then the Bengal Iron Works Company was set up near

Kolkata in 1874. The British government of India supported it by contracting to buy one-third of the output at 25 percent more than the market price. Yet, due to faulty planning this venture also collapsed. The government then bought the company and ran it from 1881 to 1889.

In that year the Bengal Iron and Steel Company was incorporated in England by an Englishman. This company took the Indian firm and ran till the First World War. Around this time, Jamshedji Tata was busy promoting Tata Iron & steel Company (TISCO). Despite considerable official assistance locally, Tata was not able to get financial support for TISCO in London. However, he was able raise the same money in Mumbai which, at that time, was "engulfed by an enthusiastic Swadeshi agitation to which the Tatas appeals in their prospectus." Thus, despite a conflict of interest with the steel makers of Manchester, the British government of India supported a Tata venture which owed its success to the Swadeshi agitation against that very government! The Tatas, who were shipbuilders to the East India Company, acquired the necessary expertise and soon became industrialists in their own right.

The first jute mill was established by an Englishman, George Acland, in 1855. However, gradually Indians began to take over this industry. One such Indian was Keshoram Poddar. He had started his business as an under broker to Mitsui, a leading Japanese firm in India. He went no to become a sugar broker to Rallis, the pre-eminent European firm in Kolkata. He borrowed heavily from Japanese banks to finance his business. By 1981, he had made enough money to buy a cotton mill from Andrew Yule. He also bought a colliery and a flour mill.

Harduttrai Chamaria had started his career as a broker to an Englishman. His sons set up two jute mills in the 1930s. Others made speculative profits in opium trade to finance their acquisitions of jute mills. The Birlas were among them.

Indian businessmen who took over these industries had often started their careers as surrogates to the British. However, as they gained confidence, they started acquiring the industrial units of their superiors. These businessmen also became the supporters of the Independence movement. For example, the Indian National Congress paid a special tribute to Jamshedji by passing a resolution expressing appreciation of his support.

The response of the Indian industrialists becomes even more noteworthy when the conditions are considered. The political supremacy of England was unquestioned. In the early 1800s, according to historian Bipan Chandra, while the English market for Indian goods was progressively narrowed through prohibitions and high tariffs, the Indian market was thrown open to British goods. While foreign capital was helped by all sorts of concessions, the native capitalists were asked to fend for themselves. Also, the stores purchase policy of the government discriminated against indigenous manufacturers.

The technological superiority of England was unquestioned. One of the leaders of the Nationalist movement, Justice Ranade, said: "We have to import freely foreign skill and machinery, till we learn our lessons properly and need no help... we have now to turn our apt hands to new work and as we learn it or spurn it we shall win or lose in the contest."

The nationalist leaders did not stop at mere exhortations. They actually participated in the creation of Indian industries. Dadabhai Naoroji became a partner in the commercial firm established in London. Ranade helped establish the Metal Manufacturing Company, a paper mill and a cotton textile mill. Pherozeshah Mehta started a soap factory. Tilak opened a cotton-ginning factory with two partners. These nationalist leaders lent both moral cover and respectability to the efforts of the Indian businessmen.

The parameters of the Indian response in the nineteenth century can now be delineated. The initial establishment of the modern industries in India was done by foreigners with support of the British government of India. The Indian businessmen recognised the technological superiority of the modern industry. They were at a disadvantage because the political supremacy of the British was working in favour of British capital. But they were encouraged by the nationalist leadership to break the stranglehold of foreign capital.

The situation today is almost similar. The technological superiority of the North is unquestioned. The political supremacy of the U.S. is being fully utilized to promote the interests of foreign capital. Frequently, Indian capital has to satisfy itself with a minority stake which is nothing but the modern form of a surrogate status.

As in the past, Indian business have outgrown this surrogate status and expelled foreign capital in areas such a telecom. They are now set to do the same on a global scale as evinced by Tata's acquisition of Corus.

Reality Check on Indian Ambitions

The discussion above related to the situation prevailing in the twentieth century. What about the situation towards the beginning of this century? It appears preposterous to project an 'Indian century'. India is beset with myriad of problems like poverty, illiteracy, and bad governance that attainment of such a position seems unlikely. But countries of East Asia, Latin America and Europe are beset with at least one of the three problems—export dependence, large scale foreign investment and welfare state. Their prospects will be limited. Among major economies, the U.S. and India alone are free of this drag. Of these the U.S. will score over India for some time because of its technological edge and inflows of profits from foreign investment. No other country can beat India in the coming times.

The first problem is that of export-oriented economic growth. This approach is okay as long as the world demand is buoyant but becomes a liability once the world economy slows down. As of today the U.S. is the buyer of last resort. The U.S. demand, however, is not stand-alone. Capital inflows from other countries are sustaining this demand. The Indian, Chinese and Japanese central banks are investing money in U.S. Treasury Bonds and providing the U.S. with the purchasing power to buy their goods. This will continue only as long as the U.S. economy is perceived to be strong. A stampede may take place to get out of dollar investments once the U.S. is perceived to be shaky. The U.S. will not then have the purchasing power to buy goods of the world and countries dependent on export markets will face trouble.

The East Asian countries, Mexico and China have all taken this export-oriented route. The share of foreign trade in their GDP is rather high: China 40 percent, Mexico 42 percent, Indonesia 51 percent, and Thailand 83 percent. These countries are likely to come under severe pressure as soon as the world investors stop providing funds to the U.S. economy.

The second problem is that of foreign investment. This route to growth works well as long as fresh investment continues to come. The foreign exchange received from new foreign investment is used to repatriate the profits of earlier investment. The problem starts when new investment ceases to come. Then the foreign investment becomes a drain on the economy. Thus we see that countries like Ghana which received high levels of foreign investment in the seventies are in dire straits today.

The third problem is of welfare state. This issue is significant for Russia, Europe and Japan. The Soviet government had taken upon itself the responsibility to provide food, clothing and shelter to its people. The strategy worked as long as her economy was protected behind the iron curtain. The high cost of production due to welfare expenditures could be sustained as long as imports were restricted. Not after opening its borders. Now Russia is caught in a no-go situation. If it reduces the welfare expenditures it faces social unrest. If it continues with those expenditures, it has no money left to invest. If it takes the foreign investment route then it sinks deeper into the problem in the long run.

Europe too is weighed down by the welfare state. In the nineteenth and twentieth centuries it excelled in looting other countries of the world. That money was used to finance the welfare state. As a result, European goods were cheap while the living standards of their workers were high. Now that loot has virtually stopped flowing in. If it dismantles the welfare stage there is social unrest. If it imposes taxes to finance it then its industries are rendered uncompetitive in a global economy.

The role of the welfare 'state' was discharged by the companies in Japan. In the sixties Japan pioneered an export-oriented economy. This is no longer possible as other low-wage countries like Thailand and India compete with Japanese products in the world markets. Thus Japan's own economy has turned placid and welfare activities can no longer be sustained.

Other than the U.S. and India all the major economies of the world face one problem or the other. China, East Asian and Latin American countries face the problems of export-orientation and heavy burden of foreign investment. Europe and Japan are faced with the problem of welfare state. Their social problems will become pronounced as they reduce this drag on the economy.

In comparison, the U.S. and India are not beset with any of these problems. The role of exports and foreign investment in India is comparatively small. The U.S. and India do not have bloated welfare state either.

Of the two the U.S. will continue to stay ahead for two reasons– technological advantage and profits from earlier foreign investments. Thus Indian may be expected to rise to the No 2 position soon.

This Chapter is adapted from the following articles:

"A Goldcn Trade Rule," The Economic Times, June 14, 1994.
"Trade is Trumps, not technology," Baltimore Sun, July 16, 1996.
"Hearken to History," The Economic Times, April 5, 1994.
"Turning the Tables," The Economic Times, May 17, 1994.
"Emerging economic power," The Daily, August 5, 1999.

9

Make Cartels and Regional FTAs, not Free Trade

The mainstream thinking is that free trade will lead to welfare of our people. India has comparative advantage in many items such as software. We can gain from exports of these items. In this section it is shown that this is not true. Instead, making cartels or regional blocs will be more advantageous. A corollary of this is that high price of oil will be beneficial for us by strengthening the power of developing countries vis-à-vis the developed countries.

Cartels of Resources, not Monopoly of IPRs

Mainstream economists concede that the present globalization is unfavourable for the poor countries but they contend that we must participate in the unfair game and extract as much concession as we can since there is no alternative. We should save as much of our life as we can when the demon has caught hold of us. This thinking is a result of mental slavery. We have assumed that the demon has caught hold of us and we are doing his bidding though really it is only a shadow of the demon.

We have no opposition to globalization. The Indian mantra is of Vasudev Kutumbakam—the whole world is one family. Our objective is to secure the welfare of all living beings on this earth. Globalization also means that the whole world is one market. Our opposition is to the present model of globalization, which is leading to illfare of large numbers.

The basic inconsistency of the WTO is that it provides protection to the monopolistic control of technologies but prohibits the monopolistic pricing of natural resources. The WTO requires that greater patents protection be provided to holders of new technologies. Monopoly of owners of technology is recognized—even encouraged. The underlying principle is that technological knowledge is a tradable 'good' and the holder is entitled to price it monopolistically.

The poor countries own eighty percent natural resources of the world such as water, soil, forest, oil, mineral, sea, etc. The monopolistic control of the poor countries on their natural resources stands on a similar footing as monopolistic control of the rich countries on technologies. Both are marketable commodities. We would argue that technology is not marketable and natural resources are a global heritage that should not be left to the whims of the market. But this view emerges from a different philosophical orientation hence we leave it here. For the discussion here let us consider both technologies and natural resources as marketable commodities. Let us consider the consequence even if we treat both as marketable commodities.

The option of monopolistic pricing of technologies available to the rich countries should, therefore, also be available to the poor countries for their ownership of natural resources. Microsoft has the freedom to charge high prices for its Windows software. In a similar way India should have the freedom to recover high prices for its bauxite and manganese ore. The inconsistency in the present globalization is that monopolistic pricing of technologies is permitted but monopolistic pricing of natural resources is prohibited.

The poor countries should resist this unfavourable situation. They should initiate an alternative model of globalization which places all commodities—technologies and natural recourses—on the same footing.

One argument against this is that monopolistic pricing of new technologies encourages more invention. No such advantage accrues from monopolistic pricing of natural resources. It is ignored here that natural resources have to be discovered and managed in the same way as new technologies. There is no value to a diamond lying in the field unless one has the necessary knowledge to recognize its value. The knowledge of diamond lying in the field and a molecule having cancer-curing property are similar. People of the poor countries have discovered these natural resources and maintained them for all these years. It is well recognized, for example, that topsoil is generated by years of dutiful cultivation. It is not merely a 'gift' of nature. The poor countries are, therefore, entitled to price their soil and crops produced from it monopolistically as much as the MNCs have a right to charge high price for their drugs.

Another argument is that IPR protection is provided only for a limited number of years hence it is self-extinguishing. It cannot be compared to monopolistic pricing of natural resources which would be perpetual. Indeed, technology has a tendency to spread while natural resources have a tendency to constrict themselves. Many efforts are afoot to duplicate Microsoft's Windows software. The Windows software has a tendency to spread itself. The tendency of natural resources is exactly the opposite. They tend to reduce and get exhausted with time instead of spreading. The availability of diamond in a mine is less with every passing day. The oil deposits of West Asia are depleting.

The question here is whether monopolistic protection should be provided to technology or to natural resources—to a commodity that spreads or to one that constricts. It seems that protection should first be given to the commodity that constricts. The commodity that tends to exhaust itself should be protected. What is the benefit of giving protection to a commodity that is growing?

It can be said that not providing protection to technologies will put an end to research and development. But what is the purpose of new R&D if they do not reach the people? Mankind has not waited for patents' laws to discover telegraph and a host of other technologies. There is no reason to believe that technological advances will come to an end without patents.

Developing countries should make cartels of their natural resources and indulge in monopolistic pricing like OPEC is doing for oil. They should openly violate the TRIPS agreement and copy advanced technologies. The rich countries will retaliate by imposing high import duties on our exports and deny us new technologies. Both these steps will meet with a failure though. High import taxes will be as harmful for them as for us. America will have to buy expensive garments from other countries if it imposes high taxes on cheap garments produced in India. Ultimately they will have to buy our cheap cloth in their own self interest just as they had to unilaterally withdraw economic sanctions imposed after the Pokharan explosions.

The fear regarding access to technologies too is without any basis. A study undertaken by Veena Jha for UNCTAD, quoted elsewhere in this book, found that poor countries are finding it more difficult to obtain new technologies after the making of the WTO.

More Gains in Cartels than Free Trade

India is trying to enter into a free trade agreement with East Asian countries. Such agreement may indirectly help us vis-à-vis the developed countries by the creation of an implicit trade bloc, it would be better if we explicitly formed cartels with them.

Free trade theory holds that each country should manufacture that item at which it is the best. If India has comparative advantage in producing tea and Thailand in the production of cameras, then the former should export tea and import cameras.

The difference in resource endowments determines the extent of gains that would accrue from free trade. For instance, if both India and Sri Lanka grow good quality tea, free trade between the two will not benefit either much. But free trade between India and Iraq, for instance, would be beneficial, as India can get cheaper oil and Iraq can get cheaper tea.

The resource endowments of Asian countries, barring Japan, are largely similar to India's. Hence, the gains from free trade with ASEAN will be minimal. Gains from cartelisation will be greater. Eighty percent of the world's resources are found in developing countries, yet they account for only 20 percent of global income. Going by free trade theory, developing countries, endowed with land, water and mineral resources, should have a greater share of the global income.

But this is not happening for two reasons. One, the developing countries have 80 percent of natural resources but less share of knowledge resources or human capital. Two, knowledge resources are granted monopoly in the WTO while natural resources are required to follow free trade. This is leading to skewed income distribution. Monopolies, not free trade, particularly in knowledge, are determining the flow of world wealth. World trade may be thought of in terms of a 'monopoly sector' and a 'competitive sector'.

The competitive sector would include producers of coffee–India, Brazil and Vietnam–and automobiles–Mexico and Thailand. These countries battle with one another to supply cheaper products to the rich countries. Indeed, the most efficient among these would gain. India may score over Brazil in coffee and the reverse may hold true for sugar but gains from such competition would be minimal because of the profit margin would reduce in the process. Thus, there is a double advantage for rich countries. On the one hand, their monopoly pricing of technology is getting them higher incomes, and, on the other hand, competition among the poor countries is providing them cheaper products.

There are limited synergies between India and ASEAN. There may be some synergy in minerals, but the share of these in their trade basket is small. While ASEAN countries can import services such as software and entertainment from India, this will hardly alter the rich-poor asymmetry. Thus, India-ASEAN co-operation will have to take a different direction.

We will have to co-operate in making resource-based monopolies to counter the technology-based ones of the rich countries. If Boeing and Airbus can co-operate to sell aircraft at high prices, India and Thailand should do the same, jacking up paddy prices, for instance. Formation of a Free Trade Zone between India and ASEAN can be helpful only if it lays the foundations of a trading bloc vis-à-vis the developed countries. The creation of a free trade bloc implies that these countries together will have a common barrier to entry from the developed countries. That *de facto* makes an Indo-ASEAN bloc against the developed countries. But this is a roundabout and uncertain route especially because the tariffs of this bloc vis-à-vis the developed countries are also kept at low levels in keeping with the principle of free trade. The need is to create a tariff barrier against the developed countries and to jack up the price of produce of the Indo-ASEAN bloc by formation of cartels.

Economic theory recognises cartels. Trade Unions are cartels of suppliers of labour. Trade Unions are sanctioned because they lead to an increase in income of the poor workers. A similar result is obtained by resource-rich developing countries forming cartels. India and ASEAN should, therefore, keep their eyesight focused on raising product prices vis-à-vis the developed countries. India could form cartels with Bangladesh (for jute), Sri Lanka (tea), Thailand (rice), Vietnam and Brazil (coffee), and so on. Only then will poor countries be able to garner a greater share of the global income. They could use this income to generate parity in knowledge in the next cycle.

Regional Trade Blocs are Better than Global Free Trade

The breakdown of WTO talks at Cancun marks a watershed in the process of globalisation. The movement towards the formation of a global market has been arrested. It is expected that countries will increasingly pursue their efforts to form regional trade bloc like NAFTA (North America), MERCOSUR (South America) and ASEAN (East Asia). Some observers believe that this will be harmful for world trade. But there are positive features of regional trade that should not be overlooked.

The Asian Development Bank had pointed out some advantages of regional trade agreements in its *Asian Development Outlook 2002*. The Bank had said that these agreements provide flexibility to the poor countries to protect their sensitive sectors. Let us say India stands to lose much from opening its agricultural sector to imports. It is afraid that cheap wheat from Australia may hurt its farmers. In the WTO India has little choice of preventing such an opening. India cannot get access to the textile markets of Germany without giving access to Australian wheat because all agreements come in one single package.

Regionalism makes it possible for India to enter into a regional agreement with Germany for the supply of textiles and imports of machinery without bringing in the issue of wheat imports from Australia. India and Germany would benefit from such an agreement without India having to compromise with Australia, which can reach a separate agreement with Germany for the supply of wheat and cheese without India having to become a party to it. Thus ADB says regional agreements "Can be more palatable than multilateral arrangements as they allow countries to clarify sensitive sectors while integrating with countries that will not create strong competitive pressures."

Second, regional economic zones can be made among countries sharing cultural affinity without having to provide the same preferences to culturally different people. The ADB cites many such examples: "The Johor-Riau-Singapore growth zone brings together semi-skilled labour from Malaysia, and capital from Singapore. The Brunei-Darussalam, Indonesia, Malaysia, and Philippines East ASEAN Growth Area (BIMPEAGA) focuses on sector cooperation in mineral, forest, and marine resources.

In this approach, countries can make up for each other's deficiencies in specific areas without opening themselves to harm that arises from global opening: "In the case of the four-country East-West Economic Corridor, for example, the Thai sub-region is relatively abundant in skilled labour, while southern Myanmar, Savannakhet in the Lao PDR, and central Vietnam have a scarcity of skilled labour but an abundance of natural resources." These countries partially opened their borders for each other with which they have some cultural affinity. They would probably not have liked to open to skilled labour from India or Pakistan. Regional agreements make it possible to capture regional complementariness while protecting one from unwanted cultural factors.

Third, it may be possible to achieve deeper integration through regional agreements. For example, India gives duty-free access to products from Bhutan and Nepal because of her historical relationship with these countries, their politically friendly regimes and land-locked nature. India would certainly not like to give a similar duty-free access to all the countries of the world in a multilateral regime like that of the WTO.

On the other hand, regional trade agreements will certainly not be the best from the point of view of the global economy. It is possible that Vietnam may produce coffee cheaper than Brazil. Yet Vietnam may not be able to sell its coffee in U.S. because Brazil may have a regional agreement with the U.S. Thus regional agreements will not lead to the maximum efficiency of the global economy.

To quote ADB, the "opponents of regionalism rightly point out that patterns of specialisation in Preferential Trade Agreements are not necessarily those that would occur if a country had opened its borders to the world economy. Most empirical and theoretical work indicates that the effects of PTA-enhanced trade are not as beneficial for welfare as more general trade liberalisation. First, the product variety in the world. Second, a PTA-created market, as the product of an agreement among a few countries, is obviously smaller than the world market." Third, competition from other PTA members may push countries into specialisation that does not reflect their comparative advantage relative to the rest of the world.

But the difficulty is that it is not guaranteed that every country will have global competitive advantage in some area. Take the example of Sri Lanka which produces tea, rice and garments. It is possible that India may produce cheaper tea, Thailand may produce cheaper rice and Bangladesh may produce cheaper garments than Sri Lanka. In that case Sri Lanka would be left high and dry in a multilateral regime. It would have to reduce the wages of its people to compete with these countries. Globalisation would then turn into a disadvantage for Sri Lanka.

There is a fundamental flaw in the theory of globalisation. It proceeds on the assumption that every country has comparative advantage in some area. That may not be true. Therefore, regional trade may be a better tool than multilateral trade. Regional trade will not provide all the gains that are possible from global economic integration but it can help them avoid the costs that come with global regime. In the end a regional trade agreement may be more beneficial. Multilateral trade under WTO auspices is good for the world economy but only for those countries that have clear-cut global comparative advantage. Thus many poor countries have seen decline in their growth rates after the formation of the WTO.

Regional agreements provide less economic benefits but come with the flexibility of being able to protect one's sensitive sectors. Multilateral agreements provide the highest efficiency but make countries politically and culturally vulnerable and also impose unrelated economic costs.

Increase Imports, not Exports

The Government is committed to secure an increase in exports, which means that we want to give away our resources in larger quantities to other countries. We will pack more labour of our engineers into software programmes and give it away to richer foreign countries that have the purchasing power. We want to pack more of our soil and water into grain and send it away. This is like telling the poor that his stomach will be filled by giving away the bread in his plate to the rich man.

Exports and imports are, generally speaking, equal. We export software and rice and import computer chips and phosphate fertilisers with the money earned. It is truly good to engage in such foreign trade as both the trading countries stand to gain. The question, however, is why so much talk is made of increase in exports, and not of increase in imports? The reason is that Western economists have brainwashed us into willingly giving away our wealth. We invest more in facilities required for sending our goods to foreign countries and less in bringing-in their resources. The British rulers of India invested in a huge network of railways so that they could take away our cotton and sugar to England easily. They did not establish a railway line from Nagaland to reach its cheap bamboos to Bihar. They did not make many dams and bunds in Bihar which would have led to higher incomes for the people. Farmers of Bihar exported their sugar at low prices offered by the British traders. Such investment in export-oriented infrastructure was suitable for the British Raj as it wanted to extract our resources and keep us bound in chains of poverty. We would build a railway line in Nagaland if the objective was economic development of our people.

The nature of investment follows the objective that we set before us. We would invest in technology parks if we put the objective of increasing imports of computer chips before us. By placing the objective of exports, we ignore such investments and instead invest in railway lines to transport our sugar to the ports.

Second, our attention drifts away from the high price of imports. Our Government has set up many organisations like APEDA and CAPEXIL to promote exports of commodities such as agricultural goods and chemicals. These institutions provide information to our exporters about the tenders and prices in the importing countries. This is good as it enables our exporters to get higher price for the goods. Similar benefits would be obtained by us if we were to set up organisations to promote imports. A "Computer Chip Import Development Agency" would provide information about the availability of computer chips to our assemblers. Such an agency would search the world for cheap supplies of computer chips. In absence of such information, we do not pay attention to the prices charged by the Western countries for their exports. The Western countries are able to sell their goods at high prices because we are busy exporting or produce.

Another idea behind export-led growth is that purchasing power lies with the developed countries and will continue to be so.

We should make profits from the capacity and willingness of the American people to pay high prices for our Basmati rice and Haldiram Bhujia. But, in the process, we get distracted from the task of increasing the purchasing capacity of our people. In focussing on export-led growth, we spend money in developing the consumption of Basmati rice in America instead of developing bamboo consumption in Bihar. We first pack our water and soil into the rice and give it to the Americans to consume. Then we deposit the dollars earned with the Federal Reserve Bank of America at low rates of interest for safe custody to maintain high level of forex reserves. As a result, America benefits twice. It gets cheap rice as well as a free supply of dollars.

Another argument for increasing exports is that it helps in attaining global standards of efficiency. But exports in small quantities are sufficient for the purpose just as one small reception is sufficient to establish the entry of the bride into the family. The correct route is to produce efficiently, reduce the quantity- and increase the price of our exports and consume more of our goods ourselves. But we have been taught that eating coarse rice ourselves and exporting basmati rice will beget us prosperity.

The mentality of export-led growth assumes that we are more dependent on imports hence it is obligatory for us to maintain dollar reserves to pay for our imports. Clearly, that is not the case. The West is importing more from the developing countries than they are buying from them. They need to hold as many rupee and Yuan reserves for payments to our exporters as we need to hold dollar reserves for payment to their exporters. But the psychology of export-led growth makes us believe that we are more dependent on their markets than they are on ours. Consequently, we maintain huge dollar reserves to manage both our exports and imports. Instead, we should ask the Western countries to maintain reserves in rupees so that they can pay for imports from India.

It is time we abandoned export-led- and embarked upon an import-led growth strategy. Import growth would indirectly lead to growth of exports just as export growth indirectly leads to growth of imports. We should focus directly on acquiring more resources of the foreign countries by increasing our imports. We should invest in infrastructure which enables us to import goods from foreign countries. A pipeline from Kandla to Jagdishpur is a better proposition than a pipe line from Tehri dam to Haldia.

Singapore Issues

The developed countries tried to include four new issues included in the agenda of WTO—labour standards, environment standards, competition policy and government procurement. For the present these issues have been thrown out agenda due to the opposition of the developing countries. However, danger remains since the developed countries may try to bring them into the agenda later.

The developed countries are trying to establish new monopolies through the inclusion of the 'Singapore issues'. We let them include patents in the trade mechanism in the Uruguay round and conceded to their monopoly over technology. Now they want to enlarge their monopolies by labour and environment standards, and other issues.

The record of the WTO so far is not so rosy. According to World Bank data, the world GDP has grown by $2,355 billion between 1995 and 1999. Of this $1,177 billion–nearly one-half–has been captured by the high-income countries. That will hardly lead to global equality.

Many developing countries have been losers. Ukraine's GDP was $80 billion in 1995. It fell to $42 billion in 1999. Similarly, Thailand's fell from $167 to $123 billion, Malaysia's from $85 to $74 billion and South Africa's from $136 to $131 billion. Major countries like Pakistan, Peru and Argentina have seen no growth in their GDP in these post-WTO years. Free trade is not leading to global equality.

Gains from High Price of Oil

Mainstream thinkers hold that developing countries stand to loose from the high price of oil. No doubt oil prices will be a burden on our economy. But if we should make other cartels of tea, jute and rubber, then we would be able to neutralise that impact. The developed countries, however, would then be doubly hit. They would have to shell out more money both for oil as well as rubber. We should emulate OPEC instead of joining the developed countries in lamenting them.

The belief is that an increase in the price of oil will harm us. History, however, tells us that developing countries have less to fear. Consider the oil price rise of the early 1970s. According to World Bank data, the growth rate of "low-income" developing countries before the price rise in the decade of the 1960s was 4.6 percent. In the 1970s it remained unchanged at 4.5 percent; rose to 6.6 percent in the 1980s and further to 7.3 percent in the 1990s. Their growth has not been affected by the increases in the price of oil.

Not so for the "high-income" developed countries. Their growth rates had been 5.1 percent in the 1960s and have followed a downward course since then, falling to 3.0 percent in the 1970, 3.1 percent in the 1980s and 2.1 percent in the 1990s. The impact of high prices of oil has indeed been negative on the developed countries.

The high price of opium leads to less consumption of that item and a decline in the capacity of the addict. Relatively, it improves the ability of the non-addict in competition. Likewise the high price of oil strengthens the competitiveness of developing countries that consume less oil vis-à-vis developed countries that consume more.

America was generating an income of 4.0 dollars per kg oil in 2001 according the *Human Development Report* of UNDP. China was producing 4.2 dollars and India 4.4 dollars. Indian economy is 'oil-efficient' compared to America and China. Thus, there will be less negative effect on India if oil becomes expensive.

The difference in the per capita consumption of energy is much greater. According to the UNDP an average Indian consumes 561 KwH energy equivalents in a year, Chinese 1139 KwH and American 13,241 KwH. These data show that an increase in the price of oil will hit at the developed countries more than us. It is, therefore, a weapon for more equal distribution of world income.

Another belief is that high price of oil will affect world economic growth adversely. It is not understood how. Such a price rise only transfers world's income from oil consumers to oil producers. The total world wealth or capital remains unchanged. Only the centre of growth shifts from America and Europe to West Asia.

Another factor important for India is that petrodollars enable the West Asian countries to import large number of goods and workers from India. The remittance sent by these workers cancels out the drain due to high price of oil. According to the RBI Annual Reports, our oil imports are nearly equal to the Invisible Transfer receipts. Part of the money that we pay to Saudi Arabia for oil comes back to us via such remittances.

The developed countries are more dependent upon us for the natural resources than we are upon them for technologies. If, for example, we had not got the technology of airplanes from the West, we could still run our trains on coal. But Europe and America would come to a grinding halt if oil were to be denied to them. OPEC has recognised this dependence of the developed countries and exploited it exactly in the same manner that developed countries have exploited our technological dependence upon them.

The ability of the developed countries to ward off OPEC-like cartels depends upon their ability to divide and rule over the developing counties. If the developing countries were to form a cartel of jute producers, the developed countries could certainly shift to HDPE bags. But if the price of petroleum products were increased simultaneously, then such substitution would not be possible. In order to extract high prices of our natural resources we would then need not just cartels for specific commodities but a series of them. Two cartels of tea and coffee working in tandem would leave little space for the developed countries to play one against the other.

We have two routes to increase our share in the world income. We could make OPEC-like cartels for our exports such as jute, tea and rubber and nullify the adverse impact of price rise of oil made by OPEC; or we could join the developed countries in berating the increase in oil prices. Which of the two we adopt depends upon our conception of the world.

In the war of Lanka, Lord Rama was under severe pressure at a particular point. He was then reminded of the *brahmastra* lying in his armoury. Thereupon he took it out and used it to vanquish the enemy. A similar awareness that the developed countries are dependent on us for natural resources can change the tables.

Do not Insulate Indian Economy from High Price of Oil

While speaking to the National Italian American Foundation, Washington, DC on October 15, 2004 the then U.S. Federal Reserve Board Chairman, Mr. Alan Greenspan, said: "The higher prices of the 1970s brought to an abrupt end the extraordinary period of growth in U.S. oil consumption and the increased intensity of its use that was so evident in the decades immediately following World War II. Between 1945 and 1973, consumption of petroleum products rose at a startling 4.5 percent average annual rate, well in excess of growth of real gross domestic product. However, between 1973 and 2003, oil consumption grew, on average, only 1/2 percent per year, far short of the rise in real GDP." Resisting the rise in the price of oil would have prevented such a fortuitous adjustment of the U.S. economy.

The producer is always adjusting his business according to the prevailing price situation. The availability of relatively cheaper LPG has made a large number of rural people switch from gobar gas and fuel wood leading to conservation of soil and forests. The same applies to the price of oil–in reverse. The high price of oil will lead to more use of gobar gas and other sources of fuel for conservation of economic prosperity. This is the natural adjustment that must happen.

Tax relief on oil means that non-oil consuming sectors will be taxed at a higher rate to make up for the shortfall in revenues from oil consumers. Software would be taxed to subsidise steel. Those not consuming oil will be taxed to subsidise those who consume oil. This will encourage greater consumption of expensive oil. Sectors that are oil-efficient will be sacrificed to support those that are oil-inefficient. It is like taking the tyre from the new car to replace that of the dilapidated one. The government can turn this crisis into an opportunity. It can say that world prices are high hence domestic prices will be high. Then it can increase excise duty on domestic production of oil to skim part of the higher price realised by them. The government can invoke the high price of imported oil to convince the consumers of this policy.

This Chapter is adapted from the following articles:

"Alternative Globalization," *Janata,* July 4, 2004.
"Free trade means lower living standards," *The Japan Times,* January 24, 2000.
"More gains in cartels than Free Trade Zones," *Businessline,* December 15, 2005.
"The Positive Side," *Swadeshi Patrika.*
"Oil price hike: A blessing in disguise," (Probably) *Businessline,* February 11, 2004.
"Increase imports, not exports," *The Pioneer,* August 24, 2004.
"Regional Trade," *The Statesman,* September 29, 2003.
"Fuel the crisis," *The Pioneer,* September 26, 2000.

10

Limits of Technology

In the chapter on TRIPS in the previous section we have explored the adverse impact of control of frontier technologies by the developed countries. We have shown that the dominance of the developed countries rests on their control of these technologies. There are limitations to their dominance, however. History tells us that new technologies may not be developed *ad infinitum*. Technological innovations have occurred in spurts followed by long periods of hiatus. In this chapter we explore whether a similar hiatus may be emerging. The evidence is not conclusive but it gives us a way to look at and understand future developments.

This aspect has a bearing on our global economic strategy. We have to think of ways of creating new technologies or acquiring them if the development of new technologies is likely to take place continuously. We need not expend our energies in this direction if technology development is likely to hit a plateau on its own.

Over Development of Technology

Most of the important technological innovations of the last century have been made in the United States. These include the motor car, atom bomb, jet air plane, personal computer and the internet. These technological advances are the base of American economic strength. In 1997, of example, the American economy was facing a downturn. The Asian crisis was, in part, a result of this. American companies were not able to export the produce of countries like Thailand to their home in absence of strong domestic demand; nor were they able to make investments in those countries. The result was that the east Asian "Tigers" were deprived of both their export markets as well as capital inflows. This led to a decline in their currencies and resulted in the crisis.

This downturn in the U.S. was arrested by the dotcom boom. Suddenly, euphoria was created in the U.S. stock markets. It came to be believed that a "new economy" was being created. The share prices of Cisco Systems and Microsoft rose dramatically. The consequent buoyancy affected capital flows of the world. Investors in Europe and Japan put their money into American stock markets. America could import goods produced by Asia with this money. American MNCs were able make more foreign investments as well. Once again the world economy was on a growth path. This change from a downturn to upturn was led by the development of the dotcom technologies.

The secret of the U.S. being the growth engine of the world lies in its ability to continuously develop new technologies. The question is whether such development of new technologies can continue to take place unabated. History tells us that technological developments have taken place in spurts with long period of hiatus in between. The development of bronze metallurgy in 3000BC was followed by about 2,500 years of technological stagnation of about 2,000 years till the Mongols developed gunpowder. There are some indications that every frontier technology developed in the recent times has not delivered.

British Airways and Air France have phased out their supersonic jet Concorde which was heralded at one time as the model of future technology. The marvellous technology notwithstanding, the Concorde resulted in heavy losses for the European airlines. Notably, the American airlines refused to buy this airplane. They had made the correct economic assessment and were saved of losses.

British Telecom had heavily invested in third generation "3G" telephony. This new generation of mobile phones can receive faxes, send or receive large email messages, download maps and help in navigation, browse the web, undertake video-conferencing and even show TV programmes. But it was not able to start these services. It had borrowed heavily for this investment. It had to sell off its investments across the world from Japan to Spain simply to stay afloat. Other European telecom players have incurred similar losses. Services based on 3G technology did not make a profit anywhere in the world till 2003.

The increasing speed of personal computers is no longer attracting new buyers. PC users are finding that the high speed does not make an appreciable change in their work. A report in the *New York Times* says that "Computers have reached a point where they are already more than fast enough to suit a typical home users' needs–web surfing, email and word processing." As a result PC-makers are having a hard time selling their faster machines.

Similar experience can be seen in the fields of bioinformatics (genome sequencing has hardly produced any economic returns yet), biotechnology (the Bt Cotton is proving to be a failure at places) and space exploration (a second moon walk has not been undertaken). There appears to arise a point where "over-development" of technology occurs. The technology is unquestioningly superior but it is not commercially viable. The money invested in its development then becomes a waste.

New technologies are today being developed in the areas of satellite imagery, space exploration, genome sequencing, cloning, superconductors, solar photovoltaic systems and human organ transplants. The future course of the world economy will depend upon whether these technologies become commercially viable in the sense of the dotcom boom.

The task before India is to acquire those technologies that are commercially viable while not fretting about getting all the new technologies. We have to walk on the knife's edge. We may face a situation like that of Iraq if we fail to adapt the new technologies. At the same time, however, we cannot afford to meet the fate of the Concorde. It is necessary, therefore, of us to develop a commercial assessment of new technologies.

Biotechnology: Limits to Development of Technologies

The slowdown of the late 1990s was broken by the dotcom boom. Biotechnology is often said to have the same potential in the new century. Whether this potential is realised would depend upon whether the biotech corporations can come up with an inexpensive product which can lower the cost of food or drugs in the same manner as IT has done for information.

The signals so far are mixed. In an article 'Addressing biotech's cycles of hope' posted on stephan.herrera@redherring.com, Mr. Stephan Herrera reminds us that in 1980 a small biotech company, perhaps the first, called Genertech's stock skyrocketed from $35 to more than $80 in less than an hour of being listed on the New York Stock Exchange. It closed the day at $71.25 on a hefty 104 percent premium. But since then the exuberance appears to have died down.

An advisory on biotech stocks from the First Trust Portfolios says: "The demand of biotech stocks diminished of various reasons, including a limited supply of products." This implies that new products are not being generated. Corporations are undertaking research but are unable to produce marketable products. Yet the First Trust is hopeful. It points out that over 130 biotechnology drug products and vaccines have already been approved by that U.S. Food and Drug Administration. There are more than 350 biotech drug products and vaccines currently in clinical trials targeting more than 200 diseases, including various cancers, Alzheimer's disease, heart disease, diabetes, multiple sclerosis, AIDS and arthritis. If some of these biotech drugs are successful it would have a positive impact on the share market.

Mr. Herrera is likewise positive. He says that despite the disappointments of the last 25 years there have been some remarkable successes. In June 1997, Med Immune was trading at

$18. A year later, its drug for premature infants, Synagis, was approved. By the end of that month, the stock was trading at $49. A year after that, shares had climbed to $140. Also in 1997, Immunex was trading in the $20s. In November 1998 its rheumatoid arthritis drug, Enbrel, was approved. Just a few months later its shares were trading at $156.

The million dollar question is whether these isolated successes would become a torrent leading to the kind of impact on the share markets that the dotcoms have had in late 1990s. There are many reasons that give hope. According to Mr. Herrera, the human genome has been sequenced and consequently the number of drug targets will expand from somewhere in the neighbourhood of 500 to 10,000. But, why the earlier known targets have not led to success? Gene mapping only increases the size of the playing field. If does not explain why there have been few successes on the smaller field.

Second, Mr. Herrera says that new software tools will improve the chances of making a successful drug. The U.S. Food and Drug Administration is now speedier in disposing of the applications. The question, however, is about significance of these factors. The internet reduced the cost of mail dramatically from Rs five per letter to merely less than a paisa per email. Biotech is likely to do nothing of the type. Quicker approvals only reduce the interest burden of the period of delay. What matters is the rate of success.

Vice Chairman of the Illinois Biotechnology Industry Organisation Michael Rosen is hopeful that new drugs targeted to an individual's genetic structure provide an exciting opening. But we have seen that there have been few takers of the commercial space tickets. The cost of such products is prohibitive and the trouble one has to undergo is substantial. On the other hand, the very future of genetically modified food itself is uncertain.

Mr. Marc Kaufman of the Washington Post Service writes that one woman developed reactions after eating Star Link corn. She had finished a chicken enchilada lunch with co-workers when she began to swell and she was having trouble breathing. Her colleagues called an ambulance. Several days later she learned that taco shells and other corn products had been recalled nationwide because they were found to contain a genetically modified type of corn called Star Link. The corn had been approved of only animal consumption because of concerns it might trigger dangerous allergic reactions in people. She complained to the Food and Drug Administration and reported that she might have had an allergic reaction after eating corn products that contained Star Link.

These reports indicate that biotech is still in doubtful territory. The industry has failed to deliver since the late 1970s. The chances of its making a turnaround would depend upon whether the success rate increases. 130 GM products have been approved and 350 are in the pipeline but the question needs answer is why the 130 drugs already approved have not let to corporate euphoria? Few isolated successes in a series of failures do not augur well.

Biotech will most likely not become the engine of global economic revival because it does not transform the health scene in any fundamental way. We may see some astounding successes. But that will be no different than Reliance having made a success in Vimal suiting while others drowned. A boom occurs when a sector undergoes structural change like the assembly line made by Ford transformed the nature of the transport industry; or the internet transformed the nature of information service. Biotech does nothing of the sort. It only provides a particular new type of drug within the larger drug sector. The drug sector is already on the downside. Thus the few successes in biotech drugs will most probably be overshadowed by the losses of others.

Technology is Source of American Wealth

The ability of the U.S. to sustain a huge army and to provide it with modern weapons is ultimately based on economic strength. This strength, in turn, is based on (1) natural resources, (2) hard work and (3) technological innovation.

A small country like Kuwait has a per capita income of $18,000 because it has lots of oil. The Kuwaiti people are rich like a person who finds pot of gold hidden in his kitchen. South Africa has gold, Zimbabwe has copper, and Malaysia has timber and so on. The U.S. is likewise a resource rich country. It has oil, gold and vast expanses of agricultural land. Remember the gold rush of the Wild West?

The second source of American wealth is the hard work of its people. The employees can be hired and fired at will. They have to work hard to retain their jobs. Most university professors are employed on a five year contract. They are shown the door if they do not innovate and create knowledge and wealth. Hong Kong and Singapore have similarly created wealth through hard work. These countries have few natural resources yet their per capita incomes compare favourably with that of the U.S.

These two sources of wealth, though important, have been replicated by other countries. What stands America apart is its ability to make technological innovations. The U.S. has been the 'innovator of the world' for the last hundred years. The motor car, atom bomb and nuclear power plants, jet airplanes, computers and internet are all American innovations. These innovations give monopolistic power to the pioneers. The Ford Motor Company was at one time the only producer of motor cars in large numbers in the world. It could have charged a high price for those cars. A few decades ago the main manufacturers of jet airplanes–Boeing, Lockheed and McDonnell Douglas–were all American companies. They charged high prices for their airplanes. Microsoft presently has a huge margin on its software products because of its dominance of the software market. The income from such technological innovations sets the U.S. apart.

Technological innovations create huge profits. The innovator company attracts investment from across the world. The dotcom boom of the late nineties has already been explained above. In 1997 the dotcom boom took place. Investors across the world flocked to buy shares of Cisco and Microsoft. There was a huge inflow of money into the U.S. economy. This led to an increase in the demand for dollar and the price of the dollar rose.

A dollar was worth 0.80 euros when it was launched. Gradually the value of the euro declined and one dollar was buying 1.20 euros. The increase in the price of the dollar further encouraged people to buy more dollars. Currency traders like George Soros bought dollars and sold Pound Sterling and German Marks. The developing countries too bought dollars in large amounts to maintain adequate levels of foreign exchange reserves. The American economy was flush with funds supplied by the rest of the world. Conversely, the value of the dollar is declining against the euro since 2004. This is the period when no important technological innovation has been made in the U.S. The absence of commercially viable technological innovations heralds a spontaneous decline of the U.S. economy.

Technology-led U.S. Growth—the Case of IT

Ten years ago economists like me had predicted that the U.S. economy would soon be in trouble. That has not happened but the decline of the U.S. economy is nevertheless inevitable. It has only been temporarily delayed by the advent of information technology.

Truly speaking, globalisation is a headache for rich countries. They cannot impose restrictions on imports of cheap cloth, software and education produced in developing countries like India. The wages of U.S. workers will have to decline to lower levels—closer to the global minimum.

This central tendency is suppressed temporarily by technological innovations. Pioneers who invent new technologies make huge profits like those made by farmers who grew Sugar Baby watermelons first. But these super-profits evaporated as soon as others adopted the new technology.

The current account deficit (excess of imports over exports) of the U.S. was $80 billion per year in 1990-96. This shortfall was being made up by inflow of foreign investment into the U.S. Japanese companies were purchasing prime properties in Manhattan and this money was being used to finance the imports. The situation came under pressure around 1997. The transfer of manufacturing to East

Asia led to less employment in the U.S. economy. There was less purchasing power to buy imported goods.

The situation changed abruptly in 1998. Advances in IT led to a boom in the shares of companies like Cisco Systems and Microsoft. World capital began to flow once again toward the U.S. This inflow of capital made it possible for U.S. to make huge imports once again and the U.S. economy was saved.

The IT bubble burst in 2000, but the U.S. economy did not collapse. Mark Olson, Governor of the Federal Reserve, explained in the Frazer Lecture delivered in November 2004: "By late 2000, that boom had come to an end, and businesses abruptly curtailed capital spending. Against this backdrop, the Federal Reserve reduced the... (interest) rate sharply....to head off a more serious deterioration...This monetary policy stance, coupled with simulative fiscal policy, was generally successful. Consumers took advantage of falling mortgage rates to buy new homes...or to finance spending on other things."

Let us understand Mr. Olson's logic. The decline in the prices of shares of dotcom companies meant that the paper wealth of the U.S. stock holders evaporated into thin air. They were left with debt they had taken in anticipation of huge returns from their stocks. The decline in stock prices thus implied slowdown in consumption in the U.S. economy. The U.S. Federal Reserve Board correctly foresaw the problem. It started to reduce the interest rates which reduced the burden of debt-service upon the U.S. consumers. The interest rates were continuously reduced from about 6 per cent to about 1 per cent. The availability of cheap credit allayed the fears of the U.S. consumers and they continued with their high levels of consumption.

The fundamental problem of the U.S. economy was very much there but it was suppressed by artificially induced consumer spending. There are limits to the efficacy of such short-term policies, though. There never would be a recession if it were possible to create growth by such policies. The debt incurred for increase in consumption has to be repaid soon. The problem resurfaces at that time. Debt-led growth of consumption and economy is like a bankrupt person taking a loan.

There are indications that this policy option was exhausted by 2006. Consumer spending and value of the dollar were both declining and the U.S. Federal Reserve Board had no options left to revive the U.S. economy. The talk then was how to attain a 'soft' landing instead of a hard one.

The decline was due in 1996. It was first suppressed by the IT boom and again by artificially induced consumer spending. But the day of reckoning must come. Former Chairman of the Federal Reserve, Alan Greenspan, speaking at the European Banking Congress, Frankfurt in November 2004 said: "It seems persuasive that, given the size of the U.S. current account deficit, a diminished appetite for adding to dollar balances must occur at some point. But when, through what channels, and from what level of the dollar? Regrettably, no answer to those questions is convincing." Mr. Greenspan's comments indicate that the dollar has to decline. The question is only about the pace and its extent. The new technology-led leadership of the U.S. will spontaneously come under pressure as the development of new commercially viable technologies falters.

Ruling the World through Control of Technology—Case of the Internet

The internet is now managed by a non-profit American company ICANN which was established by the U.S. Department of Commerce in 1998 to assign names to internet users. This was consequence of the fact that the internet was invented in America, partly with funding from the American government. Initially the use of internet was limited to that country hence there was no difficulty in the American government regulating it. But now the internet has got a global reach. Yet ICANN continues to assign names globally and is accountable only to the U.S. Government.

For example, the U.S. Government made a unilateral announcement that only five of ICANN's 18 directors would be elected from among the internet stakeholders. The four directors who had initially formed the company would continue to hold office without having to retire or be re-elected. There are no shareholders or members of ICANN. No meeting of share-holders takes place where the directors could be made accountable. The only court of appeal against actions of ICANN lies with the American government or, at best, the American judiciary.

Thus South African President Thabo Mbeki said that the world community should discuss ICANN's powers, "otherwise the world continues to be governed by California law." The suggestion came soon after South Africa took legal control of its country domain, .sa, without seeking ICANN approval. In the same tone, China had threatened some years ago that it would set up a parallel internet system if Chinese characters were not accepted by ICANN.

The U.S. Government acquires immense powers from its control of the internet. It can block selected e-mail id or websites. Hans Klein, chairman of Computer Professionals for Social Responsibility says, "The U.S. might remove from central database the domain names for countries deemed sponsors of terrorism, essentially kicking them offline." This could also be done for those who opposed other American interests. The U.S. Government can, so to say, put a person in solitary confinement by blocking his e-mail id. ICANN can refuse to divulge the address of the server on which my e-mail account is located. I would then not be able to receive any mail. It is like the post-office deleting from its records the name of a town. No one would know where to send mail addressed to such a city.

It is possible for the U.S. Government to track the information being exchanged through the internet. The U.S. Government can overhear the messages just the postal departments opened mail to catch spies during the Second World War. The internet can also be used for commercial espionage. Robert Guerra, director of Computer Professionals for Social Restructuring, says intellectual property protection is necessary within the internet, so that developing countries do not get ripped off of their indigenous knowledge by big companies in the West.

The U.S., however, is reluctant to hand over control of the internet to any multilateral organisation—even one that may be established under the United Nations. It says that governments like those of China have had a poor record of providing freedom of information to their people. *The Economist* wrote, "America is wary of a completely inter-governmental approach, since it might jeopardise the internet's capacity for free speech and technical innovation. Some of the countries that want more of a say—China and several Middle East and African nations—have dubious records on transparency, human rights and press freedoms. They do not seek more power nor to preserve the internet's character as an open medium, but to control it better within their borders."

It must be accepted that the U.S. has not imposed many restrictions on the use of internet till now while the Chinese government has often blocked the websites of opponents like Falun Gong frequently. Indeed, the objective of the Chinese government may be to seek more powers to regulate the internet for its non-democratic objectives. However, this does not mean that the U.S. may appoint itself as policeman of the world. It is not for the U.S. to determine the kind of control the people of China should have. The people of a country have the right to decide what kind of government they want. If a people do not oppose a dictatorial government then we must assume that it is what they want. The alternative of handing over control to the U.S. is worse.

If a foreign government is given the moral right to interfere in the affairs of another nation for restoring democratic rights, the same unilateral action can be undertaken to restore dictatorial rights. It is well known, for example, that Saddam's Iraq was more democratic than other Arab states. China, South Africa, India and Brazil have, therefore, correctly challenged this control of the internet by the U.S. They want the internet to be managed by the International Telecommunications Union, a multilateral organisation which manages telephones, telegraph, radio and TV across the world allotting wavelengths, telephone numbers, etc. The argument is that what applies to the telephone also applies to the internet. But America prefers the status quo.

It would be futile to ask the U.S. to give up its control of the internet. Power is taken, not given. The only way is for the countries like India to beat the U.S. is by excelling in future developments of the internet. David J. Farber of People for Internet Responsibility says in an open letter to the Global Internet Community that "an intensive, international study be started at once, with a mandate to propose detailed and meaningful paths for the internet's developments, operations and management. The goal of this study would be to help guide the formation of purpose-built representative organisations and policies that would be beneficial both to established internet stakeholders and to the wide variety of organisations and individuals who are effectively disenfranchised in the current internet policy environment."

The Indian Government, in collaboration with other developing countries, should immediately launch a serious study of the future course of the internet. India should start an ambitious programme of developing the next generation of internet.

This Chapter is adapted from the following articles:

"Technology must pay for itself," June 26, 2003.
"Doubtful Starter," *The Pioneer,* August 19, 2003.
"Dollar has to decline," *New Indian Express,* February 23, 2005.
"Control of the Internet," *The Statesman,* April 1, 2004.

11

The U.S. Economy in Decline

Spin masters of the West try to convince the developing countries that economic supremacy of the West, the U.S. in particular, is somehow inherent and longstanding. Truly, this supremacy is built on technological innovations. We have shown in the last chapter that these innovations are faltering. The underlying cause of U.S. supremacy is slowly petering out.

The developing countries should take note of this change and push the already-crumbling U.S. economy into a collapse. That will herald the emergence of their economies as global leaders.

The spin masters of the West try to hide this reality. They have persuaded the developing countries to voluntarily cede to U.S. supremacy. The developing countries are mindlessly providing the U.S. economy with funds in (1) Accumulation of unnecessary forex reserves; (2) Export-led economic growth; and (3) Endorsement of technology monopolies under TRIPS agreement. These factors have already ceased to operate in the real economy. There is no real basis for the continuation of the U.S. supremacy any longer. The developing countries should recognize this change in the real economy and push the U.S. economy into a collapse.

U.S.' Growth Propelled by Developing Countries

There are limits to the growth of the U.S. economy towards the beginning of this century because it is a predicated on a corresponding decline in the developing countries. Its growth is akin to the growth of the landlord who has grabbed all the land of the village. He alone has purchasing power. He has forced others to sell their vegetables grown in kitchen gardens cheap to him. The landlord's prosperity is a reflection of the poverty of others. More prosperity of the landlord implies more poverty for the small farmers. So is the situation of the U.S. The spin masters of the West, however, propagate that increased prosperity of the U.S. will beget better economic conditions for them. The objective is to persuade the developing countries to voluntarily give away their wealth to the U.S. and accept economic subservience.

The revival of the world economy towards the beginning of this century is said to be dependent on increased consumer spending in the U.S. The buoyant stock market of the late nineties and the continued purchase of U.S. Treasury Bonds by the developing countries have created a sense of euphoria among the American people. "Encouraged by their greater sense of wealth, households have increased their net indebtedness to the financial sector. Consumer credit rose by four percent in 1997, five percent in 1998 and six percent thereafter," said UNCTAD in *Trade and Development Report 1999*.

This buoyancy of the U.S. stock market is, in part, a result of inflow of global capital into the U.S. economy. Normally, such inflow of foreign capital should 'overheat' the U.S. economy and lead to inflation. But this is not taking place because the price of imports is declining. For the developing countries as a whole the terms of trade fell by more than five percent per annum during the 1980s. The more favourable trend around the mid-1990s has been more that offset by large losses since 1996, said UNCTAD. The stable prices have enabled the U.S. to maintain low interest rates and sustain a buoyant economy.

The buoyancy of the U.S.- and world economy towards the beginning of this century, therefore, is based on (1) the willingness of U.S. consumers to incur debt; (2) inflow of global capital into the U.S.; and (3) declining terms of trade against the developed countries. Can this formula be replicated by other countries? The answer is in the negative.

Japanese, European, Chinese and Indian people do not appear inclined to borrow to consume. Thus they cannot replicate the U.S. approach built on heavy consumer spending.

Second, a buoyant stock market in Japan and Europe will require an inflow of global capital. If that were to take place, Japan's gain would be America's loss. If stock prices and consumption increases in Japan, it will fall in the U.S. There will be no global revival.

Third, the developing countries cannot help. Their terms of trade are becoming adverse. If this was to be reversed and the prices of their exports were to rise, then there could be a revival in their economies. But, in the same breath, the terms of trade of the U.S. will become adverse and growth will suffer there. The gain of the developing countries will be loss of the U.S.

The conclusion is that the U.S. economy is more like that of the landlord's. It is buoyant precisely because Japan and Europe are depressed (due to outflow of their capital to the U.S.); and developing countries are depressed (due to fall in their terms of trade).

The U.S. growth towards the beginning of this century is not likely to sustain. First, the declining of prices of commodity imports cannot go on indefinitely. Second, the flow of Japanese, European, Chinese and Indian wealth into the U.S. cannot take place indefinitely and consequently equity prices in the U.S. cannot remain ever buoyant.

In this circumstance there are two alternatives. One, we can persevere with the strategy of free trade which has led to declining terms of trade. This has not yielded results for the developing countries so far. Two, we can reject free trade, resort to the formation of cartels and try to improve our terms of trade.

U.S. is mortgaging its future

The U.S. economy, despite a sharp slowdown, is preventing the world economy from slipping into a global recession. Americans are borrowing globally and using the money to consume the goods of the world.

The U.S. is the buyer of last resort because the world's investors continue to put their wealth into U.S. securities. This money increases the liquidity of the U.S. banking sector. It becomes possible for U.S. banks to cut interest rates. The U.S. consumer is able to borrow and import goods with this cheap money. The U.S. pays for Chinese imports with the money it has borrowed from China. At the end of the day, the U.S. will have to redeem the securities it has sold to China after the imported goods have been consumed.

The longevity of this cycle depends on the willingness of the foreign investors to put their money in U.S. securities. Investors could be betting on the U.S. either because they feel that U.S. industry is efficient and will be able to hold out against a global slowdown, or that the accumulated wealth of the U.S. is so huge that they will be able to get their repayment even in a recession.

The distinction is similar to buying a car with earned wages or with a mortgage on the family silver. If foreign investment is taking place due to the efficiency of U.S. industry, it's like buying a car with earned wages. Such a cycle can be prolonged indefinitely. If the investment is taking place because of the hugeness of present U.S. wealth; it's like mortgaging the family silver. That will last only as long as silver is in the house. The ever-increasing debt will sooner or later catch up with the value of U.S. assets.

This situation can be understood in two ways. One, rest of the world's economies are weakening while the U.S. is chugging along, even if a bit slowly. Two, the rate of growth of the U.S. economy is declining. Which of the two is the real trend is the central question.

The buoyancy of the U.S. economy appears to be more the result of domestic consumption than efficient production. Efficiency doesn't count in real estate and banking sectors that are booming. If U.S. industries were indeed efficient, jobs and exports would have increased, not declined. The rising levels of unemployment and the high trade deficit implies that the U.S. economy is not competitive.

The real story appears to be that of the sale of family silver. The U.S. is unquestionably still the world's biggest economy. It has vast natural resources. It has been the technological leader in most of the last century and has sucked in the wealth of rest of the world by selling its Boeing airplanes and Microsoft software at high profit while buying tea and coffee cheap. It has huge foreign investments across the world. The global investor is putting his money into the U.S. because he feels assured his money will not disappear as it is backed by enormous wealth.

The U.S. is mortgaging its wealth to borrow from the rest of the world and using that money to import consumer goods. It is "selling" the family silver to have a good meal. That explains the buoyancy in home prices and car sales, despite pessimistic projections of profits and more layoffs.

The situation is like that prevailing at the time of the 1997 Asian crisis. At that time the information technology boom was in the making. The global investor was putting his money into the U.S. because he expected the NASDAQ to deliver. There is no IT boom now. The money is flowing into the U.S. only because it has a lot of family silver waiting to be mortgaged.

This borrowing can be sustained only as long as the accumulated U.S. wealth is sufficient to bear the burden of the debt. It is only a matter of time before the debt collector knocks at the door. And that will precipitate a fall in the dollar.

One saving feature may be a boom in bio-technology or some other sector. If biotech companies can convince global investors that they can deliver profits like the IT companies did in 1998, then global capital once again will flow towards the U.S. The decline of the dollar will be then delayed.

Another saving feature for the U.S. would be mental slavery of the developing countries. The developing countries can support their domestic industries and prevent huge profits by MNCs. They can invest in the acquisition of latest technologies and prevent payment of huge royalties. They can stop investing their hard-earned monies in the accumulation of unnecessary forex reserves and stop providing oxygen to the U.S. economy. But they may not do this if they believe that U.S. economic strength is real.

Decline of the U.S. Economy is Good for the World

The declining fortunes of the dollar are becoming a global concern. The U.S. is earning less from exports than it needs to pay for her imports. The U.S. trade- and budget-deficits are increasing. The dollar has been falling while the euro, yen, yuan and rupee are rising. There is a possibility that this may lead to dumping of dollars in a big way and bring the U.S. economy down. Many developing countries are dependent on the U.S. market. The U.S. economy will pull down these countries along with it. Thus, it is being said that the whole world, in its own self-interest, should rescue the dollar by continuing to buy it. The dollar's fall will lead to a shrinking of consumption by the U.S. citizens which, in turn, will harm developing economies that are dependent on exports to the U.S.

This viewpoint is correct, but only in the short run. The long run results of the decline of the U.S. economy will be very different.

A businessman may feel comfortable selling goods to a buyer against dubious promissory notes. But such comfort will disappear when the promissory notes remain unpaid. The developing countries are doing this today. The U.S. economy is dependent on the purchase of its Treasury Bonds by other countries so that it can continue to import their goods. The U.S. is like a buyer asking for more supplies against a cheque which should not be presented for payment.

It will be better to sell the same goods to another buyer at lower price but whose cheque is good. It follows that the rest of the world should develop other markets instead of continuing to buy U.S. Treasury Bonds of dubious value and exporting to the U.S.

The U.S. buys Chinese goods with money borrowed from China. But if China has to sell her cloth to the U.S. with her own money then why should it not empower its domestic buyers to buy that same cloth with that money? The Chinese Government could lend money to its people and they could buy that same cloth which is presently being exported to the U.S. against the dollar-denominated Treasury Bonds of dubious value.

This "lending" can be done by giving out unemployment compensation or by making greater investment in food-for-work schemes that also create productive assets. Such an approach will have two consequences. One, the cessation of purchase of dollar by the developing countries will lead to that currency falling rapidly and the U.S. economy will collapse. The decline of the dollar will reduce cost of imports and raise the standard of living of the Chinese people. Two, the standard of living of the people of China will rise by the consumption of more cloth due to income from food-for-work or other schemes.

The Chinese economy will remain unaffected by collapse of the U.S. economy because domestic market will replace U.S. market. Buying U.S. Treasury Bonds and propping up the American economy is not the only option before the developing countries. However, this is promoted because the developing countries are awed by the U.S. hegemony. The truth is that the collapse of the dollar and the U.S. economy can lead to better standards of life for our people and also create a multipolar world.

Precipitating a Dollar Crisis is Good Military Strategy

A global economic war is taking place today between India, China and developing countries on the one hand, and the U.S., European Union and Japan on the other. The result of a war is often determined by a decisive event like the conquest of Tiger Hill in the Kargil war. Wars are not won gradually and in an organised fashion but with speed and decisive action. This applies to economic warfare as well.

America has already lost the war. Indian businessmen are more efficient than their American counterparts. The exports of developing countries to America are more and imports are less. Conversely, America's imports are more and exports are less. This is the pattern of America's trade. The American economy should have collapsed spontaneously in this situation. However, it surviving only due to the support it is getting from India and China. We are buying U.S. Treasury Bonds with our forex earnings in large quantities and preventing the collapse of the American economic empire. China and India must stop buying these bonds. That will precipitate a steep fall in the American dollar, defeat America and create a multipolar world.

It is accepted by most economists that a decline in the value of the dollar is necessary and inevitable. The question is whether this decline should be precipitated by a decisive action or be secured gradually. Military strategy requires that we speedily attack the opposite camp at its weakest point and inflict a decisive defeat. The World Bank in its *Global Development Finance Report 2005*, however, gives many false arguments in favour of a gradual approach.

Argument 1: A global recession can take place if the dollar declines fast. Our exports will be adversely affected if the American economy collapses. The argument is false. Our exports to America will certainly be affected in but it is not necessary that our economy will be affected adversely. The money we are giving to America through the purchase of U.S. Treasury Bonds can be provided by the Reserve Bank of India to our citizens or to other countries as loan or aid. These recipients will purchase those same goods and our economy can remain robust.

Argument 2: Foreign capital presently being obtained by developing countries through foreign investment will shrink in a global crisis. The truth, however, is exactly the opposite. We are not receiving foreign capital at all. Part of our own money going to America through the purchase of U.S. Treasury Bonds is coming back to us as foreign investment.

Argument 3: Global interest rates will rise in the event of the American economy facing a crisis. That would increase the cost of borrowing for the developing countries and deprive them of much needed capital for investment. This argument does not hold water. It is true that banks look inward in a crisis but one hardly looks inward when the house is on fire. The same banks may buy rupees and sell dollars when the dollar collapses. This is the secret of the Bull Run in our share markets in 2006. Foreign investors will find the shares of Indian companies even more attractive in crisis. Thus a decline in the U.S. economy may actually lower the cost of capital for us.

India should not get distracted by the false arguments given in favour of a gradual adjustment of the U.S. dollar. We should boldly sell U.S. Treasury Bonds, break the facade of a strong American economy and start the process of making a new world order. We should not fear those birth pangs.

President Bush and the Decline of the American Empire

President George W Bush is leading the U.S. in an aggressive attempt to conquer the world economically and militarily. Mr. Bush sees terrorism as a military problem which can be solved by armed intervention. Mr. Bush also believes that out-sourcing will make American companies stronger and it ultimately is beneficial for the American people though they may have to suffer for a short while during the period of readjustment. The rise in the U.S. stock market after Bush victory is ample proof of the positive impact of outsourcing on American companies.

It is accepted that the immediate impact of outsourcing on the U.S. economy will be negative. The crucial question from India's point of view is whether this decline will be short or long? The final outcome, it seems, will depend on the ability of that country to make new technological innovations. The present indicators are that new inventions are faltering hence there is greater likelihood of the short run decline due to outsourcing continuing in the long run.

Henry Ford made cars on the assembly line. Thereafter, atom bomb, jet airplanes, computer and Internet have all been American inventions. American companies benefited mightily from these innovations. The decline of the U.S. economy will be short-lived if this stream of technological innovation continues into the future and it will be of long term if this stream dries up.

It is difficult to predict the course of technological innovations. However, indications are that there is a pause in the stream of technological innovations. The price of shares of biotechnology companies is flat. Scientists have not been able to generate commercially viable uses for cutting edge technologies such as superconductor, supercomputer, hydrogen fuel solar energy and genome sequencing. I feel, therefore, that decline of the U.S. economy will continue in the long run.

The aggressive military activities undertaken by Mr. Bush will only deepen this decline. The U.S. Government has had to run up a huge budget deficit to finance its war in Afghanistan and Iraq. The U.S. has taken huge loans from the global investors for this purpose. The central banks of Japan, India, China and other developing countries have purchased U.S. Treasury Bonds in large quantities. Mr. Bush's victory means that the U.S. military expenditure will rise and with it the dependence of the U.S. on these countries to finance its deficit. The condition of the U.S. economy today is akin to that of the Roman Empire that looted other countries to provide high standards of living to its nobility.

Mr. Bush's policies present a golden opportunity for India. His soft attitude on outsourcing could see more hi-tech jobs such as those in research and development coming to India. This will lead to improvements in the country's technological capabilities even if immediate profits accrue to American companies for whom

Indian scientists work. After some time, however, some of these employees will become competitors to their erstwhile employers.

The U.S. will need more money to finance its military expenditure. The Reserve Bank of India held Foreign Currency Assets to the tune of $170 billion in 2006. A substantial portion of these holdings were in the U.S. dollar. The Government of India was planning to use part of these reserves for increased public investment in infrastructure such as import of electric turbines and so on. If this was done, India will hold less forex reserves and the U.S. will not get India's wealth for free and the dollar will decline fast. The decline in the U.S. economy will be speedier if India is able to persuade countries such as China to use their reserves for domestic investment.

Two thousand years ago the Roman Empire ruled the world much like the U.S. rules today. The Roman army was the best. Prosperity of Rome was based in large measure upon loot obtained from military expeditions. However, Rome had two failings. One, it could not come up with new technologies. Two, it imported luxury consumption goods in huge quantities.

Indian traders exported dancing girls, speaking parrots, incense and other such goods including lions for the games of the Roman Emperors. The wealth brought by the Roman army from conquest of other countries found its way to India through the trade. India became the "Golden Bird" while Rome went bankrupt. The treasury of the Empire was empty when Barbarians attacked. That was the end of the Roman Empire.

India is in a position to repeat that story vis-à-vis the U.S. today. Mr. Bush is engaging in aggressive military action while the U.S. technological lead is slackening. The U.S. is importing large quantities of luxury consumption goods. Its treasury is empty. It is possible, therefore, that under Mr. Bush's leadership the U.S. Empire will decline and India may become the "Golden Bird" once again.

The Outsourcing Pincer

The wages of Indian workers are a lot less than that in the U.S., where a blue-collar worker is paid some $10 an hour or Rs 3,600 per day. In India a worker earns only about Rs.200 per day. American companies have to pay higher wages if they employ local labour. That makes their products costlier in the world market. Conversely, products of Indian companies, which pay lower wages, are becoming more competitive.

An Indian pharmaceutical major would pay Rs 200 per day to its workers against Rs. 3,600 by an American MNC. American companies cannot truly compete with those in India, and are making profits only because they have monopoly over certain technologies. An American MNC may produce a drug at higher cost than the Indian company, but it can still pay Rs. 3,600 a day to its workers and sell the drug at a high price if it has the exclusive rights to make the drug. But the number of products protected by patents is limited. It has become necessary for the American MNCs to pay less to its workers in order to compete with the developing countries in the non-patented products segment. The same applies to other sectors. Thus, American companies are transferring many activities to Indian contractors. General Motors has to reply to thousands of customer queries everyday. Customer calls are transferred to Gurgaon or Bangalore and replied to by Indian operators. American patients can consult Indian doctors and psychiatrists through e-mail. The fees are paid through credit card. Similarly, insurance claims can be processed by Indian offices. Thousand of Americans and Europeans who were doing these jobs earlier are becoming unemployed.

Few American States like New Jersey are in the process of enacting laws that prohibit outsourcing of government contracts. However, the impact of these laws is will be minimal because government accounts for only 2 percent of outsourcing.

The U.S. may be losing its technological advantage forever. Indian software experts were allowed to work in the U.S. for only for six years under HIB visas. They were required to go back to India thereafter in order to stop them from immigrating. This policy has backfired on the U.S. They acquired the knowledge of frontline technologies as well as the requirements of American customers within the permitted period. They were forced to take this knowledge back with them to India and some have started supplying the same services through Internet to their earlier clients directly at a fraction of the American price. America has transferred the frontline technologies to Indian experts in its anxiety to prevent them from immigrating into America!

Many American experts are now afraid that the outsourcing or research activities will lead to the transfer of next generation technologies to Indian scientists and erode America's lead of the present. American companies are transferring their frontline knowledge in areas such as biotech to their research outfits located in India because Indian scientists cost less to hire. In the process, Indian scientists are gaining frontline knowledge. They can use this knowledge to develop the next generation products. America may soon loose its lead in these emerging sectors as well.

Outsourcing is not new. Companies such as General Motors have been getting parts made in Asian countries for many years. America has been outsourcing nearly all of its requirements of shoes, clothes and toys. However, this did not have a negative impact on American people for two reasons. One, such products had to be physically packed and transported which took both time and money. Thus, certain jobs were retained in the U.S. because of the time taken to obtain supplies and the cost involved in the process. Two, more and better paid jobs were being simultaneously created in new areas such as computers, biotech and the Internet. The Americans were losing low-paying blue-collar jobs but getting better jobs in the newly emerging sectors.

This strategy had been successful in the last 30 years because America had the lead in the creation of new technologies. It is this lead that is now getting eroded. The transfer of hi-tech jobs to India opens up the possibility that the next technological advances will be made here.

The U.S. does not have a solution to this problem. The products of American companies will be more expensive if outsourcing is prohibited. They will be ousted from world markets and the American people will lose their jobs from the closure of their companies. On the other hand, if the U.S. allows outsourcing to continue then the American companies will transfer many jobs to India in order to retain their competitiveness. The American people stand to lose in either situation.

Mr. George Bush understands this dilemma. He has said that he will place no restrictions on outsourcing. This way, at least, the American companies will be able to maintain their competitiveness even if the American people lose their jobs. American companies can pay dividends and taxes in America. Some benefits can be provided to the American people with this money.

The alternative of prohibiting outsourcing is worse because the American corporations will be killed along with their workers. Thus, America has taken the path of lesser evil and permitted outsourcing. But this means that American economy is likely to decline in absence of a decisive technological innovation taking place. Restrictions on outsourcing will not lead to a solution. The U.S. Chamber of Commerce has said that restrictions on outsourcing will lead to higher cost of production of goods and services in the U.S., lower tax revenues from corporations and heavier tax burden on the taxpayer. Secondly, U.S. companies will lose out in global competitiveness. If rivals in Europe, Japan, and Korea could employ cheaper workers in developing nations, they would have an advantage over U.S. firms.

American companies are trying to convince American voters that outsourcing will be beneficial for them. The U.S. Chamber of Commerce Report of 2004 shows that only 3-5 lac jobs have been exported to countries such as India in the last three years. It has quoted Forrester Research to the effect that about two lac jobs are likely to the outsourced every year. This loss is small in comparison to the number of jobs created in the U.S. economy in the same period. The effort is to convince the U.S. public that outsourcing is beneficial for them. But the long term trend will be more important in determining the final result. It is likely that the export of jobs is stable and likely to increase while creation of new jobs may be short-lived.

The U.S. citizens will loose in both situation—whether outsourcing is allowed or not—but the U.S. corporations will be saved if outsourcing is permitted. Then, the U.S. worker will lose jobs to cheaper workers in India. But the U.S. companies could remain competitive by employing the cheap Indian workers. If outsourcing is prevented, the U.S. Corporation will lose their competitiveness and sink along with the U.S. worker. The U.S. worker has to loose either way. The U.S. Chamber of Commerce is correct, therefore, in saying that restrictions on outsourcing will be counterproductive for the U.S. corporations and economy. But it is wrong in asserting that outsourcing will be beneficial for the U.S. worker. He will loose anyway except that taxes paid by the U.S. corporations may make it possible to pay him some nominal social welfare benefits.

This is what the U.S. citizens should have expected in the first place. Globalisation also means globalisation of wage rates—to their lowest levels. Technological advances in transport and communication have reduced the sustainable wage differentials to the barest minimum. It will not be surprising if the U.S. becomes the strongest votary of protectionism in the times to come.

This Chapter is adapted from the following articles:

"Fragile hegemony," *News Time,* June 9, 2003.
"Bush victory: Golden Opportunity for India," *Businessline,* November 11, 2004.
"Outsourcing to India: No other option for the U.S.," *Businessline,* December 19, 2003.
"U.S. economy: Contradictory Signals," *Businessline,* May 11, 2004.
"Limits of Growth in the U.S.," *Hindustan Times,* October 7,

1999.
"U.S. mortgaging wealth before recession," *Japan Times,* August 18, 2001.
"Why the dollar should fall," *Businessline,* February 11, 2004.
"Making of a multipolar world order," *New Indian Express,* May 4, 2005.
"Room at the top," *Pioneer,* March 2, 2004.

12

Outward FDI from India Heralds our World Conquest

Indian economy was heavily protected and state-centered till the eighties. The Government tried to simultaneously liberalize domestic and external sectors during the economic reforms of the early nineties. The Government tried to attract large amounts of FDI. This would be disastrous for the Indian economy by debilitating domestic industries and creating a long term outflow through profit repatriations, and interest and royalty payments. However, resistance by the Swadeshi and Left lobbies led to slow opening of the external sector, and failed the Government's policy that would have enslaved the Indian economy.

Times have changed much since then. Indian businesses have attained international competitiveness and are acquiring foreign businesses in a big way. Indian MNCs are in the making. This heralds India's world conquest.

Swadeshi economists opposed FDI since it would lead to extraction of our wealth through profit repatriations. Now the tables have turned. India can apply the same strategy against the developed countries. Indian MNCs can send profit repatriations to India. India has to encourage outward FDI in order to conquer the world.

The long term objective of this conquest should be the creation of a just world order in keeping with our philosophy of Vasudev Kutumbakam. That aspect we shall discuss in the next section where we discuss the future challenges before the Indian economy.

The FDI Danger has Passed

The reason for opposing foreign investment in the past was that the government's focus had shifted away from promoting domestic investment. The government got busy organising road shows for attracting foreign investors rather than removing bottlenecks of domestic investment. This encouraged MNCs to buy out Indian companies. Now this danger has passed. Few Indian companies are being bought by MNCs and the latter are unable to face competition from Indian companies. For example, Tata's Indica is giving Western car manufacturers a run for their money. Thus there is no need to cry hoarse everyday about the dangers of foreign investment anymore.

The second reason of opposing foreign investment in the past was that the money inflow was being used to finance government profligacy. Foreign investment inflow were leading to increased liquidity in our money market and enabling the government to borrow at low rates of interest. Now our banks are flush with funds anyway. Foreign investment inflow is only one contributory factor to this liquidity. Basically, there is less demand of credit from the businesses in comparison to the availability of funds with the banking sector. This liquidity will remain even if foreign investment inflows are less. The government's borrowing programme is not dependent on the liquidity caused by foreign investment inflow. Therefore, less foreign investment will not lead to less borrowing or expenditures by the government.

The third reason of reviewing this opposition is that more foreign investment is coming through portfolio inflow and less as direct investment. The impact of the two types of foreign investment on Indian business is quite different. FII strengthens Indian businesses against Western MNCs. For example, the purchase of equity of Telco by a Korean pension fund helps the Indian company buy out another Korean auto manufacturer. FII enables Indian companies to buy foreign entities with foreign money. FII is Indian business-friendly and should be welcomed.

The problem of volatility due to FII inflow has to be managed by maintaining adequate forex reserves and imposing short-run capital gains tax on FIIs. Our strategy should be to encourage FII inflows so that Indian companies can stand up to MNCs. Government borrowing and waste should be reduced by increasing accountability of government expenditures rather than by discouraging FII inflow.

The fourth reason of opposing foreign investment was that it could lead to a run on our currency. The natural corollary of foreign investment is that we also accept free outward movement of our capital. Our businesses are also eager to invest abroad. The outward FDI from India is rising fast. Previously our investors were sending their money to the U.S. and that money was being used by American MNCs to buy out Indian companies. Now the game has reversed. Indian companies are using money obtained from FIIs to make foreign acquisitions. Foreign investment is the route to multi-nationalisation of Indian business.

But there is a need to be careful because this favourable climate could prove to be short-lived. Countries like Argentina lost many billion dollars of forex reserves every day during their crisis. The price of Peso was falling. Foreign investors and banks were selling the peso in huge amounts and withdrawing their money from that country. Domestic depositors also started to withdraw their peso-denominated deposits and started converting them into dollar-denominated deposits. The result was that the "huge" forex reserves evaporated in a matter of a few days. Our forex reserves of $170 billion-plus could similarly evaporate in a few weeks if Indian citizens start sending their money out in a big way. Thus we should limit outward foreign investment to Indian companies that are making acquisitions abroad lest it lead to a run on our currency.

The fifth reason of opposing FDI in the past was that the long-term impact due to repatriation of profits was negative. For example, declaration of dividend of 200 percent buy a MNC like Hindustan Lever means that twice the money invested by Lever Brothers is being repatriated *every year*. Organisations like UNDP have drawn attention to this long-term danger. The danger from repatriation of profits by Morgan Stanley Mutual Fund, Citibank or Hindustan Lever is as serious today as it was earlier. But now the converse is also true. Our businesses may soon be repatriating profits to Indian in a big way.

Previously we had to worry only about the outward repatriations of profits. Now we also have to contend with inward repatriation of profits as well. This is a tricky problem. We cannot morally encourage outward FDI by Indian MNCs. The solution to this dilemma requires that we frame rules of conduct of outward FDI. We should encourage migratory outward FDI and pass on capital and technology to other developing countries without seeking repatriation of profits. Let this be India's contribution to world welfare. We could also make laws to discourage profit repatriations by western MNCs. With such a system in place we should have no difficulty in opening to inward and outward FDI.

A question arises about the objective of businessmen. Why should they be interested in making migratory outward FDI? We need to understand the objective of the businessman in making profits to answer this question. The businessman at this level does not seek more profits to better his lifestyle. He wants to make profits to conquer the world of finance. Just as a professor enjoys presenting a paper in an international conference or a sportsman enjoys winning a medal in the Olympics, so also the businessman enjoys the power of money—his ability to swing the fortunes of countries or industries. This he enjoyment he can get with migratory FDI even more than repatriable FDI. He will have more financial power if he is accepted as a friend in the host country on the strength of his migratory investments. The need is to communicate this dimension to the businessmen.

India Beats China in Outward FDI

It was feared at the time of the acquisition of Tomco by Hindustan Lever that India Inc would be taken over by the Western

MNCs. Nothing of the sort has happened. On the contrary, Indian business houses have announced major foreign acquisitions.

This is likely to increase. Critics say that this newfound confidence among Indian businessmen shows how out of sync the *Swadeshi* economists have been. But the reality is otherwise. The argument of the *Swadeshi* economises was that the long-term burden of repatriation of profits of foreign investment was more than the short-term gains. The government was inviting FDI not to expose domestic businesses to international competition but to get easy money for its borrowings. Indiscriminate opening of the economy to MNCs would not get us new technologies.

This resistance by *Swadeshi* and Left economists slowed the opening of the economy. Foreign investment in the insurance sector, for example, was restricted to 25 percent equity because of such resistance. The success of Indian companies is facing MNCs owes itself to the slowing of opening of Indian economy to FDI. This slowing provided breather to Indian companies to upgrade and face Western MNCs. The success of India Inc is, therefore, not a proof of wrongness of the Swadeshi argument. On the contrary, it is a proof of correctness of the Swadeshi resistance.

Happy results are now visible in outward foreign investment by Indian companies. The level of inward FDI flows appears to have reached a plateau; both in China and India, around 1996. The outward FDI flows, however, show an altogether different trend.

China's outward FDI has remained stagnant, at around $3billion per year since 1991. In India's on the other hand, shows a steep increase in the last three years from $80 million to $500 million a year. This trend appears to be gaining ground.

This indicates that Indian businessmen have been able to meet the MNC challenge in India. They are now emerging out of their shell and taking on the MNCs on their home turf. The battle has been won.

The new challenge is that India should not follow the MNCs' footsteps in debilitating the domestic economies of host countries.

Western MNCs had made huge investment in Africa in the 1960s and 1980s and in South-East Asia in the 1990s. All these countries' economies are in bad shape today. Africa has become a basket case. Latin Africa is going through its second 'lost decade'. East Asia is mired in low growth rates.

The challenge before India is to espouse an altogether different type of MNC culture. The objective of Western MNCs has been to extract money from the developing countries through profit repatriations, royalty payments and transfer pricing. Their objective is not to continually reinvest their earning and help the host countries grow. Our objective should be to plough back most, if not all, earnings into the host country perpetually. The purpose of Indian MNCs' foray abroad should be to help the host countries develop their entrepreneurship and multiply their wealth and retain it within their borders.

Indian businessmen of the present should contribute to the enrichment of the poor countries of the world rather than their impoverishment as the Western MNCs have done. Only that would be in keeping with the vision of "welfare for all," or *Vasudev Kutumbakam.*

Convertibility is Beneficial Now

As of 2007, rupee is convertible only on current account for the payment of items like foreign travel and import of raw materials. Rupee cannot be converted into foreign exchange for making foreign investments such as purchase of shares on the New York Stock Exchange or property in London. This will be permitted if rupee is made fully convertible. Full convertibility is an indicator of the currency's strength and stability.

Writers like this have been opposing full convertibility in the past. But circumstances have changed. Indian businesses have become strong. The successful resistance by Swadeshi Lobby and Left Parties has prevented Finance Ministers like Man Mohan Singh and Yashwant Sinha from providing free entry to MNCs. Indian businesses have generated the capacity to face foreign competition in this incubation period. We are no longer threatened by the MNCs. The proof is high level of portfolio investments coming into our share markets. The inflow of FII in 2006 has been about $10 billion against inward FDI of about $6 billion. Clearly foreign investors have greater confidence in our domestic companies than in the MNCs seeking to invest in India. Foreign investors are more inclined to buy shares of Tata Motors on the Mumbai Stock Exchange and less inclined to buy shares of Ford Motor Company on the NYSE.

Another proof of the emerging strength of Indian businesses is growing outward FDI. There was one-way flow of FDI in the nineties. MNCs were investing in India, albeit slowly, while Indian businesses hid in their hollows. Beginning 2006, Indian businesses were buying establishments in foreign countries in a big way. Outward FDI was about one-half of inward FDI. More importantly, outward FDI was rising while inward FDI was flat.

Convertibility of the rupee was troublesome in the past. MNCs could enter in a big way and smother Indian businesses. That danger no longer exists. Conquest of the world economy requires us to make huge outward FDI which will be encouraged by full convertibility. It will also become possible for Indian investors to make investments in New York and London and capture global wealth. The creative energy of the country at the ground level will get a chance to play in the world markets.

Another reason for opposing full convertibility in the past was the danger of large outflow of our capital. The value of the rupee was declining then—from Rs 15 to a dollar in 1991 to Rs 49 in 2000. It was profitable for Indian investors to send their capital to foreign countries then. This danger no longer exists. The rupee is rising—it rested at Rs 44 to a dollar in 2007. Indian investors are bringing back money lying in foreign countries. This rise of the rupee is likely to be stable because it is based on the global competitiveness of our service industries. In this circumstance, the outflow of our capital will partially neutralize the harmful effects of large inflows. It will also lay the foundation of our global conquest.

England had conquered us by investing in India. Now it is our turn to repay in kind. Full convertibility appears to be justified in these changed circumstances.

The problem of the common man remains, however. The benefit of convertibility will accrue to the upper 1 percent of the country's population. The common man could, if at all, get minor indirect benefits. Some employment may be generated in the services sector. However, such benefit is suspect because most investment taking place presently is capital-intensive. The number of jobs in the organized sectors has been declining since 1997 despite high growth rates. Or, Indian companies may pay more tax in the country from incomes earned abroad.

Free movement of labour will be more beneficial for the common man. The wages of unskilled worker in the U.S. is about Rs 4,000 per day. Migration of labour from India would enable Indian workers to benefit from these. Thus, India should demand free movement of labour along with free movement of capital. The free movement of capital must now be embraced even if it does not lead to benefit to the common man because India's ability to secure free movement of labour will be enhanced by our global conquest. Benefit to the common man can wait since we have no means to secure it at present anyway.

The second problem with convertibility is of justice. East India Company invested in India and impoverished us. MNCs invested in Mexico and Southeast Asia and pushed these countries into crisis. Increasing outward FDI from India indicates we will inflict such punishment on other countries. Purchase of a truck manufacturing plant in Korea by Tatas is likely to be beneficial for India and harmful for Korea.

Indian culture does not permit such behaviour. Our principle is "Let all be happy." Outwards FDI stands against this principle. Indians were seen as greedy, unfair and evil in countries like Uganda and Fiji. We may be perceived in this manner if we allow large outward FDI by our businesses. We have to conquer the world, not to exploit others, but to provide them prosperity and justice. This can be done by imposing a condition on outward FDI that large part of the profits will be reinvested in the host country perpetually. Then Indians will not be seen negatively across the world.

Face Wal-Mart Challenge Head-on

Indian government has opened the retail sector to big Indian companies like Reliance in 2006 and is slated to do the same for foreign players like Wal-Mart. There is much opposition to Wal-Mart back home in the U.S. The labour unions allege that Wal-Mart pays much less than other retailers of similar size. A study by University of California, Berkeley found that Wal-Mart was paying average wage of $9.70 per hour in comparison to $14.01 paid by other big retailers. Wal-Mart does not tolerate labour unions. An Associated Press report tells that Wal-Mart chose to close down a store rather than negotiate with its unionised workers. The store in Saguenay, Canada, whose employees formed a union, was first deprived of merchandise supply. The shelves were empty. The store began to loose money. It was then closed.

The second group opposing Wal-Mart is that of local stores. They allege that Wal-Mart is able to procure directly from China due to its size. The local stores have to purchase from importers. They cannot compete with Wal-Mart and would have to close shop. They allege that Wal-Mart provides a few hundred jobs but kills many more by forcing closure of small stores.

Economist Larry Mishel of the Economic Policy Institute sums up the problem as follows: "If people were only consumers, buying things at lower prices would be just good. But people also are workers who need to earn a decent standard of living. The dynamics that create lower prices at Wal-Mart and other places are also undercutting the ability of many, many workers to earn decent wages and benefits and have a stable life."

The problem of Wal-Mart is really the problem of globalization. Wal-Mart has 'globalised' retailing. In the process, it is forcing the U.S. wages in the retailing sector to global minimum levels. Globalisation implies globalisation of not only goods but also wages. The mainstream economists, on the other hand, have misinformed the public that globalisation will create more jobs, open new markets and lead to better wages. But that is clearly not happening and cannot happen since the global supply of labour is huge. Markets will be supplied by cheap goods produced by cheap labour in poor countries.

We face the same predicament as the U.S. Wal-Mart will create problems for our kirana stores. But we also have to provide our consumers with the cheapest goods. If our worker buys a pressure cooker for $70 while the Wal-Mart provides the same to our competitor in, say Thailand, at $17, then our cost of production will be high and we will be priced out of the global market. Our consumer and worker will be 'poorer'.

Preventing the entry of Wal-Mart would mean that the large number of 'middleman' engaged in distribution such as transporters, warehouses, wholesalers and commission agents will continue to provide 'inefficient' services. The country would be spending much money on unnecessary transport, handling ad warehousing. The consumer would have to pay higher prices of this mismanagement. The challenge before us is to place minimum burden on the consumer and provide maximum benefit to the workers. We must study various alternatives from this perspective.

Gandhian Anna Sahib Sahasrabuddhe had suggested that weaving for domestic market may be wholly reserved for the handloom sector. That would lead to high cost of cloth of the consumer but is likely to benefit a large number of weavers. The free play of market must be restricted but it has to be shown that the particular restriction, for example, of preventing entry of Wal-Mart, is the best policy. We should, therefore, compare the costs and benefits of (1) preventing entry of Wal-Mart; and (2) imposing restrictions on power looms and other alternatives. My assessment is that restrictions on power looms will provide much more relief to the workers at less cost to the consumer.

We have to balance between two contradictory objectives—least-cost production and high wages. It is possible to attain these two goals if the market is given free play in all sectors barring a few 'employment generating' sectors like weaving. We should allow Wal-Mart to open shop and provide goods in all other 'non-sensitive' sectors to our consumers at the global minimum prices.

This Chapter is adapted from the following articles:

"Swadeshi vs. FDI," *The Statesman,* March 21, 2004.
"A new mantra to remember," *Businessline,* December 8, 2003.
"Gathering Storm of Indian MNCs," *Mainstream,* September 23-29, 2005.
"Face Wal-Mart challenge head-on," *New Indian Express,* June 15, 2005.
"Welcome Convertibility," 24.3.2006

13

Large Forex Reserves are Unnecessary

The flow of money between the developing and the developed countries is, on the whole, balanced. The total remittance from developing countries equals to the total remittance by the developed countries. The developing and developed countries both need global currency to pay for the imports. Why, then should the developing countries alone maintain large forex reserves to pay for the imports?

Forex reserves are maintained by countries that are not confident of future foreign exchange earnings. India faces no such threat now. We must liquidate our forex reserves and use them for investment. There is no need to provide our hard-earned money to the Western countries for this.

We do not Need Large Forex Reserves

The Government is continuously purchasing dollars to augment our forex reserves. We have to reconsider the usefulness of this.

The need to maintain some forex reserves for day to day transactions is valid. But high levels of reserves are not necessary.

We need to hold only the required amounts. Low levels of forex reserves caused the balance of payments crisis of 1991.

The Asian crisis indicated that volatile fluctuations in short-term foreign capital flows can dislocate the economy. Foreign banks had pulled out their loans speedily and sold their equity holdings. This sell-off had led to a run on their currencies. If those countries had maintained adequate levels of forex reserves, they could have cushioned the impact of this exit. Thence was created the mantra of holding large forex reserves. High levels of forex reserves are required to insulate the economy against volatile portfolio inflows.

Forex reserves entail a high carrying cost. The World Bank says in its *Global Development Finance Report* 2004: "High external reserve holdings come with a significant interest-rate carrying cost. Most countries invest their reserves in relatively safe, short-term assets, such as U.S. Treasury Bonds. The Yields on such instruments are currently very low—well below the interest rates that developing countries pay on their debt." On the one hand, Indian companies pay around 7 percent interest on their dollar borrowings. On the other hand, the Reserve Bank of India buys U.S. Treasury Bonds and earns only about 2 percent interest on them.

The real cost to the Indian economy is much greater. Much greater benefits would have accrued to our economy if the money had been invested in public works such as highways or dams. According to the *Economic Survey* 2003-04, gross fixed capital formation by the public sector has declined from about 10 percent of the GDP in the late eighties to 6 percent in the zeros. On the one hand, our infrastructure is lagging and on the other we have put our money in low income investments abroad.

We have placed two mutually contradictory objectives before ourselves. We want to obtain large foreign investments and also to increase our exports. We receive dollars from both these activities. The total receipt form these two sources are equal to the total requirement of dollars for imports. The formula is FI +

Exports = Imports. Obviously, for a given level of imports, higher foreign investment necessarily means lower exports. In 2003-04, our imports were $65 billion, which were financed by export receipts of $53 billion and foreign investment of $12 billion. If the foreign investment was larger, then the export earnings would necessarily have to be lower. Hence we cannot have both high foreign investments and large exports.

The Reserve Bank is trying to wriggle out of this contradiction by continuously buying dollars and holding them as forex reserves. The excess dollars brought by foreign investment and exports are sucked out of the system by RBI and sent back to the U.S. In the process we incur a huge cost of depriving us of infrastructure.

A solution is to allow the rupee to appreciate and make lower exports and higher imports. The government was planning to establish a Special Purpose Vehicle to increase the level of imports for infrastructure projects. The same objective can be attained by allowing the rupee to rise. The imports will rise along with. Higher investment in infrastructure can be made by domestic public expenditure. There is not need to go through the tortuous and unnatural process of first accumulating forex reserves and then using them for imports though the Special Purpose Vehicle.

Rupee can become the World Currency

Many countries including Russia, Switzerland and Venezuela were withdrawing their foreign exchange reserves from the U.S. dollar and investing in Japanese Yen or European Euro in 2006. The United Arab Emirates sold $3 billion dollars in late 2006 and purchased Euros leading to a fall in the value of the dollar. The dollar simultaneously declined against the rupee from Rs. 49 per dollar in 2002 to Rs. 44 in 2007. Many countries want to exit from the U.S. dollar. There is an eerie perception that the dollar may collapse and investors are withdrawing before it collapses.

The purchase of dollar is being made towards the beginning of this century mostly by foreign governments like those of Japan, China and India. This purchase is motivated on the considerations of geopolitics since these governments do not want to find themselves on the wrong side of the world's only superpower. But to shift from dollar to Euro or Yen is like falling from the frying pan into the fire because the European and Japanese economies suffer from similar problems. Our rupee is a better candidate to take on the role of the world currency.

In an article titled "When Currency Empires Fall," Avinash Persuad of Agora Financial, Baltimore tells that the world reserve currency has changed many times: "International currencies in the past have included the Chinese liang and the Greek drachma coined in the fifth century B.C.; the silver punch-marked coins of fourth-century India; the Roman denari, the Byzantine solidus and Islamic dinar of the Middle Ages; the Venetian ducato of the Renaissance; the 17th-century Dutch guilder; and, of course, sterling—and now the dollar."

A study of literature and the history of these currencies indicate that the world currency must have four qualities:

(1) It should be freely convertible;
(2) It should be backed by a large economy;
(3) The economy should be growing and leading the world; and
(4) It should display sound economic management.

These qualities were present in the British sterling in the eighteenth and nineteenth centuries. But it became weak in the twentieth century when the size of the British Empire shrank. England failed to make new technological innovations like those of the steam engine and canon. Britain ceased to lead the world economy. Its growth rate faltered. As a result countries pulled out of the sterling in the early part of the twentieth century. Britain made it compulsory for its colonies to hold their foreign exchange in sterling in order to bolster the currency. But, of course, such measures failed to stem the decline. The U.S. dollar then became the world currency.

The condition of the U.S. dollar is suspect presently. The share of dollar in world foreign exchange reserves has declined from 71 percent in 2000 to 65 percent in 2006. Surely, the U.S. is the largest economy but its growth rate is weakening on a long term basis. (The high growth rates in 2003-06 were due to buoyancy in the housing sector built on loans. This growth was not from real income.) The share of the U.S. in world income was about one-half at the end of the Second World War. It has now declined to about one-fourth. The U.S. economy does not display sound economic management. Its trade- and fiscal deficits are huge. It is spending huge amounts in wars in Vietnam, Afghanistan and Iraq much the way Britain indulged in militarism in the nineteenth and twentieth centuries. The U.S. is borrowing money from across the world through the sale of Treasury Bonds and using that money to make wars or to increase consumption of its people instead of using it for investments. The U.S. remains the technology leader but it has not made any decisive technological advance like the internet in the last decade. Rather, R&D activities are being shifted to India in a big way. The future developments of technologies may take place in India rather than the U.S. For these reasons the dollar is fast losing its status as the world currency which explains the anxiety of various countries to pull out of the dollar.

The strongest contender for the world currency after the decline of the dollar is the Euro. That currency is convertible. The combined income of the European Union is more than the U.S. But the growth rate of the EU, like the U.S., is low. Europe has not contributed to the invention of new technologies in the last half-century. It also does not have a city like London or New York which can emerge as the global finance capital. The largeness of the European economy comes from merger of countries rather than from high rates of indigenous economic growth. To sell dollars and buy Euro is like withdrawing ones deposit from a drunkard millionaire and depositing it with a millionaire widow. The money may be safer with the widow but it does not make her the leader. Similarly, Euro may provide safety but it lacs the strength to lead the world economy.

The second contender is the Chinese Yuan. The growth rate of China is highest among major countries of the world. The share of China in world income is fast increasing. The Chinese government is not indulging in wasteful expenditures on wars and instead investing in projects like the Tibetan Railway. But the Yuan is not fully convertible. The price of Yuan is determined less by the market and more by the perceptions of officials of Bank of China. China lacks a transparent financial infrastructure that may beget confidence of foreign governments. China is a state-run economy. The Chinese culture venerates the Emperor. This philosophy does not match with the requirements of the global investors who want the market to determine the value of their holdings rather than some official sitting in the corridors of the Bank of China. China is also not the leader in technological developments nor is it a global financial centre. The global investor is not likely to invest in Yuan for these reasons.

The situation of the Indian rupee is better. It is moving fast towards full convertibility. India's share in world income is increasing though it is small presently. But this can change fast if the dollar declines vis-à-vis the rupee. India is increasingly becoming the global centre for technology developments. India has a long tradition of market-oriented finance institutions like the Bombay Stock Exchange. India is often described as a 'mercantile' civilization. Our traders have travelled to other lands for the last 5,000 years while China has mainly looked inward. Mumbai has the culture and infrastructure to develop into a world finance centre. There is a good likelihood that India may emerge as the global economic epicentre and the rupee may become the world currency in another ten to twenty years. We should aim at this instead of living under the awe of dollar supremacy.

FDI Recycles our own Money

Our leaders continue to harp on the need for attracting foreign investment to meet the huge infrastructure requirements of the country. The truth, however, is that India has become an exporter of capital. The *Global Development Finance* 2005 report of the World Bank says that foreign capital flows from the developed countries to the developing countries was $276 billion in 2004. This included FDI, FII and loan from the World Bank and private banks. On the other hand, developing countries have exported

$429 billion their capital. Most of this has been sent voluntarily by their central banks in order to augment their foreign exchange reserves. More money is sent illegally by Hawala. On the whole, developing countries have become net exporters of capital to the tune of $153 billion. Our government is crying hoarse that we must open the capital market in order to attract more foreign investment. But the truth is that this will open the doors for greater export of our capital. (It is a different aspect that export of our capital will be the route to our global conquest. But then we should put that objective explicitly before us. There is no need to self-deprecate ourselves by saying we need foreign investment to build our infrastructure.)

We have not received any foreign capital after 2005. The money being sent by us to hold forex reserves is coming back in the form of foreign investment. This give-and-take is doubly harmful for us. We first incur loss in holding forex reserves and again in profit repatriations from foreign investment. Our situation is like that of the farmer who gives the vegetables grown by him to the landlord and gets food grains in return. The landlord makes double profits first in buying the vegetables and then in selling the food grains. The farmer does not understand that growing food grains himself would rid him of the double exploitation.

This unholy ideology is created and promoted by the World Bank. While releasing the *Global Development Finance2005* report in Delhi, Director of the World Bank Uri Dadush admitted that India had accumulated forex reserves far in excess of the normal requirement of six months imports. India had forex reserves adequate for 14 months imports, which is less only to Venezuela. The bank official accepted that India incurs losses in various ways in holding these excess reserves.

About 70 percent of the reserves are held in U.S. Treasury Bonds giving a return rate of about three percent per year. The Government of India, however, borrows at seven to nine percent to meet its deficit.

Second, the price of the dollar is declining, and that leads to capital loss on our dollar-de-nominated forex holdings.

Third, the Government is unable to invest in highways, canals, space armaments and the like due to paucity of funds. The money sent abroad to augment the forex reserves could instead be used to meet these objectives to propel economic growth.

The officers of the World Bank, however, dismiss these costs pointing to other non-existent benefits. They say that large forex reserves help create food security for the country. We would be able to import food in case of drought or any other calamity, they say. This argument does not hold because we have adequate forex for six months imports. Holding excess reserves to augment food security is like telling a person sleeping comfortably in a heated room that a blanket would keep him warm!

The second argument is that we can face the ups and downs of world capital markets with ease. This too does not hold. The instability in the global financial markets transmits to India only if we import huge amounts of foreign capital. First, we exported our capital to hold U.S. Treasury Bonds, then we attracted foreign capital to make up for that loss and now we are saying that we need large forex reserves to ward off instability created by those capital inflows! We do not need forex reserves if we do not send our wealth and take foreign capital.

To export our capital to hold huge forex reserves and then to re-import part of that capital as foreign investment involves a double loss for the country. But our leaders are hypnotised by the World Bank and are axing their own feet. The correct policy is to use our own capital for increasing domestic investments.

This Chapter is adapted from the following articles:

"Why do we need large forex reserves?" *New Indian Express,* March 23, 2005.
"The forex problem," *The Statesman,* July 6, 2003.
"Slave of the World Bank," *The Pioneer,* April 26, 2005.
"Technology without capital," *The Pioneer,* May 8, 2001.
"Rupee can become the world currency," January 2007.

14

Emergence of the Asian Century

Slow and Steady, India Beats China

India has often been advised to follow the path of China in attracting foreign investment and making larger public investment in human capital. China has certainly done well in the last decade, but the long term success of her strategy is questionable. It can be a disaster if India followed her example. China's approach can be called "two quick steps forward, one slow step back." India's approach, in contrast, is "two slow steps forward." The end result is often that India is ahead in the long run but in the short run China appears to be ahead with her two quick steps.

Buddhist philosophy has two streams that amplify these approaches. Mahayana asks the seeker to work for the betterment of the world. The seeker is advised to dissolve his ego into the common good. Chinese governance is close to this system. Policy correctness is secured by the leader, who corrects himself as mistakes become clear, since he is driven by a deep desire to better the people's lot. The Chinese follow their leader more or less unquestioningly. This is the Chinese approach of "two quick steps forward, one slow step back." The leader takes quick decisions and backtracks when necessary.

The Hinayana, on the other hand, asks the seeker to withdraw from the world and seek individual salvation though meditation. It adds, however, that the seeker should resist the tyrannical ruler. Correctness of policy is secured by friction between the rulers and seekers—the Brahmins. Facing incessant debates by these Brahmins, leaders are unable to take quick decisions. Yet slowly there emerges a decision that is closer to the correct path. This is the Indian approach of 'two slow steps forward.'

China has a history of mighty reversals, while India has tales of slow action. In the 1950s, China's Communist government quickly organized agriculture into cooperatives. These were subsequently merged into about 25,000 communes. In many cases, even small private plots were abolished. At that time, this was heralded as a great advance. In his book *Chinese Road to Socialism* (E L Wheelwright and Bruce McFarlane, Monthly Review Press, New York, 1970), the pro-Communist author says that, "there were solid achievements by the communes and more than 16.5 million mou of land were brought into irrigation. A 30 percent increase (in agricultural production) was probable achieved." But then production faltered. Deng Xiaoping broke the land up into small private farms in the early 1980s. The quick action of cooperativization was followed by a slow partial reversal.

India's land-reform program was slow to take off. India debated for a full 10 years and then took another decade to implement the decision. Large farms were broken up and small private farms were established. The result in both cases was the same; only the approach differed.

In the mid-1950s, China embarked on an ambitious program of small-scale industrialization called the Great Leap Forward. The most exciting feature was Mao Zedong's call to make iron in every back yard. Small factories were set up to produce acid, soda, fertilizers, and pesticides and to mine coal. This effort, however, could not be sustained. Peasants found themseives overburdened with work. The quality of output was poor and the cost high. In the early 1960s, this policy was reversed. The New Economic Policy, which established large state enterprises, was put in place. These are now being privatized and China has, for the present, adopted a mixed economy.

In contrast, it took Indian rulers 10 years to make up their minds. India set up steel plants both in the private and public sectors from the very beginning. Those plants still produce steel, often at internationally competitive prices.

Chinese Mahayana-type governance has been characterized by a deep concern for the welfare of the people. It is matched by an equally strong veneration of the state by the people. The government takes a quick decision and the people follow. As the error become clear, the leadership changes course and again the people follow. Their growth occurs in spurts: two quick steps forward, one slow step backward. Quick results were achieved when land was collectivised and back-yard steel production was started. In the end, however, these policies were reversed and China reached much the same point as India–land was parcelled out in small private farms and private and state enterprises coexisted.

India's Hinayana-type governance is much slower and often appears fractured. People discuss and debate and criticize endlessly. Each follows his self-interest. The friction between the rulers and the people is an essential part of the country's style of governance.

Both approaches have sustained through five millennia. It is not, therefore, a question of either one being right or wring. It is a question of which approach suits which mind-set.

Chinese Growth Overstated

Has China really achieved double-digit growth rates in the past two decades? And is India really lagging behind? Close scrutiny reveals that India's growth rate may actually be higher.

China is said to have moved to a double-digit trajectory beginning in the early 1980s. The size of the economy at that time and 1999 is known from *World Development Reports* published by the World Bank. A simple calculation tells us the average growth rate in the period. This growth rate is much lower than the double-digit levels claimed.

China's gross domestic product was $264 billion in 1981 according to WDR 1983. By 1999, it had increased to $991 billion, according to WDR 2000/01. The compound annual growth rate works out to 7.6 percent. The claim of an average 10.1 percent growth rate in the 1980s and 10.7 percent in the 1990s made in these reports is, therefore, simply incorrect.

India's figures from the same reports, on the other hand, are consistent. Corresponding figures for India's GDP are $142 billion in 1981 and $459 billion in 1999. This works out to an average annual growth rate of 6.7 percent. India has claimed a growth rate of 5.8 percent for the 1980s and 6.1 percent for the 1990s. The discrepancy is nominal. More importantly, India has claimed lower rates of growth than those implied by the data of the two terminal years.

A similar anomaly appears in China's so-called 'spectacular' export performance. The data simply do not match. According to WDR 2000/01, China earned foreign exchange of $208 billion from exports, $42 billion from foreign investment and $4 billion from remittances or a total of $254 billion. Of this, $165 billion was used for imports and $5 billion for accretion of foreign exchange reserves—a total of $170 billion. There is no explanation as to what happened to the remaining $84 billion of foreign exchange earned. If official statistics are to be believed, China received $254 billion and remitted $170 billion. There is no explanation of what happened to the difference between the two figures. This amount is not held by China in U.S. banks because that would show on the balance sheet of the government as forex reserves. The implication is that one of the figures is fudged. Actual exports may have been only $124 billion vs. imports of $165 billion. If that's the case, then the very buoyancy of China's exports is brought into question.

In contrast, India's data on balance of payments fits. Total receipts from exports, foreign investment and remittances are reported to be $63 billion vs. outflows of $60 billion, mainly for imports.

There are reasons to believe that even the 7.6 percent growth rate for China on the basis of the two terminal years' data may be overstated since it rests on the GDP figure for 1999. Professor Thomas Rawski of the University of Pittsburgh has compared China's GDP growth rates with its energy consumption based on Government of China data. He finds that energy consumption has not kept pace with the GDP growth rate. In his words: "the figures imply that real GDP grew by 24.7 percent between 1997 and 2000. During the same three years, energy consumption dropped by 12.8 percent. The implied reduction in energy consumption seems implausible, despite the rapid growth of computer manufacturing and other activities with low unit-energy consumption. Rapid growth of energy efficiency is not a hallmark of China's economy: In 1997-98, for example, the efficiency of energy conversion in producing thermal electricity, coke and refined oil products all declined, and the 'total efficiency of energy conversion' was no better than the average for 1983/84."

He further compares the data on consumption. He finds that for the period 1997-2001, rural per capita income marginally declined by 0.4 percent while rural consumption is reported to have increased by 31.6 percent. He writes that "the difference is far too large to attribute to population growth, which is approximately 1 percent per year." Rawski estimates that China's actual rate of growth for this four-year period was about 1.5 percent a year. Therefore, even the 7.6 percent growth rate mentioned above is suspected.

Newsweek columnist Melinda Liu writes that "since 1998 nearly all Chinese provincial authorities have over reported growth rates, leading to a situation in which the sum of the parts add up to more than the whole. In statistics unveiled before the Chinese Parliament, every province but Yunan reported GDP growth rates that exceeded the national average of 7.3 percent.

It seems the actual rates of growth are low. These are surprising in view of the high rates of savings. Compare India and China. India's rate of savings in 1999 was 20 percent. It received foreign investment, or foreign savings, worth 1.3 percent of GDP. It achieved a growth rate of 6.9 percent during the year with a total savings rate of 21.3 percent. China's corresponding figures for the same year are 45 percent total savings and 7.2 percent growth rate. The total savings rate of China was double that of India, but the growth rate was a paltry 0.3 percent higher than that of India. Certainly China should have done better with double the rate of savings.

It should be remembered that the World Bank publishes data provided by governments. The data do not represent the World Bank's own assessments. It is possible that China has claimed high growth rates to create hype necessary for it to attract large amounts of foreign investment.

What needs to be explained is the huge improvement in China's infrastructure in the last two decades. It may be that these cities represent oases in the desert. India's own history is replete with massive royal grandeur juxtaposed to pervasive poverty. A similar spectacles may be haunting China. The nation's wealth has been put into building grand cities. That should not be used as an indicator of wide-spread and stable growth.

More Doubts on Chinese Growth

According to World Bank data, China received private capital of $47 billion in 2002 against India's $5 billion. China's growth rate was 7 percent year during 1990-2002 against India's 5.7 percent. But can we believe these figures?

Mr. Guy Pfeffermann, chief economist of International Finance Corporation, has argued that China's FDI was actually half of the reported levels of $40 billion. China's FDI numbers include a substantial amount of round tripping. A large amount of Chinese black-money is recycled via Hong Kong and sent back to the mainland as FDI. Round-tripping accounts for one-half of China's FDI inflows. Thus, the actual level of FDI may be about $20 billion against the reported level from $40 billion.

In contrast, India's figures of $2-3 billion do not conform to the standards of the International Monetary Fund as they exclude reinvested earnings, subordinated debt and overseas commercial borrowings which are included in the FDI numbers of other countries.

Mr. Pfeffermann's calculations suggest there is not a huge difference in the relative importance of the FDI between the two countries as is popularly believed.

If China's growth rate is higher than India's then it has to be attributed to higher rate of domestic savings, tougher anti-corruption rules, and so on, and not to higher foreign investment.

The situation regarding poverty is no better. According to an article in *China Daily* China lifted more than 200 million people out of poverty since the late 1970s. But the *Daily* says, "The speed of poverty reduction has seen a slowdown, and last year the number of people living in poverty rose by a surprising 800,000."

The World Bank sanctioned a five-year, $247 million South West China Poverty Reduction Project towards the beginning of the first decade of this century. The project aims to benefit 635,000 households in the poorest communities of 35 remote counties in Gaungxi, Guizhou and Yunan provinces. In the project villages less than half the population grew enough food to meet basic nutritional requirements. Entire households typically have cash incomes of only $15-35 per year, says the appraisal report. That would be about Rs 700 to Rs 1,600 per year. One daresay even people of the poorest districts in India would have higher incomes.

In an article titled "The Political Economy of China's Declining Growth," Rawski estimates the annual increase in formal employment plunged from 13.7 million in 1994-95 to 1.4 million in 1996-97 and then into negative territory in 1998.

These data indicate that China has not been successful in attracting "huge" amounts of foreign investment as is being claimed. The real growth rate may be less than India's. Poverty and unemployment are rising again after some initial improvement. It appears the Beijing has pushed all the country's resources into select areas which are showcased to foreign investors. China may be behind India in each of the indicators if the whole country is compared.

The true story is that the Chinese domestic savings rate is about 45 percent which is nearly double India's 23 percent. But China's growth rate may be less than India's because foreign investment is eating away half of China's savings.

The Chinese are depositing their savings in government banks. The Chinese government is pushing this money into investments in select areas. The foreign investors are being assured by this public investment-led growth. However, focus on foreign investors is debilitating domestic businesses. There is less domestic demand and with it, low purchasing power of the people.

The growth of China is like that of the former princely States in India. The Maharajas created huge palaces and beautiful fountains while the people suffered. The capital cities grew while villages became impoverished. Similarly, some economic growth appears to be taking place in select areas while mainland China remains impoverished.

Chinese Strategy Behind Cheap Yuan

No country would like to give away its resources at low prices to foreign consumers as China is doing. It is, therefore, necessary to understand China's strategy in this regard.

The Chinese economy was managed by bureaucrats of the Chinese Communist Party after the Communist Revolution of 1949. Indigenous businessmen were branded as 'exploiters' and sent to rural camps for 'retraining' and 'declassing'. The bureaucrats did not fully understand the logic of money. Gradually the Chinese economy became inefficient. In early eighties its leaders decided to modernise the economy but the indigenous business abilities had been largely extinguished. Thus China had no alternative but to invite MNCs to establish modern factories just as the helpless single mother opens up her home to paying guests. The first preference of the MNCs, of course, was to produce in China for their home markets. Wal-Mart sourced goods in China for sale in the U.S. Thus China unknowingly slipped into an export-led growth paradigm.

But America does not have the money to buy Chinese goods. Thus Bank of China is buying U.S. Treasury Bonds in large quantities and making available funds to the American economy to buy Chinese goods. China's position is like the hotel manager who gives credit to the consumer to buy dinner from his hotel.

China can give the same loan to another consumer. She could buy bonds issued by Greek or Italian government and encourage them to buy Chinese goods. Or it could place the same money in the hands of its own consumers. Instead of buying U.S. Treasury Bonds of say $100 billion, it could reduce the level of taxes on domestic consumers by that amount and place more purchasing power in the hands of Chinese consumers. Exports are not the key to Chinese economy but only a stratagem for obtaining modern manufacturing technologies.

Why should China increase consumption of U.S. consumers if it could attain the same objectives by increasing consumption of domestic consumers? It appears this is part of a well-planned strategy to put the noose of foreign debt around the U.S. economy. Just as the village moneylender enslaves the drunkard by giving him credit to buy a bottle of liquor, likewise the Chinese are enslaving the U.S. by giving it credit to buy Chinese goods.

Indian rulers for the last 2000 years have regularly compromised with foreign invaders like Shakas, Kushanas, Lodhis, Mughals and the British in order to save their skin. Chinese rulers have, in contrast, fought foreign invaders. China single-handedly fought Japanese invaders during the Second World War at the time when Gandhiji called on Indians to cooperate with the British in their war effort. China has historically preserved its sovereignty. The purchase of U.S. Treasury Bonds in large amounts should be understood in this background. It is strategy of protecting its sovereignty by gaining an upper hand vis-à-vis the U.S.

The Reserve Bank of India should develop a joint strategy with the Bank of China to first buy U.S. Treasury Bonds and then sell them in order to create a collapse of the U.S. economy. A healthy person becomes sick if provided with air-conditioned comforts for a month and then suddenly deprived of the same. So also China and India should provide cheap credit to the U.S. and then pull the rug from under their feet.

An alternative possibility is that China is unsuspectingly falling into a trap laid out by the U.S. The saying is that if you borrow Rs 1 lac then you are a slave of the bank but if you borrow Rs 100 crore then the bank is your slave. The lender becomes a slave of the borrower if the health of the lender is threatened by a default by the borrower. China's health is today threatened by the decline in the U.S. economy. China is holding dollar assets to the tune of more than $1 trillion. The value of these dollar assets will decline if the dollar falls. Thus China has become a slave to the US economy much like the Saudis.

The decline of the U.S. will necessarily affect China and vice-versa. This augurs well for the rise of India.

Indo-China FTA Needed

An India-China Free Trade Agreement (FTA) is in the works. However, a section of U.S.-based economists are opposing such a deal. Leading them is Prof T N Srinivasan of Yale University. He drew the blueprint for economic reforms for Finance Minister Dr Man Mohan Singh in the early nineties. The U.S. has already made a FTA with Mexico and Canada and European nations have formed European Union. Following the same trajectory, India and China have made eight and seven FTAs respectively with their neighbours.

Till 2004, India and China were pursuing multilateral trade liberalization under the auspices of the WTO instead of making regional FTAs. Prof Srinivasan has lamented the shift of gears by these two giants. In an article titled, "India's Unfortunate Conversion to Preferential Trade Liberalization," he says during the 1990s India remained committed to non-discrimination in trade policy. But lately India too is signing FTA agreements at breakneck speed. "If we want to maximize the benefits of trade liberalization," he says, "the ideal course is to stick to liberalization under the auspices of the Doha Round."

The argument is that bilateral FTAs are less efficient than a Multilateral Trade Agreement under the WTO. When India makes a FTA with Thailand and eliminates import tariffs for goods produced from that country, it discriminates against cheaper goods made from other countries. Say a toy is produced in Thailand for Rs 100 and allowed duty-free import into India. China produces the same toy for Rs 90 but that will not enter the Indian market because India imposes a tax of, say, Rs 20 on it. Thus Indian consumers are deprived of cheaper goods. They buy the Thai toy at Rs 100 against the Chinese toy available for Rs 90. A FTA does simultaneously two things. It provides free entry to goods from a particular country and liberalizes trade to that extent. But at the same time it creates a combined barrier of the two countries against goods from other countries. Thus a FTA provides only sub-optimal benefits.

Prof Srinivasan's argument is valid but it ignores various other costs that come along with the WTO. A FTA can be concluded only among countries sharing a common culture while excluding others. The European Union, for example, has opened borders to countries that are inhabited by whites of Caucasian race and mostly Christians. The French farmer and the Polish plumber are of the same racial stock. Free movement of persons between these countries does not create a cultural conflict. If Poland loses in the process of economic integration, the Polish people can yet migrate to Western Europe and make a living. Or India and Pakistan may make a FTA allowing for free exchange of movies because we share the same culture. A similar freedom to allow imports of pornographic movies from America or Sweden may not be acceptable. Culture-specific liberalization is not possible under the auspices of the WTO. This works as a disincentive for trade liberalization. India may not open its borders for imports of movies under the WTO even though she was willing to allow these imports from Pakistan. Thus WTO-based can lead to less liberalization. Both FTA and WTO lead to less than maximum trade liberalization—only the area is different. FTA leads to less liberalization across countries while WTO leads to less liberalization across sectors.

Second problem is of labour and environment standards, and investment. A WTO-based approach will inevitably require the consent of Western countries such as that of U.S. and Europe. These countries have been lobbying for the inclusion of these issues in the WTO. The economies of these countries are much dependent on the monies earned from the developing countries form royalties and profit repatriations. Royalties are secured under TRIPS agreement which was virtually forced upon the developing countries in the 1995 WTO agreement. The WTO route, therefore, will mean compromises on these issues. The greater benefits derived by India from greater width of trade liberalization under the WTO will be offset by the losses incurred from the inclusion of these issues in the same framework.

WTO-based trade liberalization will also not deal with the inherent inequality of the world economy. 20 percent of the people in the Western countries are consuming 80 percent of the world's natural resources presently. Historical circumstances—of colonial exploitation, in particular—have led to the concentration of wealth in the Western countries. They are able to build research infrastructure and make new innovations. The U.S. Government, for example, was able to provide huge grants for the development of the internet because the U.S. was getting huge monies from its foreign investments. Successful research requires a critical mass of investment just as conversion of milk into cheese requires a critical amount of lemon juice. The developing countries do not have this critical amount at their disposal presently. This leads to continued concentration of research in the Western countries and they are able to maintain their lead.

Free trade in such a situation is like that between a landlord and the agricultural labour. The landlord has control over the land, shop and common grazing land. How can the landless labour possibly compete with him? The solution for the landless labour is to form an association of all labourers and negotiate with the landlord as a group as done through trade unions. The same principle applies to world trade. There is little possibility of the developing countries competing with the Western countries in a free trade system. They must first from sub-regional blocks through FTAs and then negotiate with the Western countries.

The fourth problem is of monopolies. Former Chief Economist of the IMF, Prof Raghuram Rajan had made study of the civil aviation sector in the U.S. He found that the low-cost airlines succeeded because the regulators did not allow the monopolistic tendencies of the big players like PanAm to rule. In other words, the developing countries can compete with the Western countries only if there is a global regulator that restrains the monopoly of MNCs. The development of computer operating systems in the developing countries can only take place if a global regulator forces the Microsoft to open the code of its Windows platform. This issue is not even on the agenda of the WTO. Hence WTO-based liberalization will secure these monopolies and perpetuate the present inequalities.

India should beware of advisors like Prof Srinivasan. These intellectuals are paid by the Western countries. Their thinking is coloured by the interests of their paymasters. Thus Prof Srinivasan harps on the benefits of WTO-based liberalization and distracts our attention from the various costs that are built into it. India should aggressively pursue FTA with like-minded developing countries like China and ignore the misguidance emanating from the U.S.

Learning from the Mexican Experience

Mexico mortgaged its existing revenues in the hope of future gains, but slipped badly. Its story tells us the dangers of indiscriminately hitching one's wagon to the developed countries.

Mexico initiated its economic reforms in the early eighties. It was forced to borrow $40 billion from the U.S. in mid-nineties. It had to mortgage its future oil revenues as security for this loan.

During the Mexican revolution in 1917 all mineral and petroleum wealth was vested with the state. In 1938, all foreign oil companies were nationalised by the General Cardenas' Government. The strategy for industrialization relied heavily on public sector undertakings. Government controlled all major economic activities like communications, electricity, railways, ship-building, petroleum, coal and banking. It also had a significant presence in steel, airlines and auto manufacturing.

The Mexican crisis of mid-nineties has its origins in uncontrollable expansion of Government deficit. The Mexican Government as well as the International Monetary Fund, World Bank and the foreign investors felt that Mexico was invincible because of its huge oil income. These financial institutions were more than willing to lend huge amounts to Mexico. The Mexican Government had no incentive to reign in its deficit because it had access to this easy money. The result was wasteful expenditures. Public sector units employed excess labour, guaranteed them full neutralization against inflation and the Government spent heavily in grandiose projects like the Olympics. Mexican politicians, bureaucrats and businessmen siphoned money from state coffers and invested huge amounts in the U.S. and Europe.

The current account deficit reached astronomical proportions, at $28.5 billion in the early nineties. Mexico consumed away its future through these expenditures financed by deficits. It did not have a real income to justify such expenditures. But it borrowed, piled up a huge foreign debt, ate the money away or sent it abroad. This unwarranted consumption and capital flight was the root cause of the Mexican crisis.

Government expenditures, whether financed by foreign loans or printing of notes, led to excess liquidity and inflation, which was as high as 102 percent in 1983. The average rate of inflation between 1983 and 1993 was 45 percent. In order to reduce the impact of this on the people, import duties on consumer goods were reduced from 100 percent in 1982 to 20 percent in 1987 and 10 percent in the nineties. As a result, low priced imports flooded the Mexican markets. Inflation was controlled but Mexican industries came under severe pressure and employment and economic activity began to fall.

Rising imports were not matched by a corresponding rise in export earnings. As a result, the peso had to be devalued drastically. This hit foreign investors, as their peso-denominated stocks got them fewer dollars. No matter how hard the Government pleaded, the foreign investor's confidence could not be restored. They sold Mexican securities and converted them into dollars. This caused further devaluation of the peso vis-à-vis the dollar. A desperate Government had to ask for "additional sacrifices" from its people.

The net result is that Mexico is set to enter the next century poorer than it was two decades ago. The Government approached the U.S. for help. The U.S. agreed to give $40 billion against future oil earnings. In effect, Mexico has been forced to mortgage its oil, national wealth and future income to pay for the consumption and the corruption of its elite.

Why Local Rulers Want FDI

India will have to soon take a decision whether to single-handedly checkmate the developed countries or go along with them in selling the interests of their people.

There is no question of walking away from globalisation. But we want a dharmic globalisation not an adharmic one. India has historically been in the forefront of global trade. Indian traders ruled the Arabian Sea during the Indus valley civilisation. Indian traders are credited with having brought down the Roman Empire by bring all their gold home. But we also took care of our poor. That is the reason why our people supported our governments and our civilisation has survived for several millennia. The Manu Smriti says: "If the king did not untiringly inflict punishment on those to be punished, the stronger would roast the weak like fish on a spit" (7.20). The task before us is to prevent such roasting of the poor people of the world, while globalising ourselves.

The situation at the time of launch of the WTO in 1995 was that the developed countries had low import tariffs. Their incomes were coming more through technologies—royalties and foreign investment. All these factors drew strength from the technological head start that the developed countries had, and which has deepened in the last 50 years. The developing countries, on the other hand, were protecting themselves through high import tariffs.

The protection afforded to our industries was often misused by our businessmen and bred complacency and promoted second-grade production. The car industry is a case in point. Therefore, there exists a case for trade liberalisation.

But the gap between the rich and the poor countries has increased. The reason is that while the WTO has rightly prodded the developing countries to "open up" to world trade, it has re-established new monopolies of the developed countries. Patents are the most obvious one. Multinational companies can charge exorbitant prices of their produce within 'trade liberalisation'. The developed countries have nullified many gains the developing countries were to make from free trade. A scare was created by imposing a ban on our exports of women's skirts on the false ground of their being combustible. Our fish exports were banned on the grounds that equipment for turtle extrusion was not in place. While we have won these two cases, we have not succeeded in others. Our steel exports have been subjected to anti-dumping duties. The developed countries have formed regional trade blocks like NAFTA and EU and nullified the gains which were expected to accrue to us through the MFN treatment.

There is a fundamental flaw in the free trade espoused by the WTO. Free trade is beneficial only in commodities which are produced by many countries, or in which "free trade" is practicable. This applies to software, wheat, clothing, tea and coffee. The increase in global production and trade is pushing down the price of these widely-produced commodities. The benefit to the producers of items protected by patents which are produced by a single or few players suffers from no such crash of prices. The price of jet passenger planes does not collapse with competition as that of wheat does. There is asymmetry in the impact of WTO. Therefore, bulk of the gains will accrue to the developed countries.

The result is one-way liberalisation of trade. The developing countries have substantially lowered their import tariffs and liberalised imports. But the developed countries have nullified the trade liberalisation by resorting to anti-dumping duties, countervailing duties, sanitary measures, safeguards and other mechanism permitted within the WTO. The developed countries have been double gainers. The poor people of the world continue to be roasted on the spit.

The adharma of the developed countries stares in our faces today. The gap between the rich and poor countries is widening and living standards have risen little after the establishment of the WTO.

The stance of the developed countries is that further "trade liberalisation" will be beneficial to all. It is the same hype that was given to us in the Uruguay Round. We must realise that developed countries already have very low import tariffs. Further trade liberalisation, therefore, only means a further reduction in our import tariffs. But, under that ruse, they seek to deepen their monopolies in other areas. Labour and environment standards will be used to prevent imports from our countries from taking place. Investment clauses will give freedom to their monopolies to enter our countries and thwart our efforts to build up our own industries. Opening of government procurement will prevent our government from supporting domestic industries like hand made paper. What is sought to be a "give-and-take" negotiation is actually a one-sided "take-and-take" strategy.

The dharmic approach to globalisation would be: One, demand the dismantling of all measures such as sanitary standards which nullify the effect of trade liberalisation. This is part of the "implementation issues" agenda which is being rightly pushed by our government in the WTO. This will help the developing countries to expand their trade in keeping with our historical tradition. Two, we should oppose a one-way trade liberalisation and the creation of new monopolies by the developed countries.

Global Warming may Help India

We have mostly had normal monsoons since the early nineties. This fortunate circumstance owes itself partly to the rise in temperature of the earth due to global warming. But the Western countries do not like these good rains in India and are much advocating the need to control global warming. This is to be expected since it they stand to loose much from this climate change. Thus G-8 countries proclaim that human activity has contributed to global warming and there was need to reduce greenhouse gases. They promote energy efficiency and the use of cleaner fuels. It is necessary for them to take these measures to meet the adverse effects of global warming on their economies.

The Western talk is that global warming is harmful for the whole humanity. But there are indications that it is harmful for some and beneficial for other countries. Higher temperature leads to more evaporation from the oceans. Also the capacity of the air to carry moisture is increased. These result in more rains in many regions. A study by agrometeorologists at the Punjab Agricultural University reveals that in the past nearly 30 years minimum temperatures have increased while maximum temperatures have decreased in major towns of Punjab. The annual rainfall has also increased at the following rates: Ludhiana—10 mm/year; Patiala—12 mm/year; Jalandhar—11 mm/year; and Bathinda—16 mm/year. In other words, global warming is leading to less variation in temperatures and more rain in Punjab.

Global warming will impact the environment of countries differently. Prabhjyot Kaur writes in an article in *Tribune* that rainfall in latitudes approximately over 45° north and south rainfall may be enhanced by 5 percent in summer and possibly up to 15 percent in winters. However, between 30-45° north and south latitudes, summer rainfall is likely to become very limited and winter rainfall may decrease by 5-10 percent. At latitudes between 0-30° north and south, rainfall is expected to increase by about 5-10 percent. The Indian continent extends from about 8° to 36° north and, therefore, mostly stands to gain from global warming.

Many other studies support this view. Shoshana Mayden writes for UA News Services that Asian monsoon has been gaining strength during the past few centuries, possibly due to rising global temperatures. The Intergovernmental Panel on Climate Change concluded in 1994 that global warming could intensify the monsoon and increase monsoon variability.

But Western scientists ignore this beneficial effect of global warming and harp on the negative effects. In this same article Mayden quotes Jonathan Overpeck, Professor of Geosciences and Director of the University of Arizona Institute for the Study of Planet Earth to the effect that increase melt from the glaciers in the North Pole can cool down the Atlantic Ocean and lead to less rains in South Asia. Similarly, Jill McGivering writes for BBC News that Himalayan glaciers are shrinking and within 50 to 60 years they will virtually run out of producing the water levels that we are seeing now. Indeed these effects may take place. But they may be more than compensated for by the increased evaporation from the oceans as evinced by our live experience of increasing rainfall.

Further, it is doubtful whether the earth's temperature will show a long term increase. Chul Eddy Chung and V. Ramanathan of Scripps Institution of Oceanography at the University of California, San Diego say in an article that the greenhouse gases are pushing in one direction, warming the ocean and trying to make more rain, and the aerosols are pushing in another direction cooling the oceans and leading to less rain. Aerosols and air pollution, they say, forms a blanket that prevents solar heat from entering our atmosphere. They say, in some years the aerosols might win and in some years the greenhouse effect may win. But they conclude that the net effect is to drive the monsoon rain system away from South Asia into the equatorial and southern oceans. In making this conclusion they stress the negative effects of global warming and ignore the positive effects. The fact remains that monsoons have become more intense in India in the last few years.

Former scientific adviser to the Prime Minister and eminent scientist Vasant Gowarikar feels that global warming has not affected the Indian climatic system. Speaking at the inauguration of a workshop at Yashwantrao Chavan Academy of Development Administration he pointed towards the India Meteorological Departments data on cyclones and rainfall, which are indicators of global warming. If we look at the last 115 years of data on cyclones, he said, we will find that ten or more cyclones hit the country in 1893, 1926 and 1930. The highest rainfall recorded in the country was in 1917 and the lowest was in 1918. These extremes should have been closer to present if global warming contributes to them. "There is nothing to indicate the claims of warming affecting the Indian climate system," he said.

Dr R R Kelkar, the director general of the Indian meteorological department says that "India is a tropical country. We are used to hot environments, we are used to heavy rains, we are used to cyclones, and really there is no clear statistically significant trend that things are going to change drastically."

Professor SK Sinha, specialist at the water technology centre at the Pusa Institute accuses the West, in particular the U.S., of manipulating the debate on global warming. "They make the rules. In fact, they even lure people from the developing countries to substantiate or to confirm that data, not necessarily always with very valid equipments and arguments," he says.

There is a need for us to look at the effects of global warming dispassionately. It seems the Western countries are likely to be adversely affected from this change; or they may not be confident of adjusting their habitations to the changing circumstances. Thus they blow up the negative consequence of this event. Of course, there will be some negative effect on India as well. Mumbai was virtually closed down for a few days due to heavy rains. But we have to weigh the overall impact before taking a position whether global warming is good or bad for us. It is unfortunate that we often echo the G-8 hype on the negative effects of global warming.

This Chapter is adapted from the following articles:

"India rightly resists the Chinese model," *Japan Times,* May 4, 1999.

"Chinese growth miracle may be a myth," *Japan Times.*
"Is China worth emulating?" *Businessline,* August 13, 2004
"Learning from the Mexican Experience," *The Pioneer,* February 13, 1995.
"Between push and drift," *Newstime,* December 27, 1998.
"Slow and steady," *The Pioneer,* February 11, 1998.
"A crash course in globalization," *Indian Express,* November 9, 1997.
"The theme at Doha," *The Pioneer,* November 8, 2001.
"Chinese strategy behind cheap Yuan," 22.12.2006
"Indo-China FTA is need of the hour," 17.11.2006
"The good side of global warming," 4.8.2006

PART - 3

CREATING A JUST WORLD ECONOMIC ORDER

15

The Meaning of Western Values

In the previous section of 7 chapters we have discussed policies that developing countries should follow in the period of their nascent growth. These policies were indeed followed, often reluctantly, by India after the beginning of economic reforms in 1991. The Congress and BJP Governments often resisted this model but forced into the right direction by the resistance put up by Swadeshi and Left lobbies. The policies that the Government wanted to implement but could not due to this resistance included speedy opening to FDI, lowering of import taxes, and getting more foreign aid. The result is India's emergence as a global power. These policies continue to be relevant for other developing countries seeking to emulate the India story.

In this next section we discuss the main issue relevant for India as it emerges on to the global economy as a giant. Many policies that were relevant earlier are no longer so. For example, the resistance of inward FDI is now replaced with encouragement to outward FDI. Having saved oneself from MNCs, Indian companies now aim to conquer the world using their own medicine. Similarly, India has emerged as the least-cost producer in many areas such as software, gems and jewellery, etc. The task now is to conquer the industries in the developed countries and force them into a crisis.

The Western countries present values such as those of freedom, choice, rule of law, and democracy as being just. In this chapter we show that these values are often invoked selectively to further their economic interests.

Selective Adoption of Markets by the West

Americans carry with them a self-eulogising aura of promoting the values of prosperity, democracy and freedom. They promote the market being the final arbiter of human endeavours. But market is not an American invention. Englishmen were the first global readers in the modern era. What distinguishes Americans is their belief that they have prevented the government from interfering in the markets.

The reality is quite different. Take the issue of patents. The Americans led the call for the inclusion of patents in the WTO. The key concept behind patents is that the state will interfere in the market in favour of the patent holder if another copies his product and competes with him. 'Violation' of patents is the strength of the market. If a company successfully makes a drug, competition mandates that others replicate it. Patents prevent such competition. If Sugar Baby watermelons were introduced in the markets by one farmer, patents prevent others from competing with him in the next season.

Similarly consider the global labour market. The supremacy of the markets requires that labour should be free to move across countries. The market would allocate labour in a way that the maximum production could be obtained. But America, along with other OECD countries, is the forefront of preventing such market from operating. The argument here becomes that movement of labour involves cultural exchange which a people have a right to refuse. In other words, where economic interests are involved, their culture becomes supreme rather than the markets.

The second exalted American value is that of democracy. They believe that unlike 'backward' civilisations like those of the Arabia and India, the Americans give equal right to all citizens to choose their governments. Alas! This democracy too is restricted to within the country. Their record abroad is anything but democratic. Samuel P. Huntington writes in an article in *Newsweek* that people in the Muslim countries are hostile to the U.S. "As a result of Western imperialism and domination of the Muslim world for much of the 20th century." Christopher Dickey points out that dictators and emirs in the Arab world friendly to Washington moved to stifle dissent as they are sure that America cared more about bringing down the Taliban than about upholding democracy.

The constitution of the Security Council with five superpowers holding permanent veto is joke on democracy. The final authority in the United Nations lies with the Security Council, not the General Assembly. In other words, American value of democracy is to be applied only within America. It is to be freely violated elsewhere.

The successes of democracy in the Western world coincides with them exploiting the resources of the developing countries—first through colonial loot and now through WTO-sponsored provisions which protect western technological monopolies while prying open the markets of developing countries. Democracy in the West and its absence in the developing countries are reflections of each other.

The third great American value is that of anti-imperialism. It is generally true that America has not colonised or ruled over other countries like England, France and Portugal have. Americans conquered Germany and Japan but handed them back to those peoples. But this is nothing new. It is a standard prescription of statecraft to accept suzerainty in exchange for freedom. But look what the Americans did in Kuwait. They handed the country back to its anti-democratic Sheikh so that they could have their oil. The American support to repressive governments across the globe is most easily explained by their commercial interests. The IMF stops and starts aid to countries like Pakistan and India in tandem with the change of American interests.

American thinking is full of contradictions. Americans embrace the markets, democracy and freedom only within their country. They violate these same values without compunction when it comes to other ccuntries.

Technology has changed all this, perhaps, permanently. Till the collapse of the World Trade Tower, America could feel protected by the two great oceans. An attack on America by even a victorious Germany would have been hard to imagine during the Second World War. The internet, global finance, and the jet airplanes have removed much of the protection. The result is that these double standards now stand exposed. America will now have to face the ire of the oppressed if it applies these double standards. The situation is similar to that of India in the eighteenth century. We had prospered for thousands of years protected by the great Himalayas. It was the technology of the ship-mounted canon that undid us. It has taken us more than two centuries to catch up with the world. America faces a similar situation towards the beginning of this century. The challenge before that country is not to promote the values of markets, democracy and freedom. The challenge is to recognise the shallowness of these values. If they succeeded in America at all, the path lies through state-controlled, autocratic and dictatorial countries whose wealth provided the resources to buy the compliance of the American people.

Reality of 'Rule of Law'

The National Security Strategy released by President Bush in 2006 gives the U.S. an unrestricted right to override the sovereignty of nations that dare oppose its commercial interests.

Bush says that the U.S. does not need sanction of the international community and will take pre-emptive action where its interests are threatened: "The U.S. has long maintained the option of pre-emptive action to counter a sufficient threat to our national security." He adds that the "reasons for our actions will be clear and the cause just." But the justness of the cause will be determined by the U.S. itself. The U.S. is both the plaintiff and the judge.

The U.S. is not bound by the opinion of the same international community that he criticises the "rouge" states for not listening to. Bush says that "the U.S. will constantly strive to enlist the support of the international community, we will not hesitate to act alone, if necessary, to exercise our right of self-defence by acting pre-emptively against such terrorists" or against countries that, in the opinion of the U.S., support them. The U.S.'s right to act against a state is not limited by the international law or community.

Bush does not accept the jurisdiction of the International Criminal Court. He says: "We will take the actions necessary to ensure that our efforts to meet our global security commitments and protect Americans are not impaired by the potential for investigations, inquiry, or prosecution by the International Criminal Court, whose jurisdiction does not extend to Americans and which we do not accept." Thus the international law and community is to be respected only if it suits the U.S.

Bush appears committed to the spread of democracy: "We will actively work to bring the hope of democracy, development, free markets, and free trade to every corner of the world." Speaking of Russia and China, Bush says, "America will encourage the advancement of democracy and economic openness in both nations, because these are the best foundations for domestic stability and international order." But while speaking of Pakistan he forgets that the present regime has stifled democracy in that country. On the contrary, he says that the U.S.' relations "have been bolstered by Pakistan's choice to join the war against terror and move toward building a more open and tolerant society." The regime that has stifled democracy is labelled as one that is building a more "open and tolerant" society. Further, Bush has no difficulty in dealing with autocratic oil regimes like those of Kuwait and Saudi Arabia as long as they supply oil to the U.S.

Bush is hard on the terrorists. He says, "No cause justifies terror. The U.S. will make no concessions to terrorist demands and strike no deals with them. We make no distinction between terrorists and those who knowingly harbour or provide aid to them." The U.S. has admitted that Pakistan is providing aid to terrorists against India while it has joined the U.S. war against Al Qaeda. This implies that the U.S. war on terror is selective—it will be waged only when the target is the U.S.

Bush flip-flops on the relationship between poverty and terrorism. While speaking of Afghanistan he says that poverty was not the cause of growth of terrorism in that country: "Weak states, like Afghanistan, can pose as great a danger to our national interests. Poverty does not make poor people into terrorists and murderers. Yet poverty, weak institutions, and corruption can make weak states vulnerable to terrorist networks and drug cartels with in their borders." But while speaking of Africa, he says that "promise and opportunity sit side by side with disease, war and desperate poverty."

Poverty is not an issue in regard to Afghanistan because that government is already under U.S. influence. U.S. soldiers protect its President. But African leaders have yet to be brought under U.S. tutelage. Thus the U.S. will provide financial assistance when poverty is linked to terrorism. Terror in Afghanistan has to be dealt with politically by installing a stooge government. Poverty can merrily continue here. Terror in Africa cannot be dealt in this way hence poverty becomes the cause of terror. The objective in either case is the spread of American influence.

Bush says that free trade is one of the core values that he stands for, "Free trade and free markets have proven their ability to lift whole societies out of poverty—so the U.S. will work with individual nations, entire regions, and the entire global trading community to build a world that trades in freedom and therefore grows in prosperity." But he changes his tune when the same free trade affects American interests. The U.S. has provided increased farm subsidies in clear violation of the spirit, if not the letter, of the WTO. It has imposed stiff import duties on imported steel.

Bush defends these actions. He says "There is a sound statutory framework for these transitional safeguards which we have used in the agricultural sector and which we are using this year to help the American steel industry. The benefits of free trade depend upon the enforcement of fair trading practices. These Safeguards help ensure that the benefits of free trade do not come at the expense of American workers." Bush is speaking loud and clear. Free trade is fine as long as it does not hurt American workers.

This is a sample of the contradictions of the National Security Strategy outlined by George Bush. The U.S. is not interested in the spread of freedom and removal of poverty. The advocacy of freedom, democracy and liberty by that country is to promote its naked commercial self-interests.

Why Corruption does not Hurt Economic Growth

Germany-based Transparency International has found in a worldwide survey of more than 11,000 company executives that Indian companies were most corrupt in their foreign operations. Switzerland was assessed to be least corrupt while India, China and Russia topped the list. Transparency International also found that domestic corruption and foreign corruption show parallel trends. Countries ranking high in Corruption Perceptions Index (relating to domestic corruption) and Bribe Payers Index (relating to foreign operations) move in tandem. The former measures level of corruption perceived to exist among government officials and politicians while the latter measures propensity of the companies to bribe abroad. India has the distinction of topping both indices which leads to the conclusion that Indians are most corrupt among the major countries of the world. The question, however, is this: Why is our corruption not hitting at economic growth?

Generally, corruption hits at economic growth. For example, a road is constructed poorly due to corruption and wears off soon leading to high cost of transportation and lower rate of economic growth. India and China, being high in corruption, should have lowest growth rates. But the reality is exactly the opposite with these two countries logging highest growth rates at 8 percent-plus.

It seems the economic impact of corruption depends upon the use to which the bribes are put to by the bribe-taker. Say Rs 50 lacs were leaked out of a contract of Rs 1 crore given out for the making of a road. The road was made of inferior quality and affected growth rate adversely. But that leaves us with Rs 50 lacs lying with the corrupt engineer of (public works department) PWD. He can spend this money in pleasure or he can invest in the share market. The negative impact of corruption is cut if he does the latter. Say the Engineer purchased bonds of Rs 50 lacs floated by a company engaged in construction of dams and National Highways. This money is then used in the construction of highways. The final economic result of corruption is that government road was made of poor quality but a private highway was made of good quality. The negative impact of corruption is partially nullified.

Investment of bribe-money in productive purposes nullifies the adverse economic impact even though it remains immoral. This difference can be seen clearly between India and Latin American countries. Both groups of countries are highly corrupt but while Indian officers and politicians invest the bribe-money in share- or property markets, the Latin American counterparts sent it away to be deposited in Swiss Banks. The result was that growth rate of Latin American countries declined while that of India did not. One industrialist of Lucknow confided to this author that one former Chief Minister of the state has deposited a sum of Rs. 20 crore with him for safe keeping at nominal rate of interest. Such corruption does not impact economic growth adversely even though it is immoral. The money was invested in private industry instead of a government project.

Corruption can actually lead to higher growth rate. Additional income of Rs. 100 is used differently by poor and rich persons. A poor person consumes Rs. 90 and saves Rs. 10. A rich person consumes Rs. 10 and saves Rs. 90. The propensity to save is higher among the rich. The extortion of bribes by the Engineer of Electricity Boards, for example, has a positive impact on the economy. The poor person is deprived of Rs. 100 which leads to a reduction of Rs. 10 in national savings. But the corrupt engineer invests Rs. 90 out of the bribes, which leads to a net increase in national savings of Rs. 80!

Every country seeking to develop economically has to reduce its level of consumption initially. A rickshaw-wala seeking to buy an auto-rickshaw has to consume less and save more. His consumption may increase after he has bought an auto-rickshaw. This initial lowering of consumption is called 'primitive accumulation'. England undertook such reduction in the consumption of the poor during the initial phase of industrialization in the eighteenth century. That is captured in Dickens' picture of England. America did the same by reducing consumption of the black slaves imported from Africa. India is doing precisely this through corruption. Money is being extorted by the government officials from the poor and invested in share- and property markets. Surely such corruption hits at the welfare of the people. But it still becomes an engine of economic growth.

The purpose of this analysis is not to justify corruption. But here we are examining why India has a high rate of growth despite high levels of corruption. The answer is that corruption is socially and morally wrong but has little negative economic impact in the investment-oriented culture among the corrupt of our country.

Gandhiji used to say that violence is better than cowardice while non-violence is best. Gandhiji was not a proponent of violence yet he said that violence was better than cowardice. We face a similar situation with respect to corruption. 'Corruption-with-investment' is better than 'Corruption-with-consumption'. Of course, non-Corruption is best. The ground reality is that while other countries are following the 'corruption-with-consumption' approach, India is following the 'corruption-with-investment' approach which explains its high rate of growth.

Just as a student may pass an exam by cheating; or an athlete may win a race by taking drugs, similarly India is growing today by abetting corruption. This may be okay in the short run but will harm us in the long run. The student who has passed exams by cheating fails during interviews for a job. The athlete who wins a race by taking drugs is unable to maintain his record under strict surveillance. Similarly, it will be difficult for India to maintain its present high rate of growth through this process. Many problems can occur. The corrupt officers may start indulging in consumption. The government will find it difficult to steer investment in desired directions. The country may need rural roads but the corrupt engineers may invest in fancy malls. Such misallocation of resources will hurt us in the long run. We must, therefore, eschew the path of corruption and put in place strong mechanisms to prevent it even though it is not having a harmful effect on the economy presently. That said it is equally important not to be swayed by Western harangue about India being the most corrupt country. It is also most investment-oriented country as well, is it not?

That said a word of caution is in order. Transparency International is speaking about corruption by the Indian businesses. The role of Indian government has to keep tabs on this and ensure that it does not become excessive and hurting. The corruption by the government machinery—politicians and ministers—rests on an altogether different footing. There is no justification for corruption here. A poor man may have a case for indulging in theft if he has been wronged by the rich, but not the police. Likewise, the businesses may have a case for indulging in corruption in foreign countries in view of the unfair rules of international economy, but not the governments of the developing countries.

Sacrificing Health for Profit, the Indira Nooyi Way

Global soft drink giant PepsiCo has appointed India-born Indra Nooyi as its global Chief Executive Officer. Annual sales of PepsiCo are about Rs. 150,000 crore—equal to the annual income of the states of Gujarat or Andhra. But there are many apprehensions about the impact of PepsiCo products on the people's health. Consider the following:

A study of 50,000 nurses in the U.S. indicated that those who drank just one serving of soft drink a day gained weight more quickly than those who drank less than one a month. Those who drank more also had an 80 percent increased risk of developing Type 2 diabetes (*Natural Health Newsletter*, December 2004).

A study by Dr Samuel S. Epstein, author of *The Safe Shopper's Bible: A Consumer's Guide to Non-toxic Household Products* tells that soft drink companies are using huge amounts of saccharin in their 'diet' versions of colas. More than a dozen animal tests over the last thirty years have demonstrated the carcinogenic effects of saccharin in the bladder and other sites, particularly female reproductive organs. Also soft drinks have a high content of phosphates and low of calcium. When phosphate levels are high and calcium levels are low, calcium is pulled out of the bones. This leads to osteoporosis. The bones become weak and brittle and break at the slightest injury (*Natural Health Newsletter,* January 2005).

The American Beverage Association provides details of caffeine content of major American soft drinks. Most contain less than 35 mg caffeine per bottle of 8 ounces. However, some contain more. They are one drink made by Coke; three made by Dr Pepper; and five made by PepsiCo. Clearly Pepsi is not on the right side of health. Surely, people consume caffeine regularly in coffee and tea. But they do so with full knowledge. The problem with soft drinks is that caffeine is provided to an unsuspecting consumer.

A Rediff-On-The-Net report of August 1999 quotes London-based Consumers International that dyes like E-150, which gives colas their characteristic dark brown colour, have been linked to vitamin B-6 deficiency, hyperactivity and low blood glucose levels.

There is much evidence that the impact of soft drinks made by PepsiCo is not so good on the people's health. The question before us in India is this: Is it a matter of pride that a person of Indian origin is heading this organization, or is it a matter of sorrow?

The marketing strategy of PepsiCo is equally suspect. It seems the Company tries hard to get the youth addicted to its drinks. The government support to the school systems in the U.S. is dwindling in keeping with the necessities of economic reforms. One strategy the schools have adopted is to sell exclusive rights to soft drink companies to sell their drinks in the school campuses. The companies pay the school a hefty amount in exchange of freedom to create addition among the youth. In his January 2005 article Mike Adams quotes John Robbins, author of *The Food Revolution: How Your Diet Can Help Save Your Life and Our World* to the effect that in one such deal, a school district in Colorado requires teachers to push Coca-Cola consumption in classrooms whenever sales fall below contractual obligations. Teachers have been converted into sales agents for soft drinks with not-so-healthy record! In this same article Adams also tells us that PepsiCo pays manufacturers to imprint the company's logo on feeding bottles for infants. The *Journal of Dentistry* reported in 1997 that a study "found that many infants were indeed being fed soda in those bottles." PepsiCo seeks to get even infants addicted to its drinks!

But PepsiCo tries to cover up its strategy by funding programs to promote healthy lifestyles. For example, it gave $116 million to YMCA to promote healthy lifestyles. It gave a grant to Girl Scouts of America to promote healthy foods and active lifestyles. Certainly these programs would have beneficial effect. But what is the purpose of first harming the health of unsuspecting youth by feeding them with sugar, caffeine, phosphates and E-150 dye; and then seeking to promote healthy lifestyles to compensate for the harm done?

Why America Attached Iraq

The U.S. war in Iraq is sold as American intervention against tyranny and for democracy. The real purpose is to kill all resistance to American extraction of natural resources of the developing countries. Iraq has a long history of opposing British-American interests in West Asia. The present war has its origins in Iraq's consistent record in opposing British and U.S. oil interests in the region.

The Turkish Ottoman Empire had ruled Kuwait, Iraq, Jordan and Syria through local sovereigns. In 1831, Sultan Ali Riza Pasha brought Iraq directly under the administrative control of the Ottomans. Turkey entered the First World War as an ally of the Germans and Iraq spontaneously joined it on the side of Turkey-Germany alliance. Subsequently, the British attacked Iraq and brought whole of it under their control in 1918. Till this time Kuwait was a part of Iraq. The British installed Faisal as the King in 1921 after he won 96 percent of the votes in a plebiscite. But Britain did not grant independence to oil-rich Kuwait at that time.

In 1936, Iraq started building a pan-Arab movement under King Ghazi. It was interested in a treaty of friendship with Saudi Arabia. In March 1940, under the leadership of A1-Gailani, Iraq supported Germany against the British. The British thereupon attacked Iraq and defeated it in May 1941.

After the creation of Israel by the British, Iraqi forces marched against that country in May 1948 along with the forces of Transjordan. Once again it met with defeat while Jordan entered into a treaty with the British.

Iraq unequivocally supported Egypt when it nationalised the Suez Canal in 1956. In November that year when Britain, Israel and France invaded Egypt, Iraq jointed Syria and Jordan in occupying positions in Jordan. When, however, Egypt entered into a pro-Western union with Syria called United Arab Republic, Iraq denounced Egypt.

During the Arab-Israeli confrontation in 1967, Iraqi troops and planes were sent to the Jordan-Israeli border. Iraq declared war on Israel and closed its oil pipeline supplying oil to the West and broke diplomatic relations with the U.S.

Pro-West Shah was ruling Iran during the seventies and eighties. At that time Iran was instigating the Kurds in the northern regions against the Iraqi government. By the end of 1977, the Kurdish people had been granted greater autonomy and Kurdish was recognised as an official language. Till this time Iraq was anti-West while Iran was pro-West. That changed dramatically with the deposing of the Shah by Ayatollah Khomeini in 1979. The U.S. then found Iran to be the bigger enemy. Now the U.S. started supporting Iraq against Iran. A note posted by U.S. Gulf War Veterans on the internet quoted the *New York Times* of 18 August 2002 to the effect that former Presidents Reagan and Bush armed Iraq with chemical and biological weapons from 1980 to 1988 during Iraq's war against Iran.

In 1961, Kuwait was given independence by the British. Iraq's ruler Abdul-Karim Qassem immediately claimed sovereignty over it, as the Emirate was originally part of the Ottoman province of Vasra. Britain reacted strongly to this threat to its ex-protectorate, dispatching a brigade to the country to deter Iraq. Qassem backed down and in October 1963, Iraq half-heartedly recognised the sovereignty and borders of Kuwait.

In 1990, Iraq's economy was in shambles due to the war with Iran. It accused Kuwait of violating the Iraqi border to secure oil resources, of flooding the world oil market and of producing oil from the disputed Rumaila oil field. Iraq summoned American ambassador April Glaspie. Saddam Hussein outlined his grievances against Kuwait. Although, Glaspie expressed concern over the troop build-up, she seemed to give Hussein the green light he sought by saying, "The U.S. had no opinion on the Arab-Arab conflicts, like your border disagreement with Kuwait." Some people like scholar William Blum allege that the U.S. gave secret encouragement to Kuwait to be provocative and promised to defend Kuwait from the expected Iraqi reaction. This was in response to increasing Iraqi warnings about American hegemony in the Gulf region.

Shortly after Iraq's invasion of Kuwait, the organisation 'Citizens for a Free Kuwait' was formed in the U.S. It hired the public relations firm Hill and Knowlton for about $11 million with money from the Kuwait Government. This firm went on to manufacture a fake campaign, which described Iraqi soldiers pulling babies out of incubators in Kuwaiti hospitals and letting them die on the floor. Video news-releases were widely distributed by U.S. TV networks, false supporting testimony was given before Congress and before the UN Security Council. The fifteen-year-old girl testifying before Congress was later revealed to be the daughter of the Kuwaiti ambassador to the U.S. The 'surgeon' testifying at the UN was in fact a dentist who later admitted to having lied. The U.S. insisted that the only acceptable terms for peace were Iraq's full and unconditional withdrawal from Kuwait. Iraq insisted that withdrawal from Kuwait must be 'linked' to a simultaneous withdrawal of Syrian troops from Lebanon and Israeli troops from the West Bank, Gaza Strip, Golan Heights and Southern Lebanon.

Iraq thus has a long history of opposing British-American interests in West Asia. The present war against Iraq is to avenge this resistance. Iraq has espoused the cause of Arab nationalism.

Iraq has historically put emphasis on the expansion of educational facilities. As a result, much of Iraq's urban middle class was able to move from lower-class to middle and even top positions in the state apparatus and the public sector. The government provided education through a centrally organised school system. Previously, education was mostly concentrated in the city of Baghdad, which contains about one-third of the country's population. The regime under Saddam has caused a spread of education to the interior regions. Iraq was awarded a prize by UNESCO for this attainment. The health situation also improved till the sanctions were placed after the Gulf War. Women have equal rights in Iraq. Elections have been held in Iraq intermittently during the last 80 years. Compare these with the situation in neighbouring Saudi Arabia where there is no democracy or women's rights, but a regime that encourages religious fanaticism.

This is not to deny that Saddam Hussein is known to use strong-arm tactics to subdue his opponents. Reportedly, torture chambers have been found in his palaces. His two sons are reported to abduct good-looking women. But then, that is the culture of the entire region. Hence, such events should not be highlighted in the case of Iraq alone.

The war cry towards the end of the last century has its origins in the consistent record of Iraq in opposing British and U.S. oil interests in the region.

This Chapter is adapted from the following articles:

"Double Standards," *News Time,* May 28, 2002.
"Bush doublespeak," *The Statesman,* December 15, 2002.
"Its war, oil-right," *The Pioneer,* October 3, 2001.
"Iraq war," *South Asia Politics,* February 2003.
"Why corruption does not hurt economic growth?" *Daily Excelsior,* October 15, 2006.
"The meaning of being Indira Nooyi," *New Indian Express,* September 6, 2006.

16

India's Role in Sustaining the Present Immoral World Order

The present unequal world order is sustained by the developing countries' willingly accepting the suzerainty of the U.S. Indian tradition, however, advises that India must follow the path of righteousness even if it is more difficult.

Two Approaches to India's Global Dharma

Indian public opinion is in favour of America. There is talk of establishing an India-Israel-U.S. axis against terrorism. India is willing to go along with the U.S. and ignore its wrongdoings because of its superpower status. The calculation is that India should align with the superpower and climb up the ladder of global power if the superpower is somewhat "evil." Realpolitik supersedes righteousness.

Indeed, one part of the Indian tradition supports precisely such an approach. Kautilya says in *Arthasastra*, "Whoever is inferior to another will make peace with him; whoever is superior in power shall wage war" (7.1). The question of alliance is resolved here on the single criterion of superiority of strength. The righteous or unrighteous character of the superior power is not mentioned.

Again, Kautilya says, "A king who is situated between two powerful kings shall seek protection from the stronger of the two; or from one of them on whom he can rely, or he may make peace with both of them on equal terms" (7.2). India was caught between two countries, Saddam's Iraq and Bush's U.S. Kautilya clearly advocated that India should align with the more powerful of the two. Thus the mainstream Indian pro-American sentiment appears to have the sanction of our tradition.

However, there is another stream in our tradition. The *Manu Smriti* says, "A king challenged by kings of equal, greater or less power may not cease from battle remembering his duty of giving protection to his people" (7.87). The stress here is on the king's duties rather than on political expediency. Even when challenged by a superior power, the king should fight rather than compromise. *Manu Smriti* does not advise the king to make unjust peace. Again: "Whenever a king considers the enemy in every respect more powerful than himself, then having divided his army, let him seek refuge. If he perceives injury even then, he should fearlessly fight a good battle alone" (7.173-6). The stress is on doing what is right even against heavy odds. Righteous conduct supersedes political expediency here.

There is a fundamental difference in the two streams of the Indian tradition. Kautilya focuses on political expediency and places righteousness at the second position. *Manu Smriti* places righteous conduct at the first position and political expediency next.

This difference between the two texts is made clear by another example. Kautilya is quite flexible in using lower means for attaining the ends. He advocates that a king use intrigue to win over people of his enemy: "Of the three, viz. enthusiasm, power and skill of intrigue, he who possesses the quality mentioned later will be successful" (9.1). Intrigue is here placed on a higher pedestal than power. While speaking of strategies to win over local people, Kautilya advocates that one should be set against the other. He says, "A spy may tell to one person: 'Your king wants to find your heart, you should tell him the truth'. To another he may say, 'This man carries a tale to the king against you'." In this way the king should set one against the other and establish control over the people.

Yet again Kautilya says, "When a king finds that as his enemy's subjects are ill-treated, impoverished and greedy, and they can be made through intrigue to join his side, then he may keep quiet after proclaiming war (and secure his objective through intrigue)" (7.4). The focus is on getting victory by whatsoever means.

The *Manu Smriti*, on the other hand, stresses purity of the means: "Of the four methods, conciliation, bribery, dissension and force, the learned ever praise conciliation and force" (7.109). Lower techniques such as bribery and sowing dissension among people are not advocated except where conciliation and force fail.

This is not to say that Kautilya does not honour righteousness. In the opening chapter itself he says that the king should act righteously. But this element is weak in the text. On the other hand, the *Manu Smriti* also exhorts the king to conquer the weak neighbour but, at the same time, tells him not to use inferior techniques.

No wonder the Mauryan Empire built on Kautilya's thoughts rose fast and collapsed equally speedily. The reason was that Kautilya ignored the psychic aspect of governance. Alliance with an unrighteous ruler or reliance on intrigue may produce immediate results but will leave a deep scar on the minds of the affected people. They do not willingly accept such a ruler. They ever try to obstruct his works and cause failure of his schemes. This slow but deep resistance is more important in the long run. The break-up of the Mauryan Empire soon after Ashoka's death was possibly due to such a reaction among the people against a king who followed Kautilya's policies. In contrast, the Raghu dynasty and the Gupta Empire lived much longer partly because these engaged in righteous action as advocated by *Manu Smriti*.

India has a choice to make. She can follow Kautilya, join hands with the U.S., while ignoring its wrongdoings and try to quickly rise to power. The danger is that such an Indian Empire may not last very long. Those who would be wronged by us, such as the Iraqis and Palestinians, will pray and work for our collapse. Alternatively, we can take a righteous approach. We can build an alliance of countries who are variously intimidated by the U.S. We can revive the Non-Aligned Movement. Though weak, we may fight against the wrongdoings of the U.S. This approach may be tortuous presently but will put in place the foundations of a long standing Indian Empire that is loved and respected by other countries.

Preserve Nuclear Freedom

Luminaries of the Independence struggle such as Dadabhai Naoroji, Anne Besant and Ram Mohan Roy were willing to remain under British rule. They were content to seek better conditions from British rulers within the country's enslavement. Gandhi and Subhash Bose, on the other hand insisted on complete financial autonomy. Gandhi took the difficult path of "Quit India" and Bose started the Indian National Army. Both groups of leaders were "nationalists" but their approach was very different. The former group focused on immediate gains while the latter followed long term righteous policies.

Prime Minister Manmohan Singh wants to secure supplies of uranium immediately while accepting U.S.' dominance of the world nuclear establishment. He ignores the fact that in the process India will become dependent on imports for her energy requirements. His policies are akin to those of Naoroji and others and contra Gandhi.

The U.S. had entered into an agreement with India in the sixties to supply uranium for the Tarapur Atomic Power Station for 30 years. But the U.S. unilaterally stopped the supplies after Indira Gandhi made Pokharan I explosions though there was no such clause in the supply agreement. The U.S., furthermore, initiated the process of setting up the Nuclear Suppliers Group consisting of 40-odd countries to deny India access to uranium for her nuclear programme—civil as well as military. It has, accordingly, become difficult for India to obtain supplies of uranium for meeting her energy requirements.

G. Parthsarthy ("N-fuel for Tarapur power plant: India's search for self-reliance," *Tribune,* February 28, 2001) writes, "in April 1981, the then Chairman of India's Atomic Energy Commission, Dr. Homi Sethna, met American negotiators in Washington. The U.S. had signed an agreement in 1963 pledging the supply of nuclear fuel to India for these reactors till 1993. In return India had agreed to maintain IAEA safeguards on the spent fuel of these reactors. The U.S. Congress had, however, effectively nullified the provisions of the 1963 agreement in 1978. Dr. Sethna pointed out that India had accepted safeguards on nuclear spent fuel in the 1963 agreement, only in return for continued and uninterrupted supply of nuclear fuel. If the U.S. did not fulfil its commitment to supply fuel, India would feel free to revoke existing IAEA safeguards and reprocess the spent fuel. More significantly, Dr. Sethna revealed to the American delegation that Indian scientists had developed the expertise to run the Tarapur reactors on a reprocessed plutonium-mixed oxide fuel (MOX). India would proceed to do this in the event of an interruption of nuclear fuel supplies by the U.S. Shortly after these exchanges took place, the Reagan Administration agreed to assist in getting France to provide India with lightly enriched uranium."

The alternative of using MOX is open to us today. The hesitation is political rather than technical. The use of MOX will imply that we will come out of the IAEA safeguards. That might bring retaliation from the rich countries. We must be ready to face the possible political retaliation from America in order to establish a just world order.

The second alternative is to speed up research on the use of Thorium as fuel for our nuclear programme. We have known reserves of 400,000 tonnes of Thorium against only 35,000 tonnes of uranium. But the technology to convert thorium into usable raw material is yet to be perfected. There is a good chance that we may be able to achieve this breakthrough by the time our MOX stockpile is exhausted. We should consider taking this calculated risk for the alternative of accepting IAEA safeguards and importing uranium will be available when and if our MOX stockpile is exhausted. There is no need to sacrifice our raw material sovereignty upfront.

The third alternative is to step up the exploitation of our uranium reserves. Objections from the ministry of environment have led to downsizing of our only working mine at Jadugoda in Jharkhand. The autonomy granted to Tribal areas in matter of land under our Constitution is hampering the development of the Domisiat mines in Meghalaya. NGOs, many of whom are possibly foreign-funded, are leading a campaign against the development of the Pedugutta mines in Andhra Pradesh. Removal of these obstacles is within the domain of the Union government.

Yet another alternative is to forge a global alternative to the U.S.-led Nuclear Suppliers Group. Uranium is found in many countries that are not a part of the NSG. But these countries are afraid of the U.S. ire, hence have not developed their resources and are reluctant to export the same to us. We can provide nuclear power generation technology to countries like Venezuela, Brazil and South Africa and obtain uranium supply in return. There is no easy way to heaven. We will ultimately have to confront the U.S.-led unholy alliance of the rich countries that is consuming 80 percent of the world's resources. Imported uranium will make our life easy in the short term but impair our ability to secure this realignment of the world order. Let us follow Gandhi and preserve our nuclear freedom even if the path is difficult.

This Chapter is adapted from the following articles:

"Righteous politics," *The Pioneer,* May 20, 2003.
"Follow Gandhi: Preserve nuclear freedom," *Gomantak Times,* August 25, 2005.

17

Free Movement of Labour

A fundamental anomaly of globalization is that free movement of goods and capital is promoted while free movement of labour is prohibited. The argument is that free movement of capital will lead to the establishment of more industries in the developing countries and benefit their people. However, there is no reason to take this circuitous route. The benefits to the people of the developing countries as well as the world economy are higher through free movement of labour.

Gathering Storm of Indian MNCs

Tatas are an example of how Indian companies are making a space for themselves in the world economy. In the last few years the Tatas have acquired Tetley Tea in the UK, Daewoo Motors in South Korea, Natsteel in Singapore, Pierre Hotel in Manhattan and Corus Steel in U.K. Tatas are working on making large investment in energy, steel and fertilisers in Bangladesh. Indica cars made by Tata Motors are being exported to South Africa, Russia and Europe.

India is moving fast to become global economic power No.1. Businessmen and workers of rich countries are tyrannised by India. It is likely that in the next 10-20 years Indian MNCs like those of

Tatas and Lakshmi Mittal will be feared just as Microsoft, General Electric and General Motors were feared across the world in the nineties. India will acquire the same disgusting hue across the world as the MNCs of the rich countries had. Indians will be honoured with titles of cruel, greedy and exploiters. Are we ready to assume this role?

We have mostly exported knowledge and wisdom in our long history. We have not exploited other countries economically though there are exceptions. There are indications that Indians have contributed to the creation of ancient civilisations of Sumer and Egypt. Maulana Tariq Abdullah of Rampur says in his book *Now or Never* that the Sabean civilisation of Saudi Arabia in tenth century BC was exported from India. We sent Buddhist monks to the East and West. But Indian emperors never extended their borders beyond Afghanistan and Burma. The result is that other peoples have not looked upon us as evil. India was seen as a guru, friend or trader rather than exploiter like England and America are seen.

There have been exceptions, however, Pliny, a historian of ancient Rome, writes that Indian traders contributed much to the collapse of the Great Roman Empire. These traders brought speaking parrots, dancing girls, lions and tigers for royal play and items of luxury and licence like wine and scents from India. Roman emperors spent their wealth in purchase of these goods. India became the 'Golden Bird' while Rome became bankrupt. It found its treasury empty when attacked by barbarians and the empire collapsed. Such role of India has, thankfully, been an exception. Our main character has been that of love and peace; hence our culture has not faced the ire of oppressed peoples and survived for 5000 years.

We have to now redefine our image in future given the global success of our businesses. Do we want Indian businesses to establish a loving and friendly and friendly relationship with other countries? Or do we want to assume the role of exploiters? We will acquire the latter role if we give unrestricted freedom to our businessmen to acquire foreign companies and trade in 'unhealthy' items like opium, wine, tea and coffee.

We will have to define our foreign commercial relations clearly if we have to create a friendly relationship with the world of tomorrow. Perhaps the Tatas can give us a lead here too. Sixty six percent of the profits of ;the holding company Tata Sons are spent in charity Tatas are planning to make big investments in Bangladesh. Ratan Tata tells in *Newsweek* that Bangladesh is not able to attract foreign investment because there is no infrastructure; and infrastructure cannot be built unless foreign investment comes in a big way. It is necessary for some businessmen to take the lead to break this vicious cycle. Tatas may be able to jump-start the process by initiating large investments in Bangladesh.

This policy of ours needs to be converted into a code. Two points are involved here. One, a condition may be imposed that Indian companies investing abroad will not impoverish the host country by large-scale remittance of profits and royalties. At least 75 percent of income will be reinvested in the host country. Two, heavy export tax should be imposed on items that are harmful for mankind such as opium, wine, etc. This will ensure that India is not seen as a cruel imperial power in the world of tomorrow.

If Capital can Roam the World Freely, Why not Labour?

Why should a developing country in dire need of capital yet oppose the inclusion of an investment regime in the WTO? The answer is that free movement of one factor of production–i.e., capital–alone can be harmful.

True globalisation would enable both capital and labour to roam across the world. In that situation, natural endowment such as water, land and climate would determine which countries would produce what goods. Central America may produce bananas; Latin America may produce coffee, India may produce software and so on. The second factor determining the location of economic activity would be culture of the people such as work ethic and loyalty. People of Africa give more importance to the community, those of India to individual spiritual pursuits and those of America to individual material prosperity. Businesses will set up their units in areas that provide the suitable culture.

Geographical and cultural factors would determine the movement of labour and capital. So much of capital and labour would move to Central America as necessary for the production of bananas. Conversely, it is possible that both capital and labour may flow out of a country like Iceland if that country does not have a clear competitive advantage in some commodity. Yet, that would not hurt the people of Iceland. Labour would move along with capital to countries that had a comparative advantage in the global economy. The country of Iceland may suffer, but the people of Iceland would migrate and get jobs in Central American banana plantations and secure their welfare.

But free movement of labour is not easily obtained. Many countries want to preserve their own unique cultures. Islamic countries may not like to provide the free right of immigration to non-Muslims. Israel may do the same of non-Jewish persons. America wants to preserve it stress on individual right. Malaysians may wish to preserve their 'Asian values' of the importance of the family. Thus many countries do not wish to allow unrestricted entry to persons from other countries. The movement of natural persons is, therefore, restricted. That leaves us with one-half globalisation. While capital has the freedom to roam cross the globe, labour does not.

It is possible that people of Iceland or Central America may become losers in the process. Let us say only 10 million natural persons are required to produce all the bananas that the world needs. But the population of the Central American countries is 50 million. The restriction on migration of these 40 million 'excess' persons is a loss to the world economy. If they had been allowed to migrate to Canada and Russia, which have a shortage of labour, the world economy would have grown.

The loss to the people of Central America is great. Their capital may flow to Canada in the search of higher profits, as it must. But the people would be hemmed in by borders. Fifty million would be forced to eke out an existence from the work suitable to sustain only 10 million people. Thus developing countries should demand free movement of labour first and free movement of capital next.

Migration under GATS

Migration of workers is governed under General Agreement on Trade in Services (GATS) of WTO. Four modes of supply of services are mentioned in this agreement.

- *Mode 1:* The supplier supplies his services from his country without requiring cross border travel—as National Geographic supplies its TV programmes to Indian viewers through satellites.

- *Mode 2:* The purchaser of services travels to the supplier country—as Indian tourist goes to Switzerland for skiing.

- *Mode 3:* The supplier company established its office in the host country—as Citibank establishes its offices to issue car loans in India.

- *Mode 4:* The supplier natural person travels to the purchasing country to supply his services—as Indian software programmers' travel to the U.S. to write computer programs.

Modes 3 and 4 are relevant for free movement of natural persons. The difference is that a company establishes office in the host country under Mode 3 while a natural person travels to the host country under Mode 4. In both cases the supplier physically travels to the host country for the supply of services. Capital investment is made in the host country under Mode 3 while the worker alone migrates to the host country under Mode 4. Developed countries want freer under Mode 3 for their companies to open offices across the world. On the order hand developing countries want more liberal rules under Mode 4 for migration of natural persons.

India has gains to make both from Modes 3 and 4. Indian companies, particularly in the services sector, are increasingly in a position to invest in other countries hence they stand to gain from a greater opening of Mode 3. At the same time India has a large surplus of manpower which can migrate for employment in other countries under Mode 4. The question is which should be our priority?

Aileen Kwa of Thailand's Chulalongkorn University in an excellent article writes that India is putting more stress on Mode 3 as done by the developed countries:

The European Union had 'asked of authorizing at least 51 percent foreign ownership under Mode 3. The Indian proposal too asks of 'enhancement in the levels of foreign equity permitted'.

The EU proposals on Mode 4, Kwa says, were "Much more limited." The Indian proposal on Mode 4 too was limited. It only asked for more liberal rules for contractual service suppliers and independent professionals; and more relaxed rules regarding the length of stay. The discussions are restricted to migration of 'skilled professionals'. In this light, Kwa clubs Indian proposals with that of the developed countries.

India has wholly endorsed the EU stand in GATS. Instead of asking of freer migration of semi-skilled and unskilled workers that benefit of millions of our people and also of other developing countries, India is satisfied demanding more freedom of its companies to invest in other countries; and more freedom for its few professionals. The Indian Government is pushing the interests of Indian service companies like Infosys rather than of millions of its people.

India will have to decide its place in the emerging world order. Indian Government is seeking more freedom of its companies to exploit other countries just as foreign MNCs have exploited India. India is anxious to joint in the adharma of the developed countries. Our culture and heritage, however, asks us to work of the welfare of the whole mankind, nay all living beings. We should make a strong pitch of opening migration of semiskilled and unskilled workers under Mode 4. Moreover, freedom under Mode 3 should be denied until this is done. It will not be sufficient to demand movement of skilled professional alone. We should remember Gandhiji who said that the touchstone of development is what it means to the poorest person. We should work of all the poor people of the world instead of fulfilling our narrow interests..

Not all will Win from Globalization

The globalization of ideas, technologies, trade and investment is a movement forward. The end result, however, will necessarily be distributed unequally among regions. A person living in the cold climate of Laddakh may simply not be able to muster the mental agility to develop expertise in software technologies. Mexico will continue to have greater access to the market of U.S. as compared to Thailand. People located in area with rich natural resources—minerals and water, of example—will continue to have greater incomes.

This inequality can be dealt with only by globalization of labour. If it were possible for a Laddakhi to migrate freely to the U.S., then she would be able to develop her capabilities as a software engineer. If Zambia happens to have greater mineral resources, people from Rwanda could migrate there to benefit from that 'global' wealth. The carmakers of Thailand could migrate to Mexico and partake in the benefits of the U.S.' market. People from those areas which are left out by the nature of modern technologies may migrate to greener pastures. In this way, true equality between human beings will be established even if inequality between regions gets accentuated. No human being anywhere in the globe would be hemmed in artificial national borders and deprived of the benefits of globalization.

Three counterarguments are given against such a right. First, that such a right involves dilution of culture. True, but it is forgotten that economy and culture are inextricably intertwined. McDonalds and Pepsi are simultaneously economic and cultural entities. If McDonald's fast-food culture can freely come into India, then why should Osho's ashrams not freely move to the U.S.? Why not a global culture? Why not let the people have the rights to choose the culture that they wish to grow in?

The second counterargument is that the right over the natural resources of an area belong to those people. A citizen of Rwanda cannot claim the benefit of copper deposits of Zambia. But why so? The world's resources belong to the people of the world. If national borders are not to be tolerated of trade and capital, why should they be tolerated for natural resources?

Third argument is that new technologies have drastically reduced, if not eliminated, the geographical advantages of the past. The right to migrate is no longer necessary of securing an equitable distribution of the benefits. Medical transcription can be undertaken virtually anywhere in the world. Reduction of the costs of transport has made it economical to produce cars anywhere in the world. The factors of education, labour policies and infrastructure have a much greater weight than the cost of transport. Thus it is not necessary for people to move from one country to another to benefit from globalization. They can secure those benefits staying in their home country. This argument fails because geographical endowments will have a decisive bearing in determining the comparative advantage of a country. Those placed unfavourably will loose out against those placed favourably.

Equitable sharing of the benefits of globalization would take place only when all people of the world have a right to migrate to the country of their choice. The omission of this right has serious consequences. It implies that the poor countries and poor people would be condemned to remain poor in case their geography is unfavourable.

Self-employment as Human Progress

The basic ideas of socialism are indeed noble. Karl Marx was a kind soul. He was moved by the extreme conditions in which the workers of his time lived. He was perplexed as why there should be so much poverty amidst so much prosperity. The industrial revolution had brought unheard wealth to England yet the workers were whipped at work. This concern with the welfare of the common man is the centrepiece of socialist thought.

Marx had predicted that the capitalist system would collapse due to the imbalance between low wage demand and high production. With the experience of hindsight it can be said that the collapse of capitalism is no longer inevitable. There are four reasons for the same.

- The demand in the market is not generated merely from the wages. The government can tax the rich and redistribute that wealth among the poor. Distribution of dividend by companies puts money in the hands of shareholders who buy goods from the market.

- Private charity in the construction of temples and in the langars creates demand.

- The self-employed are simultaneously capitalist as well as worker. They consume profits. There would be no crisis of capitalism if all the production were carried out by the self-employed.

- The capitalists can continue to operate at zero rates of profit. They can continue to produce even if they are not making a profit.

It is not necessary, therefore, that capitalism will collapse under its own weight as Marx had predicted. The socialist approach now should be that of seeking a fair distribution of goods within stable capitalism. The focus should be especially on encouraging private charity and self-employment.

Charity is the window to a rich person's evolution. He learns to give. The richness of the rich is not evil. It is the improper use of that richness that is the problem. Socialists should seek policies that encourage the rich to give in charity.

Self-employment helps in the evolution of a person. The milkman learns to buy, produce and sell milk. There is a need to create economic policies that protect self-employment from competition of large corporations in areas such as handloom weaving, soap making and soft drinks. Such measures will provide some earning to the people. We must develop ways to secure justice within a capitalist economy.

This Chapter is adapted from the following articles:

"If capital can roam the world freely, why not labour," *The Financial Express,* November 26, 2001.

"Let there be free migration!!" *Swadeshi Patrika*, December 2005.

"Agenda for Globalization," *Eurasia Times*, March 2002.

18

Emergence of a New World Economic Order

In the previous chapters of this section we have outlined policies for attainment of equality between nations as well as individuals. In this section we discuss the contours of India's external policy to attain that objective. My assessment is that India is joining the unholy alliance of U.S.-EU-Saudi Arabia-Singapore-Japan. Instead it should develop a holy alliance of India-China-Russia-Iran-Venezuela.

Befriend China, not Japan

China and Japan have a long-standing enmity between them. We may have to befriend one and jettison the other.

Chinese civilisation is introvert. It has been repeatedly subjected to attack by neighbours from Mongolia, Korea, Japan, Vietnam, Burma and Tibet.

- The Great Wall was constructed about 2,500 years ago during the Chin dynasty to keep the tribal intruders away.
- During the Tang dynasty in the sixth century peace was bought by handing over defence to non-Chinese people and generals.

- The Sung dynasty bought peace with the tribal people in the north in the 10th century by agreeing to pay a yearly tribute to them.
- Mongol Genghis Khan captured Beijing in the 13th century.
- China was encircled by France in Vietnam, England in Burma, Russia in Manchuria and Japan in Korea before the Second World War.

Indeed, Chinese rulers have intermittently attacked these countries but that has been short-lived and bereft of imperialistic ambitions.

Japan's character is relatively aggressive.

- In the fourth century Queen Jinjo attacked and captured Korea.
- Toward the end of 18th century Japan captured Ryukyu Islands and Korea again.
- In 1931, Japan conquered Manchuria and established a puppet government there.
- Japan chose to quit the League of Nations when China raised the matter in that forum before the international community.
- Japan forged an axis with Germany and Italy during the Second World War.
- Japanese pirates have been looting ships on the eastern coast of China since the 16th century.

A comparison of the history of the two countries indicates that China has been introvert. Her effort has been to thwart exploitation by others. Japan, on the other hand, has aggressively sought to conquer and exploit others. Thus dharma is in favour of China.

The second difference relates to self-esteem. China has developed its administrative system by developing new forms suited to its situation. Confucius advocated the establishment of an independent bureaucracy based on merit rather than inheritance. In comparison, Japan has mostly copied the administrative systems of the West. Prince Iwakura of the Meiji dynasty engaged French officers to reorganise the Japanese army, British officers to reorganise the navy and Dutch engineers for construction. Japanese experts were sent to Europe and America to study their constitutions. A cabinet was formed along the lines of Germany.

The third difference is regarding the nature of external trade. China has a huge domestic market. The Grand Canal was constructed in the sixth century so that the agricultural produce of the Yangtze basin could be sent to other areas. Wagnall's Encyclopaedia notes that "commercial relations with the West were grudgingly accepted by the Manchus in the late 18th century... China, with her long history of economic self-sufficiency, was not interested in increased trade."

In comparison, Japan has tried to aggressively open up new markets. Japan started establishing modern industries after the First World War. It needed markets to sell the goods that were produced. Emperor Hirohito adopted an aggressive policy towards China after 1926.

Both countries have adopted globalisation. But there are differences that are significant. China has adopted an export-led strategy so that domestic industries can be developed in the process. Japanese companies, on the other hand, are buying American automakers and prime estate in Manhattan.

Both China and Japan are exporting their goods in huge quantities. China's exports are of low quality. It is not charging royalties for hydropower and coal. China's cost of production is therefore less. These exports will not be durable because they are based on cheap labour and squandering of natural resources. In comparison, Japan is exporting hi-tech goods like flat screen TVs and silicon semiconductors. Japanese companies are giving a hard time to Western competitors.

Presently China has nuclear weapons while Japan is an ardent supporter of disarmament. But this is an exception. Japan has been forced to accept this condition in the U.S. sponsored constitution it adopted after the Second World War. Disarmament is not the basic character of that country.

We should select our friend based on the country's basic character. China only wants us not to intrude into its borders and allow it to develop its internal economy undisturbed. Japan, on the other hand, wants to conquer our markets. We have reason to fear Japan, not China. India and China should join hands to arrest the Japanese imperialistic ambitions so that justice and peace can be established in the world.

The case for India-China Free Trade

India has to decide whether to push for an FTA with its South Asian neighbours or with those outside the region such as Singapore or China. A successful FTA can be made if the resource endowments of the participating countries are complementary. The second factor is that the countries should gain politically by joining together. Each of ten sticks becomes stronger when tied together. Similarly, ten countries should become stronger by making a FTA. Regional free trade is beneficial if these two conditions are satisfied

Japan and Singapore have capital and technology. Malaysia, Thailand and other countries have rice, rubber and labour. A FTA between these countries is mutually beneficial. Japan gets cheap rice and Thailand gets hi-tech products. The ASEAN countries are small. None have an international presence. Together they have a greater voice in international affairs. Thailand's voice will be better heard in the world as a member of ASEAN rather than alone. ASEAN is successful because both the conditions are fulfilled.

Germany has coal, France makes Airplanes and London is a centre of global finance and trade. These countries have gained by making a FTA in the form of European Union. Each of these countries is small. France, Germany, England, Spain and Italy—none have a great voice in international affairs individually. But together the EU can influence things. This was most clearly seen at Doha and Cancun where the EU, U.S. and G-20 were the three major players. Individually, France and Germany would not have such a presence.

Mexico has labour, U.S. has capital and technology and Canada has natural resources. The resource endowments of these countries are complementary hence all three stand to gain through NAFTA. In this case, Mexico and Canada do not really get much political voice through NAFTA which is dominated by the U.S. This appears to be an exception.

These examples show that a FTA is successful if there is complementarily between the resources of the member countries and they stand to gain politically by joining together.

Both the conditions are not fulfilled in South Asia. India, Pakistan, Bangladesh and Sri Lanka—all have a large supply of labour and have agricultural economies. Two farmers do not trade with each other. A farmer trades with a brick- or tractor manufacturer. Trade takes place only when one has something to sell which the buyer does not have. Such complementarity is, the main, missing among the SAARC countries. Worse, they compete with each other in the global market in their major exports. India and Bangladesh both export jute, India and Sri Lanka both export tea, India and Pakistan both export cotton. Thus they may gain more by making cartels in the global markets, not by greater free trade among themselves.

In an article "How Desirable is the South Asia Free Trade Area?" available on the Internet Jayatilleke S. Bandara and Wusheng Yu say: "Under the SAFTA scenario, India would be the only significant welfare gainer ($756 million), while small countries gain marginally. Bangladesh is even expected to lose. This is not surprising given the fact that during the last three decades India's export to other South Asian countries continued to rise, while share of export from other South Asian countries to India fell."

In another article the New Delhi-based Research and Information System for the Non-Aligned and Other Developing Countries says that SAARC is "unlikely to exploit the full potential of the regional economic integration in Asia. The extent of complementarities is limited at the sub-regional levels. The trade of South Asian countries with the East Asian countries is much larger than the intra-regional trade. At the pan-Asian level, the diversities in the levels of economic development and capabilities are quite wide, thus providing for more extensive and mutually beneficial linkages." These studies point out that the South Asian countries stand to gain little by entering into a FTA.

Some others, however, feel that there is substantial gain to be made. The Dhaka-based Centre for Policy Dialogue held a seminar on *Growth Zones in South Asia: What can we learn from Southeast Asia?* The report of the seminar states, "Nepal and the states of Uttar Pradesh and Bihar in India are hydraulic entities. It is difficult to regulate the water resources of the region to India's maximum benefit without the cooperation from Nepal. Likewise, Bangladesh has very few means at her disposal for regulating its own water resources without the cooperation from India. The whole region is locked into a particular set of common problems which can be solved efficiently only through regional cooperation. Another important potential in the region was the huge reserve of natural gas in Bangladesh and the north-eastern part of India. Besides, there was very large reserve of coal in West Bengal, Bihar, Assam and Orissa. A regional project of developing energy resources could very well be initiated for efficient and more value added use of these resources."

Imtiaz Alam, writing for the Jang group in Pakistan asks, "Why should New Delhi drag its feet from Iran-Pakistan-India gas-pipeline? Why can't Pakistan import coal from India to convert its oil-fuelled units to coal, reducing the cost of production and making non-hydel energy cheaper, in exchange for selling surplus electricity to India on which why should New Delhi have any objection?"

Certainly there are such areas of mutual cooperation among the SAARC countries. But this give-and-take is limited to few specific sectors. India and Bangladesh can enter into an agreement regarding water separately. Why should Bangladesh invite a crisis by embracing free trade in garments and jute in the process?

SAARC countries also do not improve their standing internationally by mutual cooperation. Six thin sticks tied to a heavy log do not increase the joint strength much. In fact a thin stick may have a greater recognition separately than when tied to a big log. The preponderance of India in SAARC means that smaller countries stand to lose their political voice by joining together. The situation of America is similar in NAFTA but Mexico and Canada were virtually non-existent in the world politics earlier as well and had nothing to lose. Pakistan, Sri Lanka and Bangladesh do have their independent standing in the world community hence they would be overshadowed by India in SAARC.

The basic conditions of mutual cooperation are not fulfilled in South Asia. Therefore, we should not entangle ourselves in this futile exercise. Instead we should try to make a FTA with China. India's IT and China's manufacturing base are complementary. Both our civilizations are inward looking. Both have a deep influence of the Hindu-Buddhist worldview. A rail line can be made to connect the two through Tibet. Together we speak for one-half of humanity and we can guide the world in the right direction.

Selling Asia, the Singapore Way

The Free Trade Agreement with Singapore has generally been welcomed in the country. Singapore will impose zero duty on all imports from India. India will reduce import duty on most items and eliminate duty on many. Indian accountants, architects and pharmacists will be able to provide services in Singapore. The 6,000 MNCs having offices in Singapore will be encouraged to buy Indian products. India will gain access to global markets while Singapore will get cheap goods and qualified labour from India.

But there is more to it than meets the eye. The basis of an FTA is cartelisation. We impose import duties at one single rate on imports from member countries of the World Trade Organisation under the MFN provision. We impose especially lower tariffs on imports from a partner country under an FTA. In the process, we give advantage to inefficient producers in the partner country while keeping out the efficient producers of others.

We are giving undue advantage to the inefficient producer from Singapore if we impose zero duty on computer chips imported from that country while levying a 20 percent duty on the same imports from China. We may still make the FTA if we can get bargain better with other countries. In other words, cartelisation, not complementarity of resources is the logic of the FTA. An ideal FTA would secure the benefits of both complementarity and cartelisation. We must examine, therefore, whether the FTA with Singapore helps us form a cartel to further our interests globally. This requires us to identify the main fault line of the global economy.

The main problem is that 20 percent of the people located in the U.S., the European countries and Japan consume 80 percent of world's resources. Singapore is a willing accomplice of this unholy alliance.

U.S. policy has been that of divide and rule. Munakata Naoka writes in Japanese journal *Jiji Top Confidential:* "After the Malaysian Prime Minister, Dr. Mahathir Mohammad's proposal 12 years ago to create the East Asia Economic Caucus (EAEC) met strong objections from the U.S., East Asia-wide regional initiatives remained a taboo for years. But the 1997 Asian currency crisis changed the tide. From the late 1980s through the early 1990s, when concerns mounted in the U.S. over Japan's economic power, Washington fiercely opposed the EAEC vision and attempted to reinforce and utilise the APEC framework as a tool to promote trade liberalisation in Asia... Following the conclusion of negotiations with China on its WTO accession, the U.S. has become active to drive a wedge into Asian moves toward bilateral FTAs among them. The U.S. made its first move in the fall of 2001 when it suddenly agreed with Singapore to launch FTA negotiations."

The 20/80 asymmetry requires that we build an alliance of the 80 percent people of the world who are now consuming only

20 percent of the world's resources despite most of these resources being in their countries. The U.S. is striking an alliance with the European Union, Japan and Singapore to drive a wedge among the developing countries—especially India and China. Geethanjali Nataraj writes in *The Hindu:* "It becomes imperative for India to forge ahead in its ties with ASEAN so that the adverse impact or trade diversion resulting by the creation of NAFTA and the EU can be combated by enhancing growth within the Asian region."

We must create an India-China-ASEAN bloc excluding Singapore and Japan to challenge the high consumption of the U.S.-EU-Japan group by shifting terms of trade in our favour by cartelisation just as OPEC has done for oil.

Yet Prime Minister, Dr. Manmohan Singh's media advisor holds out China as the main threat: "China looms large over the region and in the new 'balance of power' which all ASEAN member countries are trying to help shape. India, Japan and the U.S. will be increasingly viewed as checks and balances against growing Chinese economic and military power in the region." In formulating the problem in this way, he places China-ASEAN in one bloc, which is to be contained by an India-Japan-U.S. axis. But this approach does not explain how the 20/80 asymmetry will be resolved. Singapore is, really, the breaker of Asian unity. That country has signed, or is in the process of signing, FTAs with Canada, the EU, Japan, Mexico and the U.S. Japan is also negotiating FTAs with Canada and Mexico. Thus, Singapore and Japan are firmly entrenched in the U.S.-EU bloc of 20/80 division of the world economy.

True, there is complementarity between Singapore and India and an FTA makes sense from that standpoint. But this is contrary to our long-term interest of forging a Developing World Alliance against the First World to redress the basic inequality of the world economy. It appears our leaders have been swayed by the U.S. propaganda that China is the emerging treat to India.

India is making efforts to join the U.S.-EU grouping along with Singapore and maybe ASEAN to contain China; whereas the need is to create a China-India-ASEAN group against the U.S.-EU-Japan. How else will we redress the imbalance in the consumption of world resources?

We may be able to increase our consumption of the world's resources from two percent to three percent through FTAs with the U.S.-EU bloc; but to increase our consumption to 20 percent to which our 20 percent people of the world are entitled, a steep reduction in the consumption by the U.S.-EU-Japan bloc will be necessary. That cannot be secured by making an FTA with them. The Singapore FTA is regressive because it gives preferential treatment to a country that is firmly entrenched in the opposite bloc.

India-Russia-China Axis

An official of the Chinese embassy once asked me whether I considered India as a friend or foe. My intuitive response was "foe." There are 3 difficulties in India-China friendship.

China has been occupied throughout its history in keeping its empire intact from intrusions on its borders. The civilisational pain of China lies in these foreign attacks on her unity. China's relation with India is both strengthened- and weakened due to this orientation. It is strengthened because inward-looking China is not a threat to India. It is weakened because India is seen as threatening China's unity. India and China have border disputes in the North-East and Kashmir. Our support to Dalai Lama is a direct challenge to Chinese territorial integrity. India's efforts to build bridges with South-East Asian countries are a threat to Chinese dominance in the area. My assessment is that these obstructions are minor. There is a basic common perspective between India and China in the espousal of inwardness.

Another difficulty arises from the common pattern of global trade. India and China are competitors in areas such as toys, drugs and garments in the global marketplace. But there is a synergy here as well. India is more focused on services while China is focused on manufacturing. Hence they can join hands.

India is closer to Russia, however. Our territories are far apart. The global trade patterns are complementary. Russia exports minerals, oil and military hardware, which India imports. And India exports services that Russia imports.

Russian history is parallel to that of India. Russian history is that of traders. That country has always waged wars to gain access to ports on the western, southern and eastern fronts in order to promote its foreign trade. The earliest Slav tribes of eastern Russia were renowned traders. The Rurik Dynasty raided Constantinople in 911 and concluded a trade treaty. A thriving trade with Turkey was the basis of prosperity of Kiev—the capital of Russia at that time. Ivan the Great concluded several trade treaties with England. He started the process of importing foreign technical and professional experts into the country.

Russia expanded westward and captured a part of Finland in 1743 in order to get access to the Western sea. Catherine the Great conquered Crimea from the Turkish in 1774 to gain access to the warm-water Black Sea ports necessary for Russian commerce. Russia's foreign conquests have been designed, in the main, to facilitate its trade.

India's orientation has been nearly the same. We have been traders par excellence in 5,000 years of our civilisation. The prosperity of the Indus valley, the Gupta Empire and even the Mughal era was based on India's foreign trade. Thus we share with Russia a common objective of beating the West in trade. Another common feature is that of global initiative for equality. Russia had made sincere efforts in the Soviet era to assist developing countries in building their technical and economic potential. India displayed a similar orientation, for example, in Nehru's leadership of the Non-Aligned Movement.

It seems there is a natural affinity in the world view of India, China and Russia in contradistinction to that of Japan, Europe and America who can be, relatively speaking, characterised as predators. Thus an India-China-Russia axis should be possible and also beneficial for the world.

This Chapter is adapted from the following articles:

"Befriend China, not Japan," *New Indian Express*, June 1, 2005.

"Hindi Chini Bhai Bhai: India-China free trade," *Lucknow Times*, December 20-26, 2003.

"Singapore FTA: Against Asian unity?" *Businessline*, August 18, 2005.

"Russian angle," *The Pioneer*, December 17, 2002.

Index

M

N

S

T

U